Inventory Best Practices

Inventory Best Practices

Steven M. Bragg

John Wiley & Sons, Inc.

For general information on our other products and services, or technical support, please contact our Customer Care Department within the United States at 800-762-2974, outside the United States at 317-572-3993 or fax 317-572-4002.

Wiley also publishes its books in a variety of electronic formats. Some content that appears in print may not be available in electronic books.

For more information about Wiley products, visit our Web site at *www.wiley.com*.

Library of Congress Cataloging-in-Publication Data:

Bragg, Steven M.
    Inventory best practices / Steven M. Bragg.
        p.   cm.
    Includes index.
    ISBN 0-471-67625-X (cloth)
    1. Inventories.   2. Inventory control.   I. Title.
    HD40.B725 2004
    658.7'87—dc22
    2004007926

Printed in the United States of America

10 9 8 7 6 5 4 3

To Victoria, whose room resembles a warehouse

Contents

vii

Preface

This book contains almost 200 best practices related to every phase of a company's activities involving inventory—its purchase, receipt, storage, picking, and shipment. Special functions related to inventory contain so many best practices that they deserve their own chapters—production, transaction processing, planning, warehouse layout, cost accounting, and even bills of material. Further, one needs to measure a company's progress in achieving best practices, so a comprehensive list of inventory-related measurements have been added to a separate chapter. Also, a number of the inventory chapters refer to specific inventory procedures, which are helpfully detailed in yet another chapter. Given the large number of best practices presented, the Appendix summarizes them for you. If there are any concerns about the meaning of any inventory-specific terms, the glossary contains an inventory dictionary. In short, this book is the go-to source for inventory improvements.

Inventory Best Practices is designed for people in many parts of a company. The controller can use the cost accounting, inventory transactions, inventory measurements, and policies and procedures chapters to increase the efficiency of inventory accounting. The CFO can use virtually all the chapters to determine what options are available for reducing a company's investment in inventory, while the purchasing manager can use the purchasing chapter as well as the planning and management chapter to increase that department's effectiveness in procuring inventory. The warehouse manager is a particular beneficiary, with the inventory receiving and shipping, storage, picking, transactions, and warehouse layout chapters devoted to that area of expertise. The engineering manager can also benefit from the inventory planning and management and bill of materials chapters. Finally, the CEO can use the entire book to gain a sweeping view of the scope of inventory best practices on all aspects of a company.

This book is intended to be a buffet table of ideas from which one can sample. There is no clear set of inventory best practices recommended for all companies, all the time. Instead, given the wide array of industry-specific issues and inventory flow concepts in use, one should skim through

ix

the book and select only those best practices resulting in the most obvious improvements. The Appendix, which summarizes all the best practices, is a good place to conduct this review. However, a company's business plan will likely change over time, so it is worthwhile to refer back to the book from time to time to see what other best practices may have become applicable as a result of those changes.

Finally, one does not install a best practice merely by ordering that it be done. The "Make it so!" approach of Captain Picard of the *Enterprise* does not always work. Instead, read Chapter 1, "Success or Failure with Best Practices," to learn what factors will impact a best practices implementation, and how you can increase your odds of success.

In short, use *Inventory Best Practices* to improve all aspects of your company's business that relate to inventory. This can result in far less time spent recording inventory transactions, reducing the company investment in inventory, shrinking its scrap and obsolete inventory expense, improving the efficiency of the warehouse, and shortening order cycle time. Enjoy!

Steven M. Bragg
Centennial, Colorado
September 2004

1

Success or Failure with Best Practices

This chapter is about implementing best practices.* It begins by describing those situations where best practices are most likely to be installed successfully. The key components of a successful best practice installation are also noted, as well as how to duplicate best practices throughout an organization. When planning to add a best practice, it is also useful to know the ways in which the implementation can fail, so there is a lengthy list of reasons for failure. Only by carefully considering all of these issues in advance can one hope to achieve a successful best practice implementation that will result in increased levels of efficiency.

Most Fertile Ground for Best Practices

Before installing any best practice, it is useful to review the existing environment to see if there is a reasonable chance for the implementation to succeed. The following points note the best environments in which best practices not only can be installed, but also have a fair chance of continuing to succeed:

- *If benchmarking shows a problem.* Some organizations regularly compare their performance levels against those of other companies, especially those with a reputation for having extremely high levels of performance. If there is a significant difference in the performance levels of these other organizations and the company doing the benchmark-

---

*Adapted with permission from Chapter 2 of *Accounting Best Practices, Third Edition* (Steven Bragg, John Wiley & Sons, 2003).

1

ing, this can serve as a reminder that continuous change is necessary in order to survive. If management sees and heeds this warning, the environment in which best practices will be accepted is greatly improved.

- *If management has a change orientation.* Some managers have a seemingly genetic disposition toward change. If a department has such a person in charge, there will certainly be a drive toward many changes. If anything, this type of person can go too far, implementing too many projects with not enough preparation, resulting in a confused operations group whose newly revised systems may take a considerable amount of time to untangle. The presence of a detail-oriented second-in-command is very helpful for preserving order and channeling the energies of such a manager into the most productive directions.

- *If the company is experiencing poor financial results.* If there is a significant loss, or a trend in that direction, this serves as a wake-up call to management, which in turn results in the creation of a multitude of best practices projects. In this case, the situation may even go too far, with so many improvement projects going on at once that there are not enough resources to go around, resulting in the ultimate completion of few, if any, of the best practices.

- *If there is new management.* Most people who are newly installed as managers want to make changes in order to leave their marks on the organization. Though this can involve less effective best practice items like organizational changes or a new strategic direction, it is possible that there will be a renewed focus on efficiency that will result in the implementation of new best practices.

In short, as long as there is willingness by management to change and a good reason for doing so, then there is fertile ground for the implementation of a multitude of best practices.

Implementing Best Practices

The implementation of any best practice requires a great deal of careful planning. However, planning is not enough. The implementation process itself requires a number of key components in order to ensure a successful conclusion. This section discusses those components.

One of the first implementation steps for all but the simplest best practice improvements is to *study and flowchart the existing system* about to be improved. By doing so, one can ascertain any unusual requirements that are not readily apparent and that must be included in the planning for the upcoming implementation. Though some reengineering efforts do not spend much time on this task, on the grounds that the entire system is about to be replaced, the same issue still applies—there are usually special requirements, unique to any company, that must be addressed in a new system. Accordingly, nearly all implementation projects must include this critical step.

Another issue is the *cost-benefit analysis*. This is a compilation of all the costs required to both install and maintain a best practice, which is offset against the benefits of doing so. These costs must include project team payroll and related expenses, outside services, programming costs, training, travel, and capital expenditures. This step is worth a great deal of attention, for a wise manager will not undertake a new project, no matter how cutting-edge and high-profile it may be, if there is not a sound analysis in place that clearly shows the benefit of moving forward with it.

Yet another implementation issue is the *use of new technology*. Though there may be new devices or software on the market that can clearly improve the efficiency of a company's operations, and perhaps even make a demonstrative impact on a company's competitive situation, it still may be more prudent to wait until the technology has been tested in the marketplace for a short time before proceeding with an implementation. This is a particular problem if there is only one supplier available offering the technology, especially if that supplier is a small one or with inadequate funding, with the attendant risk of going out of business. In most cases, the prudent manager will elect to use technology that has proven itself in the marketplace, rather than using the most cutting-edge applications.

Of great importance to most best practice implementations is *system testing*. Any new application, unless it is astoundingly simple, carries with it the risk of failure. This risk must be tested repeatedly to ensure that it will not occur under actual use. The type of testing can take a variety of forms. One is volume testing, to ensure that a large number of employees using the system at the same time will not result in failure. Another is feature testing, in which sample transactions that test the boundaries of the possible information to be used are run through the system. Yet another possibility is recovery testing—bringing down a computer system suddenly to see how easy it is to restart the system. All of these approaches, or others, depending on the type of best practice, should be completed before unleashing a new application on employees.

One of the last implementation steps before firing up a new best practice is to *provide training* to employees in how to run the new system. This must be done as late as possible, since employee retention of this information will dwindle rapidly if not reinforced by actual practice. In addition, this training should be hands-on whenever possible, since employees retain the most information when training is conducted in this manner. It is important to identify in advance all possible users of a new system for training, since a few untrained employees can result in the failure of a new best practice.

A key element of any training class is procedures. These must be completed, reviewed, and made available for employee use not only at the time of training, but also at all times thereafter, which requires a good manager to oversee the procedure creation and distribution phases. Procedure writing is a special skill that may require the hiring of technical writers, interviewers, and systems analysts to ensure that procedures are properly crafted. The input of users into the accuracy of all procedures is also an integral step in this process.

Even after the new system has been installed, it is necessary to conduct a *postimplementation review*. This analysis determines if the cost savings or efficiency improvements are in the expected range, what problems arose during the implementation that should be avoided during future projects, and what issues are still unresolved from the current implementation. This last point is particularly important, for many managers do not follow through completely on all the stray implementation issues that inevitably arise after a new system is put in place. Only by carefully listing these issues and working through them will the employees using the new system be completely satisfied with how a best practice has been installed.

An issue that arises during all phases of a project implementation is *communications*. Since there may be a wide range of activities going on, many of them dependent on each other, it is important that the status of all project steps be continually communicated to the entire project team, as well as all affected employees. By doing so, a project manager can avoid such gaffes as having one task proceed without knowing that, due to changes elsewhere in the project, the entire task has been rendered unnecessary. These communications should not just be limited to project plan updates, but should also include all meeting minutes in which changes are decided on, documented, and approved by team leaders. By paying attention to this important item at every step of an implementation, the entire process will be completed much more smoothly.

As described in this section, a successful best practice implementation nearly always includes a review of the current system, a cost-benefit analysis, responsible use of new technology, system testing, training, and a postimplementation review, with a generous dash of communications at every step.

How to Use Best Practices: Best Practice Duplication

It can be a particularly difficult challenge to duplicate a successful best practice when opening a new company facility, especially if expansion is contemplated in many locations over a short time period. The difficulty with best practice duplication is that employees in the new locations are typically given a brief overview of a best practice and told to "go do it." Under this scenario, they have only a sketchy idea of what they are supposed to do, and so create a process that varies in some key details from the baseline situation. To make matters worse, managers at the new location may feel that they can create a better best practice from the start, and so create something that differs in key respects from the baseline. For both reasons, the incidence of best practice duplication failure is high.

To avoid these problems, a company should first be certain that it has accumulated all possible knowledge about a functioning best practice—the forms, policies, procedures, equipment, and special knowledge required to make it work properly—and then transfer this information into a concise document that can be shared with new locations. Second, a roving team of expert users must be commissioned to visit all new company locations and personally install the new systems, thereby ensuring that the proper level of experience with a best practice is brought to bear on a duplication activity. Finally, a company should transfer the practitioners of best practices to new locations on a semipermanent basis to ensure that the necessary knowledge required to make a best practice effective over the long term remains on site. By taking these steps, a company can increase its odds of spreading best practices throughout all of its locations.

A special issue is the tendency of a new company location to attempt to enhance a copied best practice at the earliest opportunity. This tendency frequently arises from the belief that one can always improve on something that was created elsewhere. However, these changes may negatively impact other parts of the company's systems, resulting in an overall reduction in performance. Consequently, it is better to insist that new locations duplicate a best practice in all respects and use it to match the performance levels of the baseline location before they are allowed to make any changes to it. By doing so, the new locations must take the time to fully utilize the best practice and learn its intricacies before they can modify it.

Why Best Practices Fail

There is a lengthy list of reasons why a best practice installation may not succeed, as noted in the following points. The various reasons for failure can be grouped into a relatively small cluster of primary reasons. The first is the lack of planning, which can include inadequate budgeting for time, money, or personnel. Another is the lack of cooperation by other entities, such as the programming staff or other departments that will be impacted by any changes. The final, and most important, problem is that there is little or no effort made to prepare the organization for change. This last item tends to build up over time as more and more best practices are implemented, eventually resulting in the total resistance by the organization to any further change. At its root, this problem involves a fundamental lack of communication, especially with those people who are most impacted by change. When a single implementation is completed without informing all employees of the change, this may be tolerated, but a continuous stream of them will encourage a revolt. In alphabetical order, the various causes of failure are:

- *Alterations to packaged software.* A very common cause of failure is that a best practice requires changes to a software package provided by a software supplier; after the changes are made, the company finds that the newest release of the software contains features that it must have and so it updates the software—wiping out the programming changes that were made to accommodate the best practice. This problem can also arise even if there is only a custom interface between the packaged software and some other application needed for a best practice, because a software upgrade may alter the data accessed through the interface.

Thus, alterations to packaged software are doomed to failure unless there is absolutely no way that the company will ever update the software package.

- *Custom programming.* A major cause of implementation failure is that the programming required to make it a reality either does not have the requested specifications, costs more than expected, arrives too late, is unreliable—or all of the above! Since many best practices are closely linked to the latest advances in technology, this is an increasingly common cause of failure. To keep from being a victim of programming problems, one should never attempt to implement the most "bleeding-edge" technology, because it is the most subject to failure. Instead, wait for some other company to work out all of the bugs and make it a reliable concept, and then proceed with the implementation. Also, it is useful to interview other people who have gone through a complete installation to see what tips they can give that will result in a smoother implementation. Finally, one should always interview any other employees who have had programming work done for them by the in-house staff. If the results of these previous efforts were not acceptable, it may be better to look outside the company for more competent programming assistance.

- *Inadequate preparation of the organization.* Communication is the key to a successful implementation. Alternatively, lack of communication keeps an organization from understanding what is happening; this increases the rumors about a project, builds resistance to it, and reduces the level of cooperation that people are likely to give it. Avoiding this effect requires a considerable amount of up-front communication about the intents and likely impacts of any project, with that communication targeted not just at the impacted managers, but also at all impacted employees, and to some extent even the corporation or department as a whole.

- *Intransigent personnel.* A major cause of failure is the employee who either refuses to use a best practice or who actively tries to sabotage it. This person may have a vested interest in using the old system, does not like change in general, or has a personality clash with someone on the implementation team. In any of these cases, the person must be won over through good communication (especially if the employee is in a controlling position) or removed to a position that has no impact on the project. If neither of these actions is successful, the project will almost certainly fail.

- *Lack of control points.* One of the best ways to maintain control over any project is to set up regular review meetings, as well as additional meetings to review the situation when preset milestone targets are reached. These meetings are designed to see how a project is progressing, to discuss any problems that have occurred or are anticipated, and to determine how current or potential problems can best be avoided. Without the benefit of these regular meetings, it is much more likely that unexpected problems will arise, or that existing ones will be exacerbated.

- *Lack of funding.* A project can be canceled either because it has a significant cost overrun exceeding the original funding request or because it was initiated without any funding request in the first place. Either approach results in failure. Besides the obvious platitude of "don't go over budget," the best way to avoid this problem is to build a cushion into the original funding request that should see the project through, barring any unusually large extra expenditures.

- *Lack of planning.* A critical aspect of any project is the planning that goes into it. If there is no plan, there is no way to determine the cost, number of employees, or time requirements, nor is there any formal review of the inherent project risks. Without this formal planning process, a project is very likely to hit a snag or be stopped cold at some point prior to its timely completion. On the contrary, using proper planning results in a smooth implementation process that builds a good reputation for the project manager and thereby leads to more funding for additional projects.

- *Lack of postimplementation review.* Though it is not a criterion for the successful implementation of any single project, a missing postimplementation review can cause the failure of later projects. For example, if such a review reveals that a project was completed despite the inadequate project planning skills of a specific manager, it might be best to use a different person in the future for new projects, thereby increasing his or her chances of success.

- *Lack of success in earlier efforts.* If a manager has a reputation for not successfully completing best practices projects, it becomes increasingly difficult to complete new ones. The problem is that no one believes a new effort will succeed and so there is little commitment to doing it. Also, upper management is much less willing to allocate funds to a manager who has not developed a proven track record for successful implementations. The best way out of this jam is to assign a different manager to an implementation project, someone with a proven track record of success.

- *Lack of testing.* A major problem for the implementation of especially large and complex projects, especially those involving programming, is that they are rushed into production without a thorough testing process to discover and correct all bugs that might interfere with or freeze the orderly conduct of work in the areas they are designed to improve. There is nothing more dangerous than to install a wonderful new system in a critical area of the company, only to see that critical function fail completely due to a problem that could have been discovered in a proper testing program. It is always worthwhile to build some extra time into a project budget for an adequate amount of testing.

- *Lack of top management support.* If a project requires a large amount of funding or the cooperation of multiple departments, it is critical to have the complete support of the top management team. If not, any required funding may not be allocated, while there is also a strong possibility that any objecting departments will be able to sidetrack it easily. This is an especially common problem when the project has no clear sponsor at all— without a senior-level manager to drive it, a project will sputter along and eventually fade away without coming anywhere near completion.

- *Relying on other departments.* As soon as another department's cooperation becomes a necessary component of a best practice installation, the chances of success drop markedly. The odds become even smaller if multiple departments are involved. The main reason is the involvement of an extra manager, who may not have as much commitment to making the implementation a success. In addition, the staff of the other department may influence their manager not to help out, while there may also be a problem with the other department not having a sufficient amount of funding to complete its share of the work. For example, an accounting department can benefit greatly if the warehouse is using cycle counting to keep inventory accuracy levels high, since there is no need for a physical inventory count. However, if the warehouse does not have the extra staff available to count inventory, the work will not be done, no matter how badly the accounting staff wants to implement this best practice.

- *Too many changes in a short time.* An organization will rebel against too much change if it is clustered into a short time frame. The reason is that change is unsettling, especially when it involves a large part of people's job descriptions, so that nearly everything they do is altered. This can result in direct employee resistance to further change, sabotaging new projects, a work slowdown, or (quite likely) the departure of the most disgruntled workers. This problem is best solved by planning for lapses between implementation projects to let the employees settle down. The best way to accomplish this lag between changes without really slowing down the overall schedule of implementation is to shift projects around within the department, so that no functional area is on the receiving end of two consecutive projects.

The primary reason for listing all of these causes of failure is not to discourage the reader from ever attempting a best practice installation. On the contrary, this allows one to prepare for and avoid all roadblocks on the path to ultimate implementation success.

Summary

This chapter has given an overview of the situations in which best practices implementations are most likely to succeed, what factors are most important to the success or failure of an implementation, and how to successfully create and follow through on an implementation project. By following the recommendations made, not only those regarding how to implement, but also those regarding what *not* to do, a manager will have a much higher chance of success. With this information in hand, one can now confidently peruse the remaining chapters, which are full of inventory best practices. The reader will be able to select those practices having the best chance of a successful implementation, based on the specific circumstances pertaining to each manager, such as the funding and time available, as well as any obstacles, such as entrenched employees or a corporate intransigence pertaining to new projects.

2

Inventory Purchasing

This chapter addresses those 23 purchasing best practices having a direct impact on inventory. As noted in Exhibit 2.1, the sequence of presented best practices begins with the involvement of suppliers and purchasing staff in the design of new products, then addresses the compression of supplier lead times, advances through the scheduling of inventory purchases, continues with a range of possible delivery best practices, and concludes with the minimization of the supplier base. In Exhibit 2.1, the implementation cost of each best practice is listed as one stack of dollars (inexpensive), two stacks (moderately expensive), and three stacks (very expensive). Also, in the exhibit, the installation time of each best practice is listed as one clock (short duration), two clocks (moderate duration), and three clocks (lengthy).

Different best practices will apply based on a company's usage of various manufacturing concepts. For example, if one is using a just-in-time manufacturing process, it is likely that kanbans (inventory move authorizations) are being used to notify suppliers of the need for more parts, so issuing purchase orders through a material requirements planning system is unnecessary. Similarly, comparing open purchase orders to current requirements is not necessary when supplier kanbans are used, or when a material requirements planning system is already automatically monitoring this information. Also, inbound split deliveries are redundant when a company has already convinced its suppliers to deliver many small shipments. Thus, the purchasing best practices noted here should be considered a buffet table of possible improvements, from which one should make selections based on the immediate needs of one's company.

11

Exhibit 2.1 *Summary of Inventory Purchasing Best Practices*

	Best Practice	Cost	Install Time
2.1	Include suppliers in the new product design process	💵	🕐🕐🕐
2.2	Avoid designing risky-procurement items into products	💵	🕐🕐
2.3	Reduce safety stock by shrinking supplier lead times	💵	🕐🕐🕐
2.4	Purchase supplier capacity	💵💵	🕐🕐
2.5	Reduce safety stocks by accelerating the flow of internal information	💵💵	🕐🕐
2.6	Buy from suppliers located close to the company	💵	🕐🕐🕐
2.7	Eliminate approvals of routine purchases	💵	🕐
2.8	Purchase based on material requirements planning	💵💵💵	🕐🕐🕐
2.9	Compare open purchase orders to current requirements	💵	🕐
2.10	Freeze the short-term production schedule	💵	🕐
2.11	Obtain direct links into customer inventory planning systems	💵💵	🕐🕐🕐
2.12	Require frequent deliveries of small quantities	💵	🕐🕐🕐
2.13	Arrange for inbound split deliveries	💵	🕐🕐
2.14	Arrange for phased deliveries	💵	🕐🕐
2.15	Adopt rolling schedules	💵	🕐🕐🕐
2.16	Adopt just-in-time purchasing	💵💵💵	🕐🕐🕐
2.17	Implement stockless purchasing	💵💵	🕐🕐🕐
2.18	Designate major suppliers as lead suppliers	💵	🕐🕐🕐
2.19	Single-source products	💵💵	🕐🕐🕐
2.20	Install a supplier rating system	💵💵	🕐🕐
2.21	Use long-term supplier relationships for strategic purchases	💵	🕐🕐🕐
2.22	Shift raw materials ownership to suppliers	💵	🕐🕐🕐
2.23	Flag changes impacting advance material requests	💵	🕐

2.1 Include Suppliers in the New Product Design Process

When the engineering staff finishes the design of a new product, it may be surprised to find that its estimated costs for some purchased components are much lower than what was actually incurred, that the materials designed into the product are not the lowest-cost alternatives, or that prices for the purchased parts subsequently increase for any number of reasons. All these issues result in a greater investment in raw materials inventory than was originally considered possible.

The solution is to actively involve suppliers in the design process. They have a level of expertise in the components they supply that the company cannot hope to match—knowledge about pricing fluctuations, imminent industrywide capacity problems, the introduction of new lower-cost materials, and design alternatives that can significantly reduce the cost of a new product. Supplier involvement does not mean an occasional contract regarding component pricing; it means direct involvement by a supplier representative in all stages of the design process.

Including suppliers in new product design work also means that the company is implicitly offering a considerable amount of new business to the supplier. Unless there is a major justifiable reason for doing so, a company cannot subsequently shift its purchases to a different supplier, or else no suppliers will waste their time in the company's design process. Also, the company must have a considerable level of trust in its suppliers, since knowledge of upcoming designs would be very helpful to competitors, and suppliers would now be in an excellent position to give them confidential information.

Cost: 💵   *Installation time:* ⚫ ⚫ ⚫

2.2 Avoid Designing Risky-Procurement Items into Products

Some product components can be purchased only from suppliers having a monopoly or near-monopoly of the market, while other components can be obtained only from parts of the world having difficult legal, exchange rate, or political problems. In both cases, obtaining the items can be either very expensive or impossible. For these items, the purchasing staff typically responds by stockpiling large quantities or entering into long-term contracts with suppliers that are typically very favorable to the suppliers. An added danger is that the company may be locked into minimum purchase levels under a supply contract that obligates it to significant purchases for many years.

A difficult best practice is to bring these components to the attention of the design engineers during the initial product design process, so they can design into the products alternative components or at least reduced quantities of them. By doing so, the company will be at much less risk of having to stockpile inventory or obtain the components at inflated prices. An added benefit of conducting this analysis during the product design phase is that the purchasing staff can spot new product components that will be difficult to procure, and act quickly to lock up supply sources before competitors arrive at the same conclusion.

In reality, this best practice will not apply to the majority of situations, since some components cannot be replaced. However, by bringing up the issue during every new product design, a company can constantly reevaluate the situation and eventually reduce its risk in this area.

Cost: *Installation time:*

2.3 Reduce Safety Stock by Shrinking Supplier Lead Times

A company goes to great lengths to reduce its internal lead times by a variety of just-in-time techniques, but it tends to accept the lead times handed to it by suppliers. These lead times frequently are not even based on the supplier's actual production capabilities, but are simply the lead times announced by the salesperson with whom a company deals. The result is excessively long lead times, which a company deals with by investing in excessively large safety stocks.

The purchasing department can shorten supplier lead times by including a reduced delivery time in its request for quotes. By specifying short lead times up front, a supplier realizes that this is an important criterion for a company, and must commit to it before there will even be any discussion of orders. This can have an added benefit for suppliers, since by being forced to revamp their internal processes to improve their lead times, they will now have a new basis on which to compete.

Sometimes an even simpler approach to reducing lead times may have a positive impact—specify the exact date *and time* of expected receipt on the purchase order. By making it clear that the company has a high expectation of receipt within a very narrow time frame, suppliers become more aware of the importance of this issue.

This best practice does not mean that one should force impossibly short lead times upon suppliers, just that lead time should be a prime focus of discussion with suppliers, rather than being blindly accepted by the company.

Cost: 💵   Installation time: ● ● ●

2.4 Purchase Supplier Capacity

When the purchasing department wants to buy items from a supplier, it must compete with the orders of the supplier's other customers. If the supplier already has a heavy backlog of other customer orders, it may be impossible to obtain materials in a timely manner. This is a particular problem when there are few suppliers of a given item, or if the company needs materials on an immediate basis. When this problem arises, a company will be faced with either paying a premium to have its order jumped ahead of other orders placed with the supplier, searching for and placing an order with some other supplier with whom the company is unfamiliar, or delaying its production until such time as a supplier delivery can be obtained.

The solution is to purchase supplier capacity. By guaranteeing a supplier payment for *all* production from a given machine or work center, a company no longer has to worry about obtaining key materials, while at the same time it can block other suppliers from obtaining that supplier capacity. The company no longer has to compete with orders placed by other customers of the supplier—it simply places orders directly into the work center that it essentially owns. Suppliers are usually more than happy to accept this arrangement, since they no longer have to worry about maximizing the capacity of their equipment. A company can also build into its contract for this service a clause to sell some of the capacity back to the supplier, who may occasionally need it for rush orders to its other customers, and which the company may not need, depending on variations in its demand.

An added benefit of this approach is that the quality of items produced by the supplier will rise, because it is using the same machines to produce the same items every time—there is no tolerance variation caused by the use of different machines throughout the supplier's facility. Along the same lines, company engineers can more easily assist the supplier with the improvement of its operations by concentrating their attention on the machines reserved for company use.

This best practice should be attempted only for the most crucial materials, and even then only the ones for which a reasonably steady demand can be predicted. Otherwise, a company may spend a great deal to reserve capacity that it rarely uses. Thus, it is *least* effective for low-volume, standard items.

Cost: *Installation time:*

2.5 Reduce Safety Stocks by Accelerating the Flow of Internal Information

A typical reordering scenario is for the warehouse manager to forward to the purchasing department a daily list of items requiring reordering. This goes by intercompany mail to the purchasing department, which places it in the department inbound work queue. After some time passes, the request reaches the top of the stack, and a purchasing person confirms the need for the item, obtains supervisory approval, and then mails a purchase order to a supplier. The total lag caused by all these activities and wait times can easily exceed a week; during this time, the inventory level continues to decline, possibly resulting in a stockout before the delivery arrives from the supplier. When this problem goes on for some time, the purchasing staff starts to lengthen the item lead times in its database, forcing the company to order sooner and sooner. The result is long lead times for many items, requiring extremely long time horizons for product forecasting, which becomes inherently more difficult when stretched further into the future.

To avoid longer lead times caused by internal communications problems, we must shrink the time required to notify suppliers of new purchasing requirements. This can involve a number of system improvements, such as having a computerized materials planning database automatically issue purchase orders to suppliers without human intervention, based on the production plan and existing stock levels, and transmitting the purchase orders by e-mail to avoid mail float. If such an advanced solution is not possible, then one can fax purchase orders to suppliers, require less supervisory approval of purchase orders, employ runners to move reorder requests more quickly within a company, and use extra staff to eliminate the queue of purchasing requests in the purchasing department.

The variety of improvement possibilities will require the active cooperation of the purchasing manager, since all the changes impact his or her area of responsibility. If there is resistance, then a senior manager must intervene to require implementation of the improvements.

Cost: 💵💵 *Installation time:* ⏺⏺

2.6 Buy from Suppliers Located Close to the Company

When a company purchases items from suppliers located far away, it is being billed by suppliers at the moment the inventory leaves their shipping docks, irrespective of how many days later the inventory arrives at the company. This means that the company has fewer days in which to use its available cash before payment is due. Also, given the considerable distances involved, the purchasing department typically orders in large quantities to reduce the transportation cost per unit shipped. This approach may reduce transport costs, but increases the company's inventory investment.

The solution is to see if purchasing only from local suppliers reduces the total supplier cost. This does not mean that all far-away suppliers must be immediately terminated, since some may have such an overwhelming cost advantage that any transport distance is worthwhile. However, by shifting to nearby suppliers, the purchasing staff has a much better chance of success in reducing order sizes and increasing the number of deliveries. The end result is a much lower investment in inventory.

The trouble with this best practice is that the best suppliers may be located far away, while local alternatives are not very good. This is a particular problem for small companies, which have no leverage over suppliers to force them to create local production or warehousing facilities. There is no good solution to this problem, unless the purchasing staff wants to work with local suppliers in an attempt to raise the quality of their deliveries.

Cost: 💵 *Installation time:* ⏺⏺⏺

2.7 Eliminate Approvals of Routine Purchases

Companies typically have a multitiered approval process for the purchase of fixed assets, which is a reasonable control, given the massive size of some of these purchases. However, it is not uncommon to see managers extend this control to a more inappropriate field—the purchase of standard inventory items. By doing so, lengthy delays can be built into the purchasing process, which increases the lead-time before a required item is received.

The only solution is to completely halt the approval of routine purchases of inventory items. In order to have managers feel that they still have control over purchases, one can certainly implement an occasional audit of routine purchases, or delve into the reasons for larger purchases after-the-fact, or (best of all) create a demand system demonstrably so accurate that there is no way an item not required by the manufacturing process could find its way into the purchasing system.

Managers can have a hard time letting go of their approval capability, so be prepared to settle for half measures, where some approvals are still required, until managers gradually become more confident of the system's ability to avoid improper purchases, and are willing to relinquish more control.

Cost: *Installation time:*

2.8 Purchase Based on Material Requirements Planning

In an unplanned environment, the purchasing staff is reduced to visiting the warehouse to visually determine what items are out of stock, as well as the production planning staff to find out what items will be manufactured in the near future. At most, the purchasers may have the benefit of a bill of materials, from which they can manually determine what items are needed for the manufacturing process, net of on-hand quantities, from which they can place orders for more items, typically with a generous dollop of extra items to cover any errors in the purchasing process. The result is consistent overordering of some items, paired with underordering of those parts the purchasers saw in stock but which were already spoken for by some other requirement.

The solution is material requirements planning (MRP), which has gradually evolved since the advent of computers into a sophisticated and reliable system for planning the purchase of parts (as well as a few other capabilities beyond the scope of this book). An MRP system multiplies the product quantities listed on the production schedule by the bill of materials for each item to produce a list of all component parts and subassemblies required for manufacture of the planned products. The MRP system then subtracts from this initial requirement list all on-hand components, less those components already reserved for other uses, plus all components already ordered but not received, to arrive at a list of items to be purchased. It then staggers the planned purchases, based on purchasing lead times stored in the item master file, to tell the purchasing staff exactly when to order components, and in what quantities. This is clearly a massive improvement over the manual calculations of the purchasing staff, eliminating many errors from the purchasing process.

MRP systems have come down substantially in price, with some low-end systems now available in the five-figure range. More sophisticated systems, especially those integrated into other company functions, still command million-dollar price tags, exclusive of implementation costs that can reach three to five times the cost of the initial software purchase.

The main problem with MRP systems is the old adage, "garbage in, garbage out." If the inventory records and bill of materials files are incorrect, the system will issue wildly inaccurate purchasing recommendations. Consequently, one should have 95 percent inventory record accuracy and 98 percent bill of materials accuracy prior to the installation of an MRP system, and ensure that these minimum accuracy levels are maintained in order to obtain accurate system output.

Cost: 💷 💷 💷   *Installation time:* ⬤ ⬤ ⬤

2.9 Compare Open Purchase Orders to Current Requirements

Between the time when a company issues a purchase order to a supplier and the date when the ordered items arrive, several problems may arise that render the original purchase order inaccurate. First, customer orders to the company may change, resulting in a modified production schedule that no longer requires certain parts from suppliers. Second, ongoing changes in the design of company products may render certain parts obsolete. Third, adjustments to recorded inventory balances through the cycle counting process may result in a need for fewer or more parts than are currently on order. For these reasons, by the date of their arrival, the amount of goods delivered by suppliers may vary significantly from a company's needs.

To alleviate this problem, one can design a report that should be run through the corporate materials planning system on a daily basis, comparing the amount of outstanding balances on open purchase orders to the company's needs, as listed in the material requirements portion of the company computer systems. A daily review of this report by the purchasing staff allows them to modify the amounts listed on open purchase orders, thereby resulting in an ongoing reduction in the amount of inventory kept on hand. This report is a standard part of any material requirements planning system, but must be created as a custom report for those companies without such a system.

Cost: *Installation time:*

2.10 Freeze the Short-Term Production Schedule

Even when a company uses an MRP system (see the previous best practice), it can suffer from recurring late supplier deliveries. The problem arises when the inventory planning staff changes the production schedule inside the lead times of purchased items or manufactured subassemblies, resulting in a scramble by the purchasing staff to obtain materials on exceedingly short notice. The reasoning behind these short-term changes is the perceived need to accept customer orders requiring immediate fulfillment.

The solution is for company management to authorize a complete freeze of the production schedule once it enters the period where a change can impact purchasing lead times. This will call for longer quoted delivery lead times for customers, which can impact customer perception of the company's service level. If this is a problem, managers should work with suppliers to reduce their lead times to the company, which in turn reduces the number of production schedule days that must be frozen.

Cost: *Installation time:*

2.11 Obtain Direct Links into Customer Inventory Planning Systems

The purchasing department usually places orders based on the requirements output by a material requirements planning (MRP) system. Though this output may appear to be precise, it is still driven by an estimate of what someone in the sales department thinks customers are most likely to purchase. Consequently, despite the appearance of a great deal of precision in the types and quantities of parts ordered, the purchasing staff's efforts may still result in excess inventory or shortages.

A solution is to actively pursue direct system linkages with the inventory planning systems of customers. By doing so, one can eliminate all estimates from the planning process and avoid considerable amounts of excess quantities for some inventory items and shortages for others.

The problem is getting customers to agree to reveal their demand information. This can be achieved by suggesting some type of shared cost savings, or by promising long-term fixed pricing, and so on—the inducement must be sufficient to attract the customer's attention, while at the same time not being too expensive for the company. Another approach is to offer the customer free software in which it can more easily place orders to the customer, which yields a less efficient manual linkage to the customer. Given the time required to achieve direct customer linkages, this best practice is usually cost-effective only for the largest customers.

Cost: *Installation time:*

2.12 Require Frequent Deliveries of Small Quantities

Suppliers like to ship in the largest possible quantities, so their delivery trucks can drop off the largest possible number of units in a single delivery. The result is not so efficient for the receiving company, which must store a larger quantity of items than it needs, invest in the extra inventory, and run the risk of never using some of it.

From the perspective of the buying company, a better approach is to order in small quantities and require frequent deliveries. In its most advanced form, a supplier can deliver several times a day, just enough to meet a company's immediate needs. This best practice is a difficult one to implement for the following reasons:

- *Too many accounting transactions.* Under a traditional accounting system, there is a separate invoice for every delivery, which requires authorization against a purchase order and receiving documentation. If frequent deliveries are implemented, the accounting staff will be crushed under a blizzard of paperwork. The solution can range from a single monthly invoice from the supplier to payments without an invoice, based on the number of items received in a given period.
- *Too much quality review time.* Frequent deliveries will not work if a quality assurance person must review every delivery. Instead, certify suppliers in advance to a quality standard, and move their deliveries straight to the production area without any review.
- *Too much receiving time.* The traditional approach is for the receiving staff to document the amount and type of each receipt when it arrives at the dock door. When there are many small deliveries, this is a great deal of work. Instead, they should accept deliveries from certified suppliers with no paperwork at all and backflush completed production to verify how many items must have been received.
- *Multiple deliveries cost too much.* If a company is charged by delivery, the freight cost is bound to increase. A solution is to obtain pricing by product weight instead of by delivery, or to have a large variety of items shipped in one delivery, rather than large quantities of just a few items.
- *The supplier refuses to deliver in small quantities.* This is the crux of the problem. Suppliers view many small deliveries as being a significant cost to them, and will resist. One alternative is to offer long-term demand for specific items with only modest fluctuation in unit volume, so suppliers have time to revise their delivery routes to be the most efficient under this scenario. This approach also eliminates the need for any planning or authorization of specific deliveries—a truck simply leaves the supplier location at a fixed time every day. Also, the supplier may be able to create a delivery route based on deliveries to the company that it can use to offer frequent deliveries to other customers.

The purchasing department should go out of its way to assist a supplier in working through these alternatives to arrive at the lowest-cost frequent delivery solution. If all these approaches do not work, a company may have to find a different supplier. This best practice may not work at all if a company's purchasing volume is too small, since suppliers will not see a viable reason to alter their delivery systems in order to accommodate a small customer.

Cost: 　　　　　　　　Installation time:

2.13 Arrange for Inbound Split Deliveries

Though the latest practices in inventory management dictate small delivery quantities from suppliers, this results in a higher delivery cost to the supplier, as well as much more frequent monitoring of company purchasing requirements. Suppliers are especially wary of such arrangements when the company issues a separate purchase order for each delivery made, since they have no assurance of repeat orders.

A possible solution is to issue a large purchase order for a fixed purchase quantity, but to have the order split into a number of deliveries. By doing so, the supplier gains a commitment to a large order, thereby making it more worthwhile to make frequent deliveries to the customer, while the customer can frequently obtain reduced per-unit pricing as well as more frequent deliveries. The company also gains by greatly reducing the quantity of purchase orders issued. The primary downside is the company's commitment to a large order quantity, so it needs to either have a rock-solid sales funnel that can absorb the inventory commitment or an escape clause built into the purchase order. Such a clause will likely require a termination payment to the supplier to cover the supplier's fixed costs related to the order, and possibly some portion of its lost profit, too.

Cost: 　　　　　　　　Installation time:

2.14 Arrange for Phased Deliveries

When a company places an order, the supplier sometimes imposes a minimum order quantity that may exceed the company's immediate needs, resulting in an investment in excess inventory when the entire minimum quantity is delivered.

Though the supplier may impose a minimum *order* quantity, it may be possible to negotiate for a smaller *delivery* quantity, so that smaller quantities are delivered more frequently. This concept works best when the supplier delivers numerous items to the supplier and can still make the same number of delivery runs—just with smaller quantities of more items in each delivery. This best practice differs from the preceding "Inbound Split Deliveries" concept in that there is no attempt to make a long-term purchasing commitment to obtain lower per-unit prices. This concept works best for high-turnover items requiring constant replenishment.

Cost: 　　　Installation time:

2.15 Adopt Rolling Schedules

As noted for Best Practice 2.13, "Inbound Split Deliveries," suppliers are unwilling to depart from a commitment to a fixed purchase quantity, since they can in turn arrange for specific quantities of their own materials, as well as production capacity, to ensure that they can turn a profit on a business arrangement. Nonetheless, a company deals with considerable uncertainty in committing to long-term fixed prices and quantities that may result in losses.

An alternative to the inbound split delivery best practice that addresses some aspects of the long-term commitment problem is the use of rolling schedules. Under this approach, the company and its supplier enter into a long-term supply agreement, but the company's forecast is updated on a rolling basis within certain min-max boundaries. By doing so, the company can still commit to approximate purchasing levels over the long term, while more closely tailoring its purchases to actual demand. The supplier still obtains a purchasing commitment within min-max boundaries, allowing it to commit to the purchase of materials and allocation of sufficient production capacity. This approach works well for high-usage items that are reordered frequently.

An added benefit is that the company can assume the same quantities will be ordered in the next forecast period by taking no action at all. Under this scenario, the company's purchasing staff does nothing—creates no purchase order or similar paperwork—if the intent is to continue the existing forecast. By doing so, the company's purchasing work is reduced.

One should be aware of the following issues when using the rolling schedule approach:

- Suppliers will be insistent on the establishment of at least a minimum purchase commitment over a fixed time frame, thereby compensating them if the company suddenly experiences a major decline in its requirements for the items in question. A company will likely have to agree to such a minimum commitment in order to attract a high-quality supplier.

- When using a rolling schedule, the company must be careful not to adjust the rolling forecast by too much, or too frequently, because this jerky approach to ordering will be reflected in the supplier's production schedule, making it much more difficult for the supplier to efficiently fill orders.

- The rolling schedule is better than a fixed long-term commitment to a specific amount, but scheduled purchases can still vary considerably from actual usage, depending on the reliability of the company's own demand forecasts.

Cost: *Installation time:*

2.16   Adopt Just-in-Time Purchasing

Though the rolling schedule is an improvement over setting fixed purchasing commitments, it still leaves a company open to the risk of being required to purchase more than it needs in a given time period, resulting in an excessive inventory investment. The core problem is the company's reliance on a demand forecast, which inherently introduces a risk of demand inaccuracy based on the perceptions of the people creating the forecast.

The only way to eliminate inventory fluctuations based on an inaccurate forecast is to eliminate the forecast. This requires the complete reorientation of the purchasing (and manufacturing) system from one that pushes materials through the production process based on a forecast, to one that pulls items from production based on actual customer orders. Under this demand-pull approach, when a new customer order is received, the manufacturing operation is authorized to build exactly enough units to fill the order, which in turn requires an order to a supplier for the exact amount of materials needed to fill the company's purchasing requirement.

This is an extremely difficult best practice to implement, even if the difficulties of manufacturing to the demand-pull methodology are overcome. Suppliers simply do not like it. It requires a constant flow of small-quantity deliveries to the company, at a high level of quality, and minimal paperwork. This concept is addressed further in the following best practice.

Cost: 💵 💵 💵   ***Installation time:*** ⬤ ⬤ ⬤

2.17 Implement Stockless Purchasing

An incoming component delivery from a supplier must survive a gauntlet before reaching the shop floor for inclusion in a finished product—a quality review, putaway in a rack, picking, and forwarding to the shop floor. At any point in this process, an incorrect transaction entry could make the controlling computer system think the delivery has disappeared, while the large amount of handling involved could damage the components.

Wouldn't it be simpler for components to be delivered directly to the shop floor by suppliers, thereby eliminating the entire list of delaying activities just noted? By doing so, all the fixed costs associated with warehousing are also eliminated. However, this is an advanced best practice requiring the completion of the following activities prior to its implementation:

- *Certify supplier quality levels.* It makes no sense for suppliers to deliver shoddy goods directly to the production department, so every supplier's production process must be certified in advance.
- *Communicate materials needs to suppliers.* Suppliers need to know exactly when materials are needed, so the company must find a way to communicate this information to them. A sound approach is to allow them online access into the company's materials planning database.
- *Alter the accounts payable process.* If suppliers bypass the receiving department, there will be no receiving documents from which to authorize

a payment. Instead, the accounts payable staff must be trained to make payments based on scheduled deliveries, as shown in the materials planning system.

- *Arrange for limited storage facilities near the production process.* If there is no room for inventory near the production department, the area will be choked with inventory deliveries. It is better to arrange for sufficient inventory storage in strategic locations, and show suppliers exactly where their deliveries are to be made.

- *Arrange for small, frequent supplier deliveries.* Storage near the production floor is likely to be limited, so suppliers must be able to make small-quantity deliveries to avoid overburdening the storage areas. This will call for frequent deliveries in order to avoid stockouts.

One must first address all five of the items just noted before stockless purchasing can be successfully implemented, so the implementation period can be quite long. Also, some suppliers will never pass the quality certification process, which requires their replacement with better suppliers or a more limited receiving function to handle their deliveries.

Cost: 💵💵   *Installation time:* ●●●

2.18 Designate Major Suppliers as Lead Suppliers

Despite its best efforts to reduce the number of suppliers used, the purchasing staff may find itself overwhelmed by the level of work needed to coordinate the deliveries of a large number of suppliers. This inadequate level of communication typically results in late or incorrect deliveries, which have a major negative impact on the ability of the production department to manufacture products on time. The materials management staff may counter this problem by keeping excess levels of raw materials on hand to protect against shortfalls.

One solution is to designate key suppliers as the lead suppliers for selected major subassemblies. These lead suppliers take the key role in creating subassemblies, which means the coordination of work by many suppliers who contract with the lead suppliers. The company's purchasing staff now has a much smaller group of suppliers to deal with, while the lead suppliers are typically eager to take on the extra work in order to garner a greater share of the company's purchases. A common added result is for the company to shift more assembly work to the best lead suppliers, so that only the final assembly is conducted by the company, thereby reducing the complexity of its production operations.

There are two problems with this approach. First, lead suppliers are in a position to demand a larger profit in exchange for their efforts, though the company can contractually lock in prices for long periods. When this happens, the lead suppliers can still improve their profits at the expense of lower-tier suppliers. The second problem is the sudden departure of a lead supplier due to bankruptcy or some dispute with the company. Given the considerable importance of a lead supplier to company operations, this can have a major negative impact on the company's ability to match its production to customer demands.

Cost: 　　　　　Installation time: 　

2.19 Single-Source Products

The purchasing department likes to use multiple suppliers for parts, because it can not only play one supplier off against another for the lowest price, but also ensure a backup source if the primary supplier is unable to ship items to the company on time or ships items having substandard quality. However, an undue focus on the lowest price tends to result in lower-quality goods or degraded service from suppliers, while the purchasing staff must also deal with extra suppliers and buy in lower quantities, which tends to yield higher per-unit supplier prices. Further, it is more difficult for the receiving staff to identify the same items coming from different suppliers, due to differences in packaging.

For all these reasons, it is frequently better to trade off a modest price increase in favor of higher quality, improved shipment reliability, and consistently identifiable packaging from suppliers. In particular, the purchasing staff will find itself using far less paperwork to place orders when it can concentrate all orders for a specific commodity with a single supplier. Multiple-supplier sourcing may still be required for key components where supplier reliability is suspect, but this is still a reliable best practice to pursue for the bulk of all items. A side benefit of single sourcing is a reduction in the amount of supplier management time, since there are fewer of them (and fewer contracts) to deal with. Also, a supplier receiving a higher volume of company business will be more inclined to accept a request for frequent deliveries of small order sizes, which was discussed earlier in this chapter as Best Practice 2.12. Further, if there is a quality problem with an item, there is no question about determining which supplier delivered it, since there is only one supplier for each item. And finally, the development of long-term relationships with a small number of suppliers can result in other benefits, such as joint product development programs and the sharing of cost-saving ideas that can benefit all parties.

Single sourcing works best when the merged level of company demand results in significantly higher purchasing volumes being offered to suppliers, since they become much more willing to work with the company to achieve its inventory goals. Conversely, very small companies will find themselves with little additional sway over their remaining suppliers, since they do not buy in large enough quantities. Also, if there is a significant risk that a supplier will go out of business, a secondary supplier must be used to ensure a steady flow of materials.

Companies implementing this best practice should devise a supplier rating system based on such items as the percentage of on-time deliveries, quality, and price in order to determine which suppliers to retain (see the next best practice).

Cost: 💵 💵   *Installation time:* ⬤ ⬤ ⬤

2.20 Install a Supplier Rating System

Suppliers will not deliver items with better quality, in smaller quantities, or more frequently unless there is an excellent reason for doing so. Their cooperation is especially unlikely without any financial inducement, since they only see more demands from the company without any corresponding increase in their own profits.

A supplier rating system is the answer, since it allows a company to determine which suppliers it really wants to use, resulting in the direction of more purchase orders to those suppliers, giving them more volume and therefore more profits. By creating a rating system and making its results available to suppliers, there will be no question about problem areas that suppliers need to address. If the company also makes it clear that it intends to single-source components from suppliers, those suppliers wanting to increase their order volume from the company will use the supplier rating system as a competitive tool to hoist themselves above other suppliers and take away their business.

The components of a supplier rating system are unique to a specific company's needs. In general, it will rank suppliers on their ability to deliver within designated time frames and to deliver correct quantities, and on the level of their product quality. Product pricing is also a component of the rating system, but tends to be weighted rather low on the scale. There will typically be additional "yes or no" ratings, such as the willingness of a supplier to alter its packaging to include bar coding for the company's receiving system. A possible outcome of a supplier rating system is, at the lowest level, a list of approved suppliers who can be used occasionally, but whose deliveries require complete inspection. At a higher level, the qualified supplier list signifies those suppliers who get preferential treatment for orders, and whose deliveries require only reduced quality reviews. The highest level of supplier rating is for certified vendors, who receive absolute priority for orders, and whose deliveries can flow straight through to the production area.

A supplier rating system can require a considerable amount of staff time, as well as its own database. Someone must accumulate information for the rating system, or alter the existing company systems to automatically extract the required data. Suppliers must be kept up-to-date on their ratings, perhaps with a periodic report card or access to a company Web site on which this information is posted. Further, there will be problems with some suppliers claiming that their rankings are incorrect or unfair, especially if they are dropped from the certified supplier list. Thus there needs to be a considerable commitment to the concept of a supplier rating system to make it a success.

Cost: 💸 💸 *Installation time:* ⬤ ⬤ ⬤

2.21 Use Long-Term Supplier Relationships for Strategic Purchases

Many companies' products include a few purchased items that are of high value relative to the entire product cost, and which are available only from a small number of suppliers. If the company treats these suppliers with indifference, it will not be accorded special treatment when rush deliveries are needed, nor will it gain cooperation from the suppliers in designing new products, obtaining price breaks, or for smaller delivery quantities. In short, these key suppliers will treat the company the same way it is treating them.

The solution is for the purchasing staff to spend a considerable amount of time building up long-term relationships with these suppliers. This will likely require repeated trips to the supplier premises, possibly involving people from other functional areas of the company (right up to the CEO). A long-term purchasing agreement may also be necessary, covering such topics as continuous improvement targets, problem resolution procedures, ownership of jointly developed products, and expected product quality levels. Of more importance is sharing the company's production schedule with the supplier to ensure good demand visibility, and possibly the supplier's involvement in new product development. In cases where an extremely tight long-term arrangement is desired, one can even consider swapping shares in each other's companies to ensure mutual ownership. This approach will gradually change the structure and purpose of the purchasing department from that of a transaction processor to a relationship builder. The end result of these changes will be such tight supplier relations that a company will be assured of a steady stream of purchased parts when it needs them.

This greatly expanded level of communication will tax the purchasing staff's time, so this level of relationship building can be achieved only if a small number of carefully selected suppliers are involved. The approach should certainly not be used for more than one company per commodity.

Cost: *Installation time:*

2.22   Shift Raw Materials Ownership to Suppliers

The raw materials portion of a company's inventory can consume a major part of its working capital investment, money that could otherwise be used for other activities. Also, the occasional purchase of excessive quantities of stock will eventually result in a large proportion of the inventory being obsolete. Further, a number of nonvalue-added transactions are required to track this inventory. These issues can have a negative impact on profits.

One way to mitigate the adverse effect of raw materials inventory is to shift its ownership to suppliers. Under this scenario, suppliers deliver goods to the company in whatever quantities they want above a designated minimum, as long as they do not exceed the physical storage area set aside for their use. The company logs these items out of the storage area when it uses them and pays the supplier for the amounts used. This has the obvious impact of eliminating a company's investment in raw materials, and shifts the burden of obsolescence to the supplier. In exchange, the supplier obtains a single-source contract with the company, ensuring itself of sales for at least one year and possibly for several, and using a pricing schedule that both parties have agreed to in advance. In addition, the supplier can park extra inventory at the customer location, thereby avoiding the cost of any just-in-time deliveries. This approach has the added transactional impact of eliminating all purchase orders to the supplier, as well as all receiving transactions and cycle counts, while the supplier can avoid making a large number of just-in-time deliveries to the company.

A variation on this approach is for the supplier to store inventory intended for a customer in a warehouse located close to the customer. The supplier controls this warehouse, but the customer is responsible for sending pick requests to it, which the supplier's warehouse staff fulfills. The warehouse staff then sends the completed pick request form to the supplier's accounting department, which bills the customer for the delivery.

Whatever the exact type of vendor-managed inventory plan, both parties should enter into a formal contract that clearly specifies the rights and responsibilities of each party. In particular, the contract should note the duration of the agreement and how the parties can dissolve it, as well as how the supplier is to bill the customer—identifying specific prices and the point in the transaction flow when invoices are to be issued. The contract should also note the replenishment schedule, and how the parties are to communicate inventory requirements and fulfillment information. Further, it should clearly describe the responsibility of the customer for supplying forecasting information to the supplier, and who is responsible for the cost of excess inventory if the customer's actual product usage turns out to be less than originally forecasted.

Unfortunately, there are several problems with this best practice that limit its practical application. First, it is generally limited to nearby suppliers who can regularly monitor stock levels at the company location (though this can be resolved through the use of the just-noted adjacent warehouse).

Second, the company must be willing to share its material requirements information with suppliers (though an unusual benefit of this approach is that suppliers can see actual demand rather than planned consumption, which eliminates any planning inaccuracies). Third, the company must be willing to sole-source large portions of its inventory. Fourth, any custom parts made or obtained by the supplier will ultimately be paid for by the company, even if it never uses them, since the supplier has no other means for liquidating the stock. Fifth, the company must be responsible for any inventory discrepancies, since these problems typically arise through the lack of knowledge of inventory-tracking procedures by its own staff. Sixth and perhaps most commonly, suppliers tend to resist this best practice on the grounds that they will incur a greater proportion of the expenses. This last issue can be partially resolved by having the customer pay for all setup costs incurred by the supplier and by contractually promising to pay for inventory not used, but suppliers may still feel that they must retain a large amount of expensive buffer stock. Within these restrictions, many companies with large raw material inventories will find that the prospective elimination of at least some of their investment in inventory is well worth the effort.

Cost:　　　　　　*Installation time:*

2.23 Flag Changes Impacting Advance Material Requests

The purchasing department must sometimes purchase items in advance of finalization of a new product design, because the lead times are so long. This practice enables a company to meet aggressive delivery targets, which is important in industries where products have extremely short life cycles. However, if the engineering department alters the product specifications after an advance material request has been made, the purchasing department has no way of knowing that goods will be eventually received that can no longer be fitted into the final product, causing an excess inventory investment that may have to be written off or at least liquidated at a loss.

Several best practices can be used to avoid the risk of "hanging" advance material requests. One is to flag all components included in the preliminary product's bill of materials that require advance material requests. By doing so, any change to a flagged component will result in immediate notification by the computer system to both the purchasing and engineering departments of the prospective change. However, this approach nearly always requires customized programming of the bill of materials software.

An alternative is to assign a purchasing department representative to the product design team who is aware of all outstanding advance material requests, and who can manually flag any product design changes that will impact the advance requests. This approach is expensive, especially if the purchasing department representative is being added to the design team for only this one purpose.

One can also have the purchasing department regularly issue a list of all advance material requests to all design teams. Though this is an easily scheduled and low-cost alternative, it is still up to someone on each of the design teams to regularly compare the report to recent design changes and notify the design team manager of problems.

Cost: *Installation time:*

3

Inventory Receiving and Shipping

This chapter addresses those 17 receiving and shipping best practices having a direct impact on inventory. As noted in Exhibit 3.1, it begins with the control of inbound materials, continues with the enhanced collection and entry of receiving information, and addresses the use of faster put-away techniques. Further, the chapter covers dock assignments to reduce material travel times within the factory, shipping using returnable cartons as well as dunnage bags to protect inventory, and several accounting issues related to the shipping function.

These best practices address a broad spectrum of receiving and shipping capabilities. For example, only an advanced just-in-time facility is likely to completely eliminate the receiving function or require supplier deliveries directly into the production area. However, many of the best practices can be implemented in less advanced environments, such as rejecting unplanned receipts, directly entering receipts into the computer system, and tracking shipper performance. Only two of the best practices require the use of advanced computer systems—a warehouse management system to assign dock doors (though this can be done manually in smaller environments) and a complete overhaul of the receiving computer system for payments based on receiving approval only. Others call for smaller levels of automation, such as automatically collecting cube and weight information. In general, the bulk of these best practices require more time than money to implement.

Exhibit 3.1 *Summary of Inventory Receiving and Shipping Best Practices*

	Best Practice	Cost	Install Time
3.1	Reject unplanned receipts	💰	🕐
3.2	Obtain advance shipping notices for inbound deliveries	💰	🕐🕐
3.3	Directly enter receipts into computer	💰	🕐
3.4	Automatically collect inbound and outbound cube and weight information	💰💰	🕐🕐
3.5	Repackage incoming items into increments ordered by customers	💰	🕐
3.6	Put away items immediately after receipt	💰💰	🕐🕐
3.7	Stage received goods for zone putaways	💰💰	🕐🕐
3.8	Eliminate the receiving function	💰💰	🕐🕐🕐
3.9	Combine the shipping and receiving functions in one area	💰	🕐🕐
3.10	Assign docks based on minimum warehouse travel time	💰💰💰	🕐🕐
3.11	Require supplier deliveries with open-sided trucks directly to production	💰💰	🕐🕐
3.12	Ship using returnable wheeled containers	💰💰	🕐🕐
3.13	Use dunnage bags to cushion outbound shipments	💰	🕐
3.14	Use shippers with the most consistent delivery performance	💰	🕐🕐
3.15	Have delivery person deliver the invoice	💰	🕐🕐
3.16	Pay suppliers based on receiving approval only	💰💰💰	🕐🕐🕐
3.17	Provide pending shipment information to the collections staff	💰	🕐

3.1 Reject Unplanned Receipts

The ideal receiving scenario is when the supplier sends a message to a company's receiving department, telling it that a shipment is on its way, what is in the shipment, and when it is expected to arrive. By doing so, the receiving staff is prepared in advance to properly log in the received item and disposition it in an orderly manner. Reality is usually a tad less efficient. Unplanned and unidentified receipts can arrive at any time, requiring the receiving staff to set them to one side for eventual identification, log-in, and disposition, which can take days and interfere with the orderly running of the receiving area. Delays can be especially long when the receiving staff has no idea who ordered something, and must conduct a Sherlock Holmes–style investigation throughout the company to identify an item's owner. Due to this delay, suppliers are more likely to encounter payment delays, while the production staff finds that necessary items are hidden amid the stack of unidentified items at the receiving dock, thereby interfering with the manufacturing process. Further, fraudulent deliveries can be received (and then billed to the company) without the company having any idea of the problem for some time, since there is no policy to reject unplanned receipts.

These problems can be overcome through the rigorous rejection of all unplanned receipts. By doing so, the receiving staff has no backlog of receipt identifications to labor through, nor is it subjected to unexpected deliveries it may have no available labor to handle.

Though this best practice sounds simple, it is extremely difficult to implement. Success in this area requires training the entire organization to understand that only authorized purchases coming through the purchasing department will be allowed at the receiving dock. This means that a purchase order number must be assigned to every single item shipped to the company; if there is no number in evidence, the item is rejected. This is a hard lesson to learn when a rush order arrives and is rejected, potentially causing significant short-term problems in a variety of departments. Nonetheless, only a hard commitment to the rejection of unplanned receipts, coupled with strong support by senior management, can achieve this best practice. It is also easy for a company to suffer a collective relapse in this area, so management must support it consistently over the long term.

Cost: *Installation time:*

3.2 Obtain Advance Shipping Notices for Inbound Deliveries

There is a great deal of in-house activity surrounding the receipt of goods, including possible cross-docking of received items to an outbound truck, the availability of dock doors, clearing of staging space, and arranging for prompt quality assurance reviews. This is especially difficult if the warehouse manager is not aware of the exact arrival time of inbound deliveries, resulting in a bedlam of unplanned activity when a delivery arrives. Given the difficulty of planning operations against uncertain delivery arrival times, there is an inherent level of inefficiency in the receiving operation.

A good approach for introducing more planning into the receiving function is to arrange for the receipt of advance shipping notices from the inbound freight carrier. This best practice is easiest to implement with the larger third-party freight haulers, several of whom have created onboard tracking systems that monitor their progress and make this information available to customers, either by telephone, proprietary network, or the Internet (mostly the last approach). If freight is not arriving by such a carrier, one can also arrange to have the supplier contact the company by any number of communication media to notify it of the approximate arrival time of a load, as well as the contents of that load. It is also possible to obtain system-to-system transparency of this information through the use of automated electronic data interchange (EDI) transactions, but this approach is moderately expensive to set up, and so is normally used only between frequent trading partners.

The downside to this best practice is the difficulty of having minor suppliers adhere to it. They tend to arrive at unscheduled times, clogging dock doors needed for scheduled arrivals. One can mitigate this problem by leaving a small number of outlying dock doors available for the use of these suppliers, or by gradually eliminating them with the cooperation of the purchasing department. Another issue is the use of third-party freight carriers by suppliers that do not offer advance shipping notice services; the purchasing department should demand the use of specific freight carriers when it places a purchase order, thereby controlling this problem.

Cost: 　　　　　　　*Installation time:*

3.3 Directly Enter Receipts into Computer

One portion of the accounts payable matching process is to physically match some evidence of receipt, usually a packing slip or bill of lading, to a supplier invoice, thereby proving that the goods being paid for were actually received. The receiving documentation usually wends its way to the accounts payable staff over a period of several days, and may be lost on the way. Once it arrives, the information may not agree with the quantities being billed by the supplier. Consequently, the matching of receiving documentation tends to be either delayed, missing, or cause for extra reconciliation work by the accounting staff.

A simple alternative approach is to enter receipts directly into the computer system at the receiving dock, rather than forwarding any receiving documentation to the accounting department. This approach has the advantage of instant communication of receipts to the accounting staff, since an entry into the accounting database at the receiving dock will be instantly transmitted to the accounting staff. The accounting software can then compare received amounts to the purchase order (which is usually entered into the computer already). All that is left for the accounting staff to do at this point is to enter the purchase order number listed on the supplier's invoice into the computer to see what quantity has been received and how much has not yet been paid. By taking this approach, the bulk of the accounts payable matching process is eliminated.

Before implementing this best practice, there are a few issues to review. One is that the receiving staff must be properly trained in how to enter receipts into the computer. If they are not, receipts information will be inaccurate, probably resulting in the accounts payable staff going back to manual matching, since it is the only way to ensure that invoices are accurately paid. Another issue is ensuring that the existing accounting software allows the receiving personnel to enter receipts information. This is a standard feature on most accounting software packages. However, some packages do not use the information once it is entered, so it is important to see if the software will match receipts to purchase orders, showing any variances that may arise. If these issues can be overcome, then it is reasonable for companies of any size or complexity to implement the direct entry of receiving information into the computer at the receiving dock.

Cost: 🖻   *Installation time:* 🌢

3.4 Automatically Collect Inbound and Outbound Cube and Weight Information

When items are received, the putaway staff either guesses at its weight and cubic dimensions, or spends time manually doing so. In the first case, items may be put away in racks or bins with excess room, while the second case simply requires more staff time. Similar problems arise when finished products are being shipped—the shipping staff must manually weigh and measure items for shipment planning and the freight manifest, which requires a considerable amount of time.

The answer can be found at www.cubiscan.com. A variety of Cubiscan products, made by Quantronix, automatically weigh and measure any item. Smaller Cubiscan units are limited to items with small dimensions and weights, but are portable, and so can be used throughout the warehouse. Larger Cubiscan versions can correctly measure large quantities of items at a high rate by using a conveyor system. The devices measure dimensions with ultrasonic and infrared beams, while weighing with either load cells or deck scales. Measurements can be uploaded to a warehouse management system for inclusion in the inventory database.

Cost: 　　　　　　　　　*Installation time:*

3.5 Repackage Incoming Items into Increments Ordered by Customers

When items arrive at the receiving dock, it is customary for the putaway crew to pick up an entire pallet load and drop it straight into a bin somewhere in the warehouse. Though this is an efficient putaway, it does not address the efficiency of downstream activities, such as breaking down the pallet to extract quantities ordered by customers, repackaging the order for shipment, and delivering it. These additional activities tend to be much less efficient, since the company is no longer dealing with full pallet loads. Also, all the repackaging work contributes to a longer interval before a delivery can be sent to a customer.

A good solution is to repackage incoming items into the increments most commonly ordered by customers, and *then* storing them in the warehouse. The first step is to encourage customer ordering of specific quantities, typically through the use of price breaks for certain quantities; an alternative is to simply not allow orders in anything but preset quantities. Then, ask suppliers to prepackage their deliveries to the company into those increments, thereby shifting the repackaging burden away from the warehouse. If this approach does not work, have the receiving crew do the repackaging work as soon as an item is received. By handling repackaging up front, there is much less work to do when a customer order is actually received, thereby increasing the speed with which orders can be filled.

The main problem with doing repackaging prior to putaway is the possibility of less efficient storage. For example, if pallet loads are broken down into quarterloads, one must either stack the loads vertically (requiring sturdy product cases) or adjacent to each other, which can substantially reduce storage density. If each partial pallet load is situated on a separate pallet, this means that the much larger number of pallets being used will increase the amount of "dead space" in the racks. Though there will be less storage space available with this best practice, one can reconfigure rack heights to eliminate some unused space, thereby reducing lost storage density to some extent. One should compare improvements in speed of filling customer orders to the loss in warehouse storage density to see if this best practice makes sense. Usually, it is most cost-effective in situations where there is already excess storage space available.

Cost: 　　　　　Installation time:

3.6 Put Away Items Immediately After Receipt

It is customary to shift goods from the receiving dock to a staging and/or quality review area from which items are eventually pulled for putaway, once there is sufficient staff time available to do so. The trouble is that items tend to build up in the staging area, which can create a considerable mess if multiple inbound deliveries build up prior to being put away. This results not only in confusion in the staging area, but also in slowdown in cross-docking, late deliveries to the shop floor for manufacturing purposes, and potential stockouts in the picking areas.

A good best practice to resolve these problems is the enforcement of a policy to put away items immediately following receipt, preferably into primary storage locations. By doing so, a company saves space by eliminating its staging areas. It also ensures that items are available for picking into job or customer orders as soon as possible, while cross-docking can be accomplished as efficiently as possible. At an advanced level, a warehouse management system can even send instructions to a putaway person's wireless terminal, noting exactly where the received item is to be stored in the warehouse in accordance with preset criteria for optimal storage efficiency.

Of course, there are a few problems with implementation, or everyone would use this best practice. First, incoming items must meet a minimum quality standard in order to avoid a quality assurance review, which calls for the preexistence of a supplier quality program. Second, there must be sufficient early notice of inbound deliveries, so the warehouse manager can have enough putaway staff available to immediately put away all received items, which requires an advance shipping notice system with suppliers, third-party delivery services, or both. Third, there should be either a barcode scanning or radio frequency identification system in place for all received items, so the putaway staff can log in receipts and putaway locations with the minimum amount of transactional activity; this also takes care of any receipt logging for the accounting department, which needs this information to approve payments to suppliers. Consequently, a fast putaway requires the existence of several other systems before it can be properly implemented.

Cost: 💵 💵   *Installation time:* ● ●

3.7 Stage Received Goods for Zone Putaways

As just noted, the most efficient approach for the putaway of received items is to shift it from the receiving dock directly to primary storage locations. However, as also noted, a number of other systems must also be in place before this best practice will work properly. Consequently, many organizations will still be stuck with a large staging area filled with received items. Is there any lesser best practice that will still improve the efficiency of the putaway function?

Yes. One can sort the staged items by putaway zone. If there is going to be staged inventory, it might as well be in some sort of order. There are several ways to implement this best practice. The easiest is to manually reshuffle the staging area. If there are already items in the staging area, this approach can be cumbersome, and involves considerable labor. A slightly more automated approach is to set up several portable conveyors at a dock door, each one leading to a separate staging area representing a different putaway zone; the receiving staff then places items on the correct conveyor for a specific putaway zone. This approach requires knowledge of putaway zones by the receiving staff, which could be a bit much to ask if there are thousands of items in the warehouse. However, if warehouse management knows about the inbound delivery before its arrival, managers can determine the contents of the delivery and warn the receiving staff in advance of which items are to be placed in a specific staging area.

Cost:　　　　　　　　　*Installation time:*

3.8 Eliminate the Receiving Function

The receiving function is responsible for entering inventory receipts into the computer system, and occasionally does not do a good job in this capacity. For example, the late or inaccurate data entry of receiving information can lead to inaccurate financial statements, as well as inaccurate information for the production planning and purchasing staffs to procure and assemble materials for the production department to use.

The solution is to eliminate the function. This is an extremely difficult best practice to implement. The concept that only a relatively small number of companies have fully implemented is to fully qualify suppliers in terms of their ability to ship goods of high quality, precisely on time, and to do so directly to the production process. This requires a great deal of advance work by the purchasing staff to find suppliers willing to do this, as well as supplier inspections by company engineers to ensure that supplier quality standards match or exceed those of the company. Only after this work has been done can a company convert to the direct delivery of goods to the production department, bypassing the receiving area.

A final problem to overcome is how to account for receipts if there is no receiving staff. The answer is to assume that parts were received if the products in which they are used as components were built. Accordingly, explode production records into their component parts in the computer to determine whose parts were used, and then pay those suppliers based on their usage records. Subsidiary problems to resolve before this payment system will work are to centralize component sourcing with one supplier per part and to eliminate all scrap from the production process. Supplier centralization is necessary because the computer system will not know which supplier to pay once it backs into the number of parts used. Similarly, there can be no scrap in the production process, or else suppliers will not be paid for the full number of parts delivered, since these parts were not included in finished products; the only alternative that will work here is to set up a scrap reporting system from which suppliers can also be paid.

Clearly, there are a large number of major issues to overcome before the receiving department can be eliminated. Though this results in fewer transaction errors for the accounting department to worry about, the improvement is dwarfed by the changes needed to bring it about.

Cost: 💵 💵   *Installation time:* 🥁 🥁 🥁

3.9 Combine the Shipping and Receiving Functions in One Area

The classic building layout for shipping and receiving is for them to be located either side-by-side or else in different parts of the warehouse. The reason for the split function is the inherently different nature of the work in each one, with receiving essentially being a putaway function and shipping requiring shipment staging and labeling activities. Traditional thinking holds that combining the two functions in front of the same dock doors would create a confusing tangle of incoming and outgoing inventory. However, this approach also leads to underutilized dock doors, since receipts are commonly made in the morning and shipments in the afternoon. Also, if the two functions are too far apart, it can be quite a journey for materials handlers if they are cross-docking received items straight to an outbound load.

A possible solution is to combine the functions in one area, thereby maximizing dock usage and eliminating travel time for cross-docking. To eliminate confusion with two different activities going on in the same area, all receiving can be conducted during the morning shift and all shipments during the afternoon shift.

This best practice does not work well if the shipping and receiving areas deal with large transactional volumes, since automated and relatively immovable materials handling systems are probably in place in each functional area and cannot be readily moved out of the way.

Cost: 💵   *Installation time:* 🥁 🥁

3.10 Assign Docks Based on Minimum Warehouse Travel Time

Some warehouses have a long row of dock doors, possibly on all sides of the warehouse. If the warehouse manager assigns docks at random, the warehouse staff may have to shift inbound items into warehouse slots on the far side of the warehouse from the trailer, which is grossly inefficient. Likewise, if an outbound order was already pre-positioned and the trailer was docked at the other end of the warehouse, extra move time is required to shift the order to that trailer.

The solution is to assign docks to trailers based on the minimum amount of internal travel time. In a small warehouse, one can estimate the dock door closest to putaway locations or staged outbound orders. It is particularly easy for outbound orders, since orders can be staged next to specific doors for immediate movement onto an outbound trailer. The problem is worse for inbound loads, since one must be aware of the contents of each inbound load and where those items are to be distributed throughout the warehouse. The best approach here is to obtain a computerized warehouse management system that can determine the optimum dock assignment based on total putaway time. For this best practice to be truly effective, one must have advance information about the contents of each inbound load, which requires the presence of an advance notification system. The warehouse management system needed to optimize dock assignments is quite expensive, and is usually only cost-effective for larger warehouse operations. The decision to purchase such a system is typically based on additional efficiencies from its control of picking and putaway routes, as well as the assignment of inventory to optimum storage locations throughout the warehouse.

Cost: *Installation time:*

3.11 Require Supplier Deliveries with Open-Sided Trucks Directly to Production

Even when a company has arranged with its suppliers to deliver goods directly from the receiving dock to the production area, they must still unload all items from the back of their delivery trucks into the receiving area and cart their deliveries into a variety of locations within the production facility. This can result in the temporary storage of inventory at the receiving dock until the supplier has completed all internal deliveries, or at least the blocking of a dock door until the supplier has gradually unloaded the truck. Further, this does not represent a good use of the supplier's time, which may make multiple deliveries through the production area from a fixed receiving point.

The solution is to create docks all around the production facility that allow for unloading from open-sided trucks. By doing so, suppliers can pull up to the dock next to whichever part of the company's production area it needs to service, unload only those parts it needs to deliver, walk them the shortest distance to the required area, and then drive around to another dock to make another delivery to a different part of the production area.

This is an expensive best practice, since creating special docks around the production building is not easy. Also, suppliers must be persuaded to invest in open-sided trucks for their deliveries, which can probably be achieved only with those suppliers having considerable delivery volume with the company. This approach is useful only if a company has already ensured that supplier deliveries have a sufficiently high level of quality that no incoming inspection is required, and that accounting procedures have been altered to allow for no logging in of receipts.

Cost: *Installation time:*

3.12 Ship Using Returnable Wheeled Containers

The standard form of transport from the production area to the shipping dock is for a forklift to pick up a full pallet load of finished goods, usually packed in cardboard cases, from the last workstation in the assembly line and shift it to the shipping dock. The forklift requires wide aisle access to pick up and move the pallet, which is a waste of space. Further, if forklifts are not readily available, a large amount of finished goods can build up next to the workstation, which also entails excess floor space. Further, the company must pay for disposable shipping containers, which add to the cost of the product.

An alternative in some situations is the use of returnable wheeled containers, which frequently are configured to look like nested egg cartons on wheels. The containers tend to be considerably smaller than the pallet loads moved by forklifts, so production workers can easily fill and move the containers themselves. The containers can also be shifted directly into a truck by hand, so excess space otherwise used for forklift travel is no longer required. Further, the containers are sent directly to customers, who then return them at a later date for refilling; this eliminates the cost of packaging. An additional benefit is that the container walls protect finished goods from each other, so in-transit damage is reduced. Further, because of the standardized container size, it is easier for cycle counters to count inventory.

This is a difficult approach to require of company suppliers if the company still uses a multitude of suppliers for each component; it is difficult to tell which containers came from which suppliers, so they are difficult to return. It is also not a useful best practice if customers insist on specific types of packaging, as is found in a retail environment. Further, there can be a significant up-front investment to switch to returnable wheeled containers, so this may require a gradual transition before they are used throughout the production area.

Cost: 💵 💵   *Installation time:* 🕭 🕭

3.13 Use Dunnage Bags to Cushion Outbound Shipments

When containers are packed into trucks or rail cars, there is frequently some unused space between the containers; if the load shifts in transit, containers can be jostled against each other, resulting in damaged packaging or goods. The result is likely to be returned goods from customers or damage claims for a credit against future orders.

A good alternative is to insert dunnage bags between containers. A dunnage bag is a paper bag constructed of varying plies of paper, surrounding a plastic bladder that is pumped up with an air compressor to fill the empty storage space. A two-ply outer wrapper is typically used for deliveries by truck, while anywhere from four to eight plies are used for railcar shipments. A two-ply bag is designed to restrain up to a 40,000-pound load, while an eight-ply bag can restrain up to a 120,000-pound load. A dunnage bag is typically much less expensive and easier to install in a load than more rigid forms of restraint, such as lumber frames. Also, if handled carefully, dunnage bags can be reused multiple times.

Dunnage bags can burst when overinflated. Also, their manufacturers are less than thrilled about reusing the bags, partially because they can burst with repeated use, and probably because this means fewer dunnage bag sales by the manufacturers.

Cost: *Installation time:*

3.14 Use Shippers with the Most Consistent Delivery Performance

Many companies properly track when orders must be shipped to customers in order to meet required receipt dates, only to receive customer complaints days later about nonreceipt. The third-party shipper has either lost or delayed delivery of the order. As a result, the company must spend time researching the issue, and possibly sending a replacement product. Further, the errant delivery may eventually turn up, requiring a return transaction to be processed by the company. In short, the shipper's problem has resulted in a poor purchasing experience by the customer and the extraction of more finished goods inventory from the company's reserves than it had planned for.

The solution is to track shipper delivery performance and gradually winnow out those shippers unable to provide consistent delivery performance. This is most easily done by tracking the shippers involved when customers complain about late or lost deliveries. One can also gain leverage with shippers by offering all of the company's delivery business to a single shipping firm. This approach works especially well when the shipper offers online package tracking, as is the case with FedEx and UPS, since the tracking number can be supplied to customers by e-mail at the time of shipment. Customers then track the deliveries themselves, resulting in far fewer follow-up calls to the company.

Cost: *Installation time:*

3.15 Have Delivery Person Deliver the Invoice

It may be possible to have the delivery person hand-carry an invoice at the time of delivery to the customer's accounts payable department. By doing so, a company can compress the mail time that would otherwise be required to get an invoice to a customer and ensure that the invoice is delivered directly into the hands of a person who is responsible for paying it. Thus, direct delivery of an invoice carries with it the advantage of reducing the total transaction time, while also ensuring that the invoice is not lost in transit.

However, having the delivery person deliver the invoice works only in a small number of situations. The key element is that the company must make deliveries with its own personnel; if not, a third-party delivery person will not hand-carry an invoice, which makes this best practice impossible to implement. Also, there must be a close linkage between the accounting department and the shipping dock, so that invoices are prepared slightly in advance of shipment and sent to the delivery person at the time of shipment. In addition, a customer may not allow delivery personnel to have access to the accounting department, resulting in the delivery of the invoice to the customer's front desk, which can cause delayed or incorrect delivery to the accounting department. Finally, there may be a problem with creating invoices slightly in advance of shipment—what if the invoice is created but the shipment never leaves the dock? The invoice must then be credited out of the computer system, which adds an unneeded step to the invoicing process. Consequently, given the number of problems with this best practice, it is best used in only those few situations where a company has its own delivery staff and the accounting department can efficiently produce accurate invoices either in advance of, or at the time of, shipment.

Though there seem to be many obstacles to this best practice, there is one scenario under which it can work quite well. If the shipping dock has a computer terminal and printer, it may be possible to create an invoice at the dock as soon as a delivery is ready for shipment. This alternative keeps the accounting staff from having to be involved in the invoicing process at all and keeps invoices from being produced by mistake when a delivery is not actually ready for shipment. This alternative requires a modification to the accounting system so that invoices can be produced singly, rather than in batches, which is the customary mode of invoice creation. The shipping staff must also be given permission to create invoices in the computer system, and must be thoroughly trained in how to do so. If these problems can be overcome, an incremental increase in the level of technology used at the shipping dock can make this best practice a viable alternative.

Cost: 💰 *Installation time:* 🕐 🕐

3.16 Pay Suppliers Based Only on Receiving Approval

The accounts payable process is one of the most convoluted to be found anywhere in a company. First, it requires the collection of information from multiple departments—purchase orders from the purchasing department, invoices from suppliers, and receiving documents from the receiving department. The process then requires the accounting staff to match these documents, which almost always contain exceptions, and then track down someone either to approve exceptions or at least to sign checks, which must then be mailed to suppliers. The key to success in this area is to thoroughly reengineer the entire process by eliminating the paperwork, the multiple sources of information, and the additional approvals. The only best practice that truly addresses these underlying problems is paying based on receipt.

To pay based on receipt, one must first do away with the concept of having an accounts payable staff that performs the traditional matching process. Instead, the receiving staff checks to see if there is a purchase order at the time of receipt. If there is, the computer system automatically pays the supplier. Does it sound simple? It is not; a company must have several features installed before the concept will function properly. One issue is having a computer terminal at the receiving dock. When a supplier shipment arrives, a receiving person takes the purchase order number and quantity received from the shipping documentation and punches it into the computer. The computer system will check against an on-line database of open purchase orders to see if the shipment was authorized. If so, the system will automatically schedule a payment to the supplier based on the purchase order price, which can be sent by wire transfer. If the purchase order number is not in the database, or if there is no purchase order number at all, the shipment is rejected at the receiving dock. Note that the accounts payable staff takes no part whatsoever in this process—everything has been shifted to a simple step at the receiving location. The process is shown graphically in Exhibit 3.2.

Before laying off the entire accounts payable staff and acquiring such a system, one must address the following problems:

- *Train suppliers.* Every supplier who sends anything to a company must be trained to include the purchase order number, the company's part number, and the quantity shipped on the shipping documentation, so

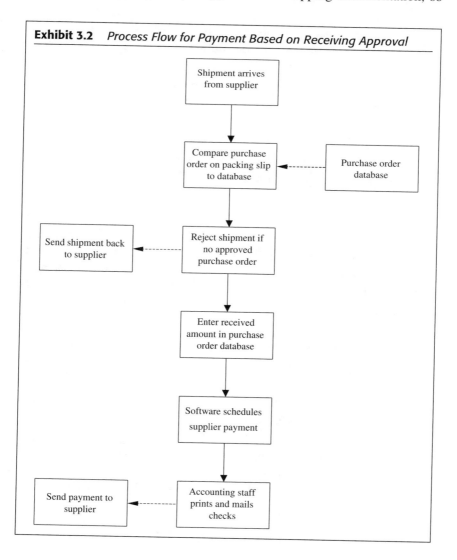

Exhibit 3.2 *Process Flow for Payment Based on Receiving Approval*

this information can be punched into the computer at the receiving location. The information can be encoded as barcodes to make the data entry task easier for the receiving employees. Training a supplier may be difficult, especially if the company purchases only a small quantity of goods from the supplier. To make it worthwhile for the supplier to go to this extra effort, it may be necessary to give each one a significant volume of orders.

- *Alter the accounting system.* The traditional accounting software is not designed to allow approvals at the receiving dock. Accordingly, one must reprogram the system to allow the reengineered process to be performed. This can be an exceptionally major undertaking, especially if the software is constantly being upgraded by the supplier—every upgrade will wipe out any custom programming that the company may have created.

- *Prepare for miscellaneous payments.* The accounts payable department will not really go away because there will always be stray supplier invoices of various kinds arriving for payment that cannot possible go through the receiving dock, such as subscription payments, utility bills, and repair invoices. Accordingly, the old payments system must still be maintained, though at a greatly reduced level, to handle these items.

- *Pay without a supplier invoice.* One of the key aspects of the reengineered process is paying based on the information in the purchase order, rather than the information in the supplier's invoice. To do so, one must have a database of all tax rates that every supplier would charge, so the company's computer system can automatically include these taxes in the invoice payments. Also, there will sometimes be discrepancies between the purchase order prices and quantities paid, versus those expected by suppliers, so an accounts payable staff must be kept on hand to correspond with suppliers to reconcile these items.

The preceding bullet points highlight the wide array of items that must first be overcome before the dramatic improvements of this new process can be realized. However, for a company that has a large accounts payable staff, this can be a highly rewarding system to install, for the savings realized can be the elimination of the majority of the accounts payable department.

Cost: 💵 💵 💵   *Installation time:*   ⬤ ⬤ ⬤

3.17 Provide Pending Shipment Information to the Collections Staff

If a customer has a large open order with a company, it is likely that the customer will be responsive to pressure to pay for open orders when those orders are put on hold. Consequently, an excellent best practice to implement is to give the collections staff current knowledge of all open orders.

Implementation of this best practice is easy for most companies; just give password access to the existing customer orders database to the collections staff. This access can be read-only, so there is no danger of a staff person inadvertently changing key information in a customer order. An additional issue is that someone must be responsible for flagging customers as "do not ship" in the customer orders database. This is a necessary step since orders will inadvertently pass through the system if there is not a solid block in the computer on shipments to a delinquent customer. However, many companies are uncomfortable with allowing the collections staff to have free access to altering the shipment status of customers, since they may use it so much that customers become irritated. Thus it may be better to allow this access only to a supervisor, such as an assistant controller, who can review a proposed order-hold request with the sales staff to see what the impact will be on customer relations before actually imposing a hold on a customer order.

In summary, giving the collections staff access to the open orders database results in better leverage over delinquent customers by threatening to freeze existing orders unless payment is made. The use of this database should be tempered by a consideration for long-term relations with customers; it should be used only if there is a clear collections problem that cannot be resolved in some other way.

Cost: 🖴   *Installation time:* 🕯

4

Inventory Storage

This chapter includes 24 inventory storage best practices. As noted in Exhibit 4.1, it begins with several techniques for avoiding any inventory storage at all, and then proceeds to a discussion of several inventory segregation techniques designed to improve the overall level of inventory putaway and picking efficiency. There are also several more subtle improvements to be made to the cases stored on pallets to improve cubic storage utilization while also reducing damage to inventory. Finally, a number of storage alternatives are covered that make the most cost-effective use of a company's particular inventory needs.

Many of the best practices noted in this chapter involve a capital investment in inventory storage systems, requiring not only cash but also a considerable investment in warehouse reconfiguration to install the systems. These include the use of carousels, gravity-flow racks, push-back racks, and multistory manual picking systems. Other best practices, such as storing by ABC classification or customer zone, require little capital investment but a great deal of staff time to move items within the warehouse.

The most commonly used (and highly recommended) best practices begin with the assignment of location codes to all inventory locations (an absolutely mandatory item), and continue with the consolidation of inventory into the minimal number of locations for each item, as well as the dispersal of some items to the shop floor and the configuration of storage space in accordance with ABC classifications. This basic set of improvements will greatly enhance the accuracy of the inventory database while also smoothing the flow of materials into and out of the warehouse.

Exhibit 4.1 *Summary of Inventory Storage Best Practices*

	Best Practice	Cost	Install Time
4.1	Drop ship inventory	💵	🕐🕐
4.2	Cross-dock inventory	💵💵	🕐🕐🕐
4.3	Move inventory to floor stock	💵💵	🕐🕐
4.4	Use temporary storage for peak inventory requirements	💵	🕐🕐
4.5	Assign unique location codes to all inventory storage locations	💵	🕐🕐
4.6	Reduce the number of inventory bin locations assigned to the same product	💵	🕐🕐
4.7	Assign fixed inventory locations to high-volume items	💵	🕐🕐
4.8	Segregate customer-owned inventory	💵	🕐
4.9	Allocate warehouse areas to specific customers	💵	🕐🕐
4.10	Segregate inventory by ABC classification	💵	🕐🕐
4.11	Store high-pick items in order fulfillment zones	💵💵	🕐🕐
4.12	Adjust case height to match cubic storage capabilities	💵💵	🕐🕐
4.13	Adjust case stacking or width to avoid pallet overhang	💵	🕐🕐
4.14	Combine out-and-back inventory moves	💵💵	🕐🕐
4.15	Use different storage systems based on cubic transactional volume	💵💵	🕐🕐
4.16	Use modular storage cabinets for low-storage volume items	💵💵	🕐🕐
4.17	Use carousels to increase picking efficiency	💵💵💵	🕐🕐
4.18	Use moveable racking systems	💵💵	🕐🕐
4.19	Use multistory manual picking systems	💵💵💵	🕐🕐
4.20	Use gravity flow racking for FIFO picking	💵💵	🕐🕐
4.21	Use pallet flow racks for pallet FIFO picking	💵💵	🕐🕐
4.22	Create double-deep racking or stacking lanes for large SKU pallet volumes	💵💵	🕐🕐

Exhibit 4.1 *(Continued)*

Best Practice	Cost	Install Time
4.23 Use push-back racks for multiple pallet storage		
4.24 Eliminate cross bracing in low weight storage configurations		

4.1 Drop Ship Inventory

A typical set of inventory transactions involves receiving items, moving them to a quality review area, checking them, moving them again to main storage, picking them for an order, assembling and packaging the order, and shipping it. Not only does this process require a large number of transactions, any of which could be made in error, but it also involves a great many "touches" of the inventory, increasing the odds of product damage.

In situations where a company is purchasing a finished product from a supplier and turning around and selling it to a customer, there is a possibility of using drop shipping. Under this approach, the supplier ships the product directly to the customer, bypassing the company's warehouse entirely. By doing so, all of the transactions and risks of product damage just noted are eliminated. This is the ultimate approach to storing inventory—there is nothing to store. It is an especially attractive option for large items, which would otherwise require special handling and take up considerable space within the warehouse.

Unfortunately, drop shipping is an option only in the minority of situations. Many suppliers are unwilling to ship directly to customers, especially if shipment sizes are smaller than full pallets; issuing small shipments increases a supplier's costs, so the company may have to accept a supplier price increase in exchange for this service. Another problem is the need for new procedures to handle drop shipments. The accounting department must be trained to accept a shipment notification from the supplier, so it can issue an invoice to customers and also have a control point in place for verifying if no shipment notification has been received. Further, the company may not want the customer to know the name of the supplier, since the customer could theoretically purchase the product at a lower price directly from the supplier.

Cost: 💵   *Installation time:* 🕰 🕰

4.2 Cross-Dock Inventory

As just noted under the "Drop Ship Inventory" (4.1) best practice, there are a great many inventory transactions and physical moves required if an item is brought into a warehouse, stored, retrieved, and shipped. All these moves introduce the possibility of creating an incorrect transaction or damaging items. Though the drop shipping approach completely eliminates this problem, it is not always possible to do so, either because suppliers refuse to ship direct, container sizes must be reconfigured prior to final delivery, or items from multiple suppliers must be combined into a single shipment.

If drop shipping is not possible, cross-docking may be an alternative. Under this approach, items arrive at the receiving dock and are immediately shifted across to a shipping dock for immediate delivery. By doing so, the only inventory transactions are for receiving and shipping, while the only inventory move is from one dock to another. There is no quality review, putaway, or picking transaction at all. Because of these missing transactions, the use of warehouse staff is kept to a minimum.

To make cross-docking work, inbound deliveries must have a high enough level of product quality to eliminate the quality assurance review, which would otherwise create a potential delay in the delivery of shipments to customers. Also, there must be excellent control over the timing of inbound deliveries, so the warehouse manager knows exactly when items will arrive. This is especially critical when some parts of a customer order must still be picked, since the picking transaction should be completed just prior to the arrival of a delivery containing the remaining items in a customer order. Further, the computerized warehouse management system must be sufficiently sophisticated to tell the receiving staff that items are to be cross-docked, and the number of the shipping dock to which items must be shifted for delivery. Finally, this approach requires a number of docks, since trailers may have to be kept on-site longer than normal while loads are accumulated from several inbound deliveries.

Cost: 💵 💵   *Installation time:* 🕰 🕰 🕰

4.3 Move Inventory to Floor Stock

The typical inventory contains a high proportion of small parts, many of which are difficult to track, are not stored in easily countable containers, and require a large amount of paperwork in proportion to their size and frequency of usage. In short, they are a pain for the warehouse staff to handle. Likewise, they represent a minor irritation for the accounting staff, since they must all be counted during the physical inventory counting process, and, because of the counting difficulty, they take up an inordinate amount of time. Further, they can easily represent one-third of the total number of inventory items, which is one-third more costing documentation than the accounting staff wants to track. Accordingly, it is safe to say that the smallest and most inexpensive parts in inventory are the root cause of a great deal of extra work for the employees of several departments.

A moderately easy best practice that takes care of this problem is shifting the small inventory items out of the warehouse and onto the shop floor, where they are treated as supplies. This approach carries the multiple benefits of requiring far less inventory handling work from the warehouse staff, fewer inventory counts during the physical inventory process, and much less inventory-costing work from the accounting staff. In addition, it brings more inventories close to the shop floor, where the production staff appreciates the easier access as well as not having to go to the parts counter to requisition additional parts. This is one of the rare best practices greeted with universal approval by multiple departments.

Though this step can be taken quickly, one should be mindful of the danger of issuing a quantity of expensive parts to the shop floor that may quickly disappear, resulting in a significant loss. For these few costly items, it may be better to leave them in the warehouse. Also, there must be a tracking system in place on the shop floor, whereby someone can check part bins and quickly determine which parts must be reordered. There are a variety of simple systems available to accomplish this, such as painting a reorder fill line in each storage tray, or using a two-bin system where parts are reordered as soon as one bin is emptied. A manual reorder system is necessary for shop supplies, since it is no longer in the inventory database, where reordering can be done automatically based on recorded inventory levels. Also, some of the parts being pulled from the warehouse may be listed in bills of material, which can be a problem if a company uses back flushing. In this instance, items will be automatically withdrawn from the quantity shown in the computer system as soon as production is recorded, so the system will show negative usage of items that are no longer there. One should carefully consider and resolve these problems before moving parts out of the warehouse and into floor stock.

Cost: 💵 💵   *Installation time:* 🕐 🕐

4.4 Use Temporary Storage for Peak Inventory Requirements

It is a rare company that does not experience occasional jumps in inventory demand beyond the long-term average demand. Some inventory planners do not ever want to be accused of stopping production or backordering customer requirements, so they tend to plan for the maximum possible inventory load. Warehouse overloading also occurs just prior to expected peaks in forecasted item demand, when materials planners stuff the warehouse in anticipation of orders. In either case, a company will fill up an excessive amount of expensive warehouse space.

A widely practiced alternative is to offload some storage into less-expensive overflow locations, such as trailers. By doing so, a company can pay less per square foot for storage, and then stop paying rent on the overflow storage as soon as its inventory requirements decline.

There are some cautions associated with this best practice. One is the difficulty of extracting needed inventory from a secondary storage location, which requires extra travel time. Even if the inventory is stored in a docked trailer, the materials handling staff must still unload the trailer to access the required item (not to mention the added problem of using up available dock space in the process!). Second, overflow storage has a habit of becoming permanent, resulting in complex materials handling problems, added storage costs, and a general ignorance of the size of a company's inventory investment (i.e., anything out of sight is not considered a problem). The solution to both problems is to make a periodic determination of the amount of excess inventory a company will stock and the duration of that storage requirement. If the duration is short and the extra demand is high, renting overflow storage is a good alternative. However, if extra inventory will be on hand for many months and the excess is not drastically greater than standard demand levels, management should give serious consideration to storing the excess quantities in the main warehouse area.

Cost: *Installation time:*

4.5 Assign Unique Location Codes to All Inventory Storage Locations

A fundamental issue is being able to locate inventory in an efficient manner. It does little good for the warehouse staff to memorize inventory locations if the staff happens to be out sick on the day when an item is needed in a particular hurry. Also, new warehouse employees must suffer through a lengthy indoctrination period of memorizing every item location. If the warehouse grows to a respectable size, the amount of search time involved becomes so great that the entire department nearly grinds to a halt.

A fundamental best practice is to assign a unique location code to every possible inventory storage location and to subsequently track inventory by these codes. A common code is to assign a letter to each aisle, followed by a number for each rack within the aisle, and a letter to each level within the rack. Thus, the location code for the third level of the second rack in the fifth aisle from the left could be E-2-C. It is important to use some kind of logical location code assignment rather than a random one, so the warehouse staff can go straight to the proper location based on the location code.

There is no downside to assigning location codes, since this is the most elementary best practice needed for the proper organization of a warehouse. Keeping several issues in mind will make the system work somewhat better. First, be sure to assign location codes to *every* possible inventory location—it does little good to have a few items squirreled away in undocumented locations. Second, consider the impact on the numbering scheme of any likely warehouse expansion. For example, if racks will probably be added to one side of aisle A, consider giving aisle A a higher letter designation to allow for the expansion. Third, if any type of real-time data entry is contemplated for inventory transactions, consider putting a large bar code next to each location label, so scanners can be used to enter location codes.

Fourth, number the racks sequentially from left to right and back again as you proceed down an aisle, so the first rack on the left is number 1, the first rack on the right is number 2, the second rack on the left is number 3, and so on. Because picking reports are usually sorted in ascending numerical order by rack number, this allows pickers to reduce their travel time, picking from both sides of the aisle until they reach the highest required rack to complete their picks.

Cost: 🖮   *Installation time:* 🕭 🕭

4.6 Reduce the Number of Inventory Bin Locations Assigned to the Same Product

When the warehouse staff picks items from stock either for delivery to the production floor for assembly or for shipment to the customer, they must sometimes travel to multiple bin locations scattered throughout the warehouse, depending on where they were originally stored and the quantity needed. If the bin locations are widely distributed, this represents a significant increase in the time required by the warehouse staff to pick the items, resulting in significant labor inefficiency. In addition, the warehouse staff must process a separate inventory move transaction from each bin, possibly requiring several move transactions just to shift one part number out of the warehouse.

The clear solution to this problem is to centralize parts into the minimum number of bin locations, preferably as close to each other as possible. One approach is to periodically schedule a bin centralization review, whereby the warehouse staff prints a list of all part numbers in the warehouse, sorted by part number and also showing the storage location of each item. The warehouse staff can use the report to rearrange selected inventory items into the smallest possible number of adjacent bin locations. Another option is to arrange the warehouse by types of parts, so that similar items will at least be stored in the same aisle, though not necessarily in adjacent bins; this approach is also useful in that rack heights in aisles designated for specific purposes can be altered to maximize the volume of items stored there.

Cost: 🖮   *Installation time:* 🕭 🕭

4.7 Assign Fixed Inventory Locations to High-Volume Items

In a disorganized warehouse where inventory items of all transaction volumes are scattered throughout the warehouse, stock pickers must use the most recent inventory report by location to determine where items are being stored, requiring not only a great deal of travel time, but also considerable research into determining the exact contents of a bin once they reach it. This is a highly inefficient approach to picking.

This problem can be resolved with two best practices. The first, physically storing the inventory by ABC classification, is covered later in best practice 4.10. Once that is implemented, one should also assign permanent storage locations to the "A" classification items. By doing so, one can prominently label each bin as being the "home" of a specific item, which stock pickers will memorize over time, allowing them to more rapidly pick parts from the "A" classification storage area.

If the receiving staff uses mobile radio-frequency terminals to guide them in putting away received items, then the assigned bin location for each "A" classification item should be entered in the item master file. By doing so, the computer system can tell the warehouse staff exactly where to store selected items.

This best practice does not mean that every storage location in the warehouse should be assigned to a specific item—far from it. If that were to happen, there would be a great deal of unused space in the warehouse, since there would always be some locations for which assigned inventory is not needed or available. Instead, continue to use the more space-efficient random-location storage approach for all other parts of the warehouse. This results in a good mix of efficient picking for high-usage items and efficient storage for low-usage items.

Cost: 🖢   *Installation time:* ⬤ ⬤

4.8 Segregate Customer-Owned Inventory

A dangerous problem for many controllers is incorrectly valuing inventory too high because customer-owned inventory is mixed into it. This problem is especially common in cases where customers frequently ship components to a company for inclusion in finished products. This situation arises when a customer has the rights to a proprietary product component, prefers to do some finishing work on selected components, or only wants a company to do final assembly on its products. When any of these situations arise, the receiving staff commonly makes the mistake of recording receipts as company-owned stock and storing it alongside all other inventory in the warehouse. As a result, the inventory can be massively overvalued, leading to incorrectly reported profits.

The best way to eliminate this problem is to institute procedures and set up segregated areas that allow one to promptly identify customer-owned products at the receiving dock and shunt them immediately to the segregated area. By doing so, one can be assured of having much more accurate inventory quantities and costs. To implement this best practice, it is critical to require a purchase order or delivery schedule on all items arriving at the receiving dock. With this procedure in place, the receiving staff can quickly identify all receipts that the purchasing department has previously noted on a purchase order as being owned by a customer. With this information in hand, the receiving staff can easily record the entry in the computer system and then move the items to a separately marked-off area. This approach results in the storage of item quantity information in the computer system so the warehouse staff can easily find the parts, but at a zero cost, meaning the accounting staff does not have the mistake of increasing the amount of company-owned inventory.

The main problem with using this methodology is that the purchasing and warehousing departments must get used to issuing purchase orders for all items received, while also rejecting all items shipped to the company without attached purchase orders. Only by closely following these procedures can one be sure of identifying all customer-owned inventory at the point of acceptance.

Cost: 🖩   *Installation time:* 🔴

4.9 Allocate Warehouse Areas to Specific Customers

A common occurrence is for a company to ship the bulk of its sales to a very small proportion of its customer base. When this occurs, the company must ensure that the major customers receive the best possible service in order to retain their business. However, if the warehouse is organized in a "democratic" manner, with all items picked from the same warehouse locations and shipped in the same manner, it is more difficult to provide exceptional service to the few customers who matter the most.

Depending on the situation, a possible alternative is to concentrate the most commonly picked items for specific customers in a single inventory location, and assign the best inventory pickers and shippers to those areas. Orders could be picked individually, rather than using the more efficient wave picking approach, in order to attain higher picking accuracy levels. Also, cycle counting could be done more intensively in these areas to ensure higher inventory record accuracy and presumably fewer stockouts. This approach does not mean that every item ordered by a customer need be segregated in one area, only the most commonly picked. Also, excess item quantities could still be stored in a general reserve storage area with other items.

The downside of allocating warehouse areas to specific customers is the inefficient use of space due to multiple stocking locations, and employee time due to single-order picking and shipping. Consequently, one should set up this inventory storage configuration only if there is clear evidence of a high level of customer profitability to offset the added expense.

Cost: *Installation time:*

4.10 Segregate Inventory by ABC Classification

If the warehouse staff is allowed to store inventory in any open space anywhere in the warehouse, stock pickers will find themselves traveling to distant corners of the warehouse for frequently used items. This greatly increases nonvalue-added travel time by stock pickers, possibly even resulting in the addition of more staff.

A good way to eliminate excess travel time in the warehouse is to cluster the inventory into ABC classifications and then store the most heavily used classifications near warehouse entry and exit points. Definitions of each category are:

- *"A" classification:* the top 20 percent of items by transaction volume, usually comprising about 60 percent of all transactions.

- *"B" classification:* the next 20 percent of items, usually comprising about 20 percent of all transactions.
- *"C" classification:* the remaining 60 percent of items, usually comprising about 20 percent of all transactions.

By organizing warehouse storage around these classifications, a company can save not only warehouse labor costs, but also fuel for forklifts and related machine maintenance. However, this can involve a significant short-term mess and a major portion of warehouse staff time as they reconfigure rack space and move loads to new locations.

Cost: 💵   Installation time: ⚫ ⚫

4.11 Store High-Pick Items in Order Fulfillment Zones

Even if inventory items with high transaction volumes are stored near warehouse entry and exit points, as was advocated in the "Segregate Inventory by ABC Classification" best practice (4.10), order pickers will still find that they must search for high-use parts within these more limited storage zones, adding excessive search and travel time to the picking process.

An enhancement is to review the transaction records to find the absolute highest-volume items in stock, and then group these items together into a small geographic cluster, preferably using a storage system that allows for easy, high-accuracy picking. For example, if a warehouse manager finds that 20 items out 500 in stock account for half of all order lines picked, it would make sense to group these items into a pick-to-light carousel where the order picker has no travel time and items are essentially brought to the picker. By creating high-volume order fulfillment zones, a company can realize extremely high levels of picking efficiency for selected items.

The order fulfillment zone concept should not be expanded to include somewhat lower-volume items, since the cost of storage systems with high picking efficiency may not present a cost-effective solution. Also, one should regularly examine the transactional volume of all items kept in an order fulfillment zone, since long-term volume variations may require some changes in the items kept in the zone.

Cost: 💵 💵   Installation time: ⚫ ⚫

4.12 Adjust Case Height to Match Cubic Storage Capabilities

The most efficient way to store inventory is to stack individual cases on a pallet and store the entire pallet in some variation of a racking system. However, if the resulting pallet height does not match the cubic volume of the existing rack space, some reduced pallet configuration must be used, probably involving one less layer of cases on the pallet. This inevitably results in some cubic storage space not being used at all, permanently reducing the total storage utilization of the warehouse.

A solution is to alter the height of the case so that the optimal pallet height can be achieved to fill all available rack space. This usually requires a small alteration in the case height of less than an inch.

There are several objections to this best practice that limit its usefulness. One is the probable increased cost of a smaller case, since it may not be a standard size. Second, the contents of each case may not allow for a height reduction. Third, other automated packaging systems in the factory may already be designed to handle the height of the existing case, and alterations would be expensive. Finally, it may be less expensive to adjust the height of the existing storage racks rather than to modify the pallets to match the racks.

Cost: *Installation time:*

4.13 Adjust Case Stacking or Width to Avoid Pallet Overhang

When the stacking configuration on a pallet results in some overhang of cases over the edge of the pallet, a company will likely experience a much higher rate of inventory damage. One reason is that a forklift will make contact with the edge of the lowermost case first before its tines reach the pallet for a putaway function. Also, if pallets are stacked, the weight of upper pallets is primarily supported by the outside walls of the cases underneath, which must support the load alone rather than be based on the pallet, since it overhangs the pallet. Thus, excessive pallet stacking can result in catastrophic failure of the underlying cases and the loss of a great deal of inventory.

There are several possible approaches to avoid this issue. One is to use a different stacking configuration on the pallet. An alternative is to reduce the number of cases on the pallet, though this will likely result in the underutilization of the pallet so that cubic storage volumes are not maximized. Finally, one can use a smaller-sized case, though this may not match the size of the stored item and could be more expensive if it is an odd-sized box.

Cost: 　 　　　　　*Installation time:*

4.14 Combine Out-and-Back Inventory Moves

When a warehouse worker shifts inventory from the receiving dock to a storage location in the warehouse, he or she typically returns straight to the receiving dock to pick up another load. This means that there is an outbound load, but no load on the return, representing staff efficiency of only 50 percent.

The solution is to combine out-and-back inventory moves, so the staff is always shifting items for other needed transactions (usually for outbound shipments that bring them back to a dock). To do so, each employee must carry a wireless terminal, and use it to notify the company's warehouse management system after completing a move transaction. The system then tells the employee via the terminal where to go for their next load in a manner that most efficiently routes the employee back to the receiving dock while still conducting another move.

Though this approach sounds wonderful, it requires a company to equip its warehouse staff with wireless terminals, and also calls for an expensive warehouse management system with the capability to efficiently route workers through the warehouse. Thus, smaller operations will not be able to cost-justify this best practice.

Cost: 　 　　　　　*Installation time:*

4.15 Use Different Storage Systems Based on Cubic Transactional Volume

It can be difficult to slot items into various inventory locations around a warehouse just based on their cubic volume, since this single criterion does not reflect the amount of moves to which each one will be subject. As a result, the warehouse staff may find largely unused items slotted near the shortest access paths in the warehouse, while high-use items are parked in the rear, causing long travel times. This is a particular problem for small parts, since there are a variety of both low- and high-efficiency storage modes available for them.

A good solution is to assign storage locations based on both an item's cubic volume and number of transactions. As a result, some high-use pallets will be stored near a major picking area, while other, less-used pallets will be kept in random storage along a back wall. Similarly, low-volume small parts may be stored in bins or storage drawers, while high-volume small parts will be stored in carousels from which picking can be done much more quickly. This approach can even extend to the height at which small parts are stored in fixed bins, with high-volume items stored at waist level for easy picking.

Cost: 💷 💷   Installation time: ⚫ ⚫

4.16 Use Modular Storage Cabinets for Low-Storage-Volume Items

The classic storage system for items kept in small quantities is bin shelving, where items are stored in a fixed volume of cubic storage space. However, because item quantities are frequently very small, they occupy only a small portion of their assigned cubic storage space. Also, because items are easily accessed, there is no security to prevent people from taking parts from the bins.

An alternative to bin shelving is the use of modular storage cabinets. They are multidrawer cabinets with varying drawer heights, the contents of which can be reconfigured with dividers to achieve the optimal amount of storage space given the on-hand quantity. Some cabinet systems can also be locked, thereby increasing item security. This approach yields excellent storage density, which may result in the consolidation of storage space.

However, modular storage cabinets are expensive, rendering them usable only for selected items. Also, it can be difficult to establish item identification within a drawer when there may be a dozen parts packed into different divided segments of the drawer, though this issue can be reduced through the use of identification labels on the dividers. Further, storage cabinets may not be high enough to take up the cubic volume in a storage area, so one should find other uses for the unused overhead space, such as secondary storage for overflow quantities.

Cost: 🖅 🖅 Installation time: 🥁 🥁

4.17 Use Carousels to Increase Picking Efficiency

In many situations, pickers must prowl the entire warehouse to locate items for their latest pick list. Not only does this vastly increase their travel time, but it also makes their supervisor's job difficult—a picker can easily hide in a remote corner of the warehouse for an unauthorized break period.

An expensive solution is to install either a horizontal or vertical carousel to house the most commonly picked, low-cubic-volume items. A carousel holds items in bins that can be rotated around an axis to the picker, who calls up items to be picked from a central control panel. Using this equipment, the picker stays in one spot and the carousel brings items to the picker. This approach virtually eliminates picker travel time, and makes it easy to supervise them.

A horizontal carousel typically reaches from the ground up to the maximum picker height, and so does not use any cubic volume above this height. A vertical carousel can be constructed that reaches up a great distance, and so is more efficient from this perspective. However, vertical carousels tend to rotate slower, since they are fighting gravity, and therefore require a more powerful drive motor.

Horizontal carousels usually contain bins that are open to anyone who can enter the warehouse, and so are considered less secure than vertical carousels, which are usually encased in sheet metal (except for the access slot currently open for picking). Consequently, higher-cost items can be more securely stowed in a vertical carousel.

A slow carousel can actually reduce the efficiency of a picker, so one must be careful to set up the carousel system to achieve the highest possible level of picking throughput. Also, carousels can be extremely expensive, and therefore make sense only when used for items being picked in high volume. Further, an excessively long or high carousel requires extra rotation time before an item to be picked arrives in front of the picker, so in these cases it may make sense to have a picker use two carousels at once in order to maximize picking speed.

For more information about carousels, contact Cisco-Eagle Systems (www.cisco-eagle.com) or White Systems (www.whitesystems.com).

Cost: 💵 💵 💵   *Installation time:* 🔴 🔴

4.18 Use Moveable Racking Systems

When there is minimal floor space available, a company must cram stock into every nook and cranny. This commonly results in excessively small and therefore overflowing storage bins, as well as items being inefficiently stacked in every possible location, no matter how difficult they may be to access. The result is considerable storage inefficiency, as well as difficulty in cycle counting and great difficulty in the putaway process, since so little space is available.

A possible solution is to install moveable racking systems. Under this approach, racks are mounted on wheels and pushed together, thereby eliminating all but one aisle. When someone needs an item from a particular bin, he or she pushes the racks apart (either manually or with a motor drive) to create an aisle, and then picks the part.

Though this solution certainly fills the maximum amount of space, it creates considerable trouble for order pickers, who must spend extra time pushing apart racks. Consequently, it is applicable only in low-picking-volume situations. Also, the stability of moveable racks is less than for fixed-rack configurations, so they are appropriate only for low-height racks from which manual picking is conducted.

Cost: 💵 💵   *Installation time:* 🔴 🔴

4.19 Use Multistory Manual Picking Systems

When high picking volumes make the just-noted moveable racking system an inadequate solution, one may still be able to build more storage space by constructing a second set of storage racks in a mezzanine configuration directly above the original storage area, thereby greatly increasing the cubic storage space, even though the square footage occupied does not change.

The main problem with this best practice is the extra time required by order pickers to ascend to and descend from the upper storage area. To minimize this inefficiency, one should store the least commonly used items in the upper level, thereby concentrating most picking time in the floor storage level. A secondary issue is the strength of the construction used to build the mezzanine area—if a low-cost addition is made with a low weight-bearing capability, one must be careful to retain all high-weight items in the floor storage area. It is also necessary to store all high-weight items in the floor area for another reason; in the absence of a conveyor or elevator system, pickers must move these items to the ground floor by themselves.

Cost: 💵 💵 💵   *Installation time:* 🕐 🕐

4.20 Use Gravity-Flow Racking for FIFO Picking

When items have a short shelf life, pickers must know where to go to find the oldest item in the warehouse and pick that item first. Even if they are aware of the exact bin in which the oldest item is located, they must root around the accumulation of items there to find the oldest one—all of which takes time.

A good way to automatically position the oldest item in front of a picker is the use of gravity-flow racking. This racking system requires putaway from the rear, where items slide down a slight angle in the rack, assisted by rollers, pushing any items in front to the front of the rack. As soon as pickers remove items from the front of the rack, the weight of items in the rear push the next-oldest item to the front. An additional feature is that putaway work can be done at the same time as picking without creating bottlenecks in the aisle, since people involved in these two functions work on opposite sides of the rack. A gravity-flow rack is usually configured to contain a large number of items so pickers can also find a great many items in a small area, thereby contributing to short travel times.

Gravity-flow racks are more expensive than standard storage racks, though not excessively so. They are not useful for pallet storage, and are useful only up to a height of about seven feet, since they are used only for manual picking. This height restriction can be overcome by installing other forms of overhead racks above them to properly utilize the available cubic volume.

Cost: 💵💵   *Installation time:* 🔔🔔

4.21 Use Pallet-Flow Racks for Pallet FIFO Picking

As noted in the last previous practice, gravity-flow racking can be used to ensure that items are used on a FIFO basis, so items with a short shelf life will be used promptly. The problem with these racking systems is that they are designed to deal in case sizes, not larger pallet sizes.

The solution is pallet-flow racks, which are the same thing as gravity-flow racks, only larger. A pallet-flow rack uses standard racks that are set at an even height, on which are built dynamic flow rails at a slight downward angle from the loading end to the unloading end. The flow rails incorporate rollers and a series of automatic brakes to slow the movement of pallets. A forklift operator places a pallet at the receiving end of the pallet-flow rack, and it slowly slides along the rails, being slowed by the brakes, until it comes to a halt behind the next pallet in line. When someone removes a pallet from the other end of the rack, the whole line of pallets automatically slides forward to fill the void. This approach is also effective in eliminating aisle space as well as pallet damage from forklifts, which tend to move pallets less using this configuration.

Pallet-flow racks are least efficient for a small number of pallets, since a considerable amount of rack space will be wasted without large quantities of the same item on hand.

Cost: 💵💵   *Installation time:* 🔔🔔

4.22 Create Double-Deep Racking or Stacking Lanes for Large SKU Pallet Volumes

The standard warehouse configuration is to have every item immediately accessible from an aisle, so there is typically an aisle, followed by a row of racks or bins fronting on that aisle, then a row of racks or bins fronting on the next aisle, and so on. This is an efficient warehouse configuration when there are modest SKU volumes. However, when there are excess pallet volumes of the same SKU on hand, there is no need to have each pallet immediately accessible from the aisle, so the standard storage system only fills up space that could otherwise have been granted to an SKU with lower on-hand quantities.

The solution to excess pallet quantities is double-deep racking. This best practice calls for two rows of racks adjacent to each other, with only one rack exposed to an aisle. Under this approach, one can store two pallets of the same item in a single storage location, one behind the other. The main benefit is the elimination of an aisle, which can instead be used to position more storage racks or bins. The result is more storage per square foot in the warehouse as a whole. If there are many pallets of the same SKU, one can also use stacking lanes in an open warehouse area where multiple pallets are stacked on top of each other without any bracing system, many pallets deep.

Double-deep racking calls for a different warehouse layout than is normally used, so it is best to incorporate this feature into the original warehouse floor plan. Also, this form of storage requires the use of specially designed forklifts that can reach deep into a rack to remove the second-tier pallet. Further, if products have a short shelf life, a company's computerized materials management system must be able to track SKU age by individual pallet, because it is impossible to manually verify this information for second-tier pallets that are blocked from view.

When using stacking lanes instead of double-deep racking, be sure to verify the amount of weight that a pallet can support, since there is a serious safety issue if a pallet stack collapses. It is a particular problem in high-humidity environments where the cardboard boxes used to contain items on some pallets can gradually lose their integrity and collapse under the strain of extra stacks of pallets. Also, though it is not usually a problem, verify that the load-bearing capacity of the floor can withstand high stacks of pallets.

Despite these issues, both double-deep racking and stacking lanes are an excellent best practice for many warehouses containing large quantities of SKUs in pallet sizes.

Cost: 🪙 🪙   *Installation time:* 🕭 🕭

4.23 Use Push-Back Racks for Multiple Pallet Storage

Double-deep racking, as just noted, is a good approach for storing multiple pallets in one deep rack, but it requires a special forklift attachment to handle the deeper loads. A company may not want to invest in these attachments, which eliminates double-deep racking as an option.

An alternative approach to double-deep racking that allows for the use of a standard forklift is push-back racks. Under this approach, two lines of racks are assembled next to each other, and short load rails are installed across the racks that are angled slightly downward toward the front. When a forklift leaves a pallet in a push-back rack, the pallet will be forced by gravity to stay at the front rack position. If another pallet is loaded, it pushes the existing pallet to the rear. When the front pallet is removed, the one in the rear automatically slides to the front.

This approach certainly eliminates the need for special forklift equipment, but replaces it with new equipment to be installed in the racks, so there is really just a replacement of one investment with another. Also, this approach assumes that shelf life is not a problem, since the last item stored will be the first one used. Pallets stuck in the rear rack position may not be used for a long time.

Cost: 💵 💵   *Installation time:* ⬤ ⬤

4.24 Eliminate Cross Bracing in Low-Weight Storage Configurations

It is a common safety measure to bolt cross braces to the back of storage racks, since this provides a significant amount of rigidity to the racks, thereby improving their safety. However, cross bracing makes it impossible to access a rack from the rear, which might be a consideration when a single-depth rack can be reached from aisles on both sides. This is a particular problem from the perspective of picking inventory in the most efficient manner, since when employees picking down an aisle on the "back" side of a rack encounter cross bracing, they must continue to the end of the aisle, turn into the aisle accessing the "front" of the rack, and proceed back to the correct point on the aisle from which they can remove items from or place them into a rack. This represents a clear waste of employee time in extra moves through the warehouse.

A possible best practice in selected situations is to eliminate the cross bracing from those racks on which low-weight inventory items are stored. As long as a maximum weight limit is not surpassed, this approach allows for rack accessibility from both sides while retaining a high level of safety for those employees working near the racks.

There is an obvious safety concern with this best practice. Even if low-weight items are initially stored on racks that are not shored up with cross bracing, one could mistakenly place much heavier items on the racks at a later date, possibly leading to rack collapse and employee injury. To avoid this, one should clearly label these racks with "Low-Weight Tolerance" or "No Cross Bracing" signs, or some similar warning label. In addition, one should add to the item master record for each SKU its pallet weight—thus, in cases where the computer system tells the warehouse staff where to store SKUs, it can use this information to automatically block the storage of excessively heavy items in those racks.

Cost: *Installation time:*

5

Inventory Picking

This chapter addresses those 16 picking best practices having a direct impact on inventory. As noted in Exhibit 5.1, they range from some simple efficiency improvements to an existing picking system, such as grouping single-line orders, through more complex zone and wave picking techniques, to expensive pick-to-light systems for high-volume picking. We also address related picking issues, like using multibin picking carts, optimizing picking locations, and avoiding picking location restocking when picking activities are underway.

Improving picking efficiency is an extremely important target, since more than one-half of all picking time can be spent traveling in the warehouse, rather than actually picking. This chapter is designed to present some level of efficiency improvement to any warehouse, so an occasional pick environment can find improvement through such changes as the use of portable counting scales, while high-volume users can gravitate toward pick-to-light or wave picking systems. While most of the best practices noted here are not particularly expensive, a few will require a significant up-front investment, particularly zone picking (if conveyors are used between pick locations), pick-to-light, and pick-to-voice. Other best practices are applicable only in carefully defined circumstances, such as issuing parts in full-bin increments (only in high-volume situations when unused items would soon be picked anyway) and optimizing inventory storage with periodic location changes (only when the presence of many picking transactions will make this time-intensive project worthwhile). The inventory picking function is an excellent area in which to apply best practices, given the high potential for efficiency improvements and reduction of employee travel time.

Exhibit 5.1 *Summary of Inventory Picking Best Practices*

	Best Practice	Cost	Install Time
5.1	Group single-line orders and pick in order by location	💵	●
5.2	Use single order picks for emergency orders	💵	●
5.3	For manual systems, pick from the source document	💵	●
5.4	Implement forward picking	💵	●
5.5	Use wave picking by grouping to consolidate transactions	💵 💵	●
5.6	Use zone picking to consolidate total transactions	💵 💵	● ●
5.7	Use zone picking with order forwarding	💵 💵	● ●
5.8	Use voice picking to record low-volume picking transactions	💵 💵 💵	● ●
5.9	Use pick-to-light to record high-volume picking transactions	💵 💵 💵	● ●
5.10	Use portable scales to pick small items	💵	●
5.11	Pick into multibin carts	💵	●
5.12	Store kitted inventory in an accumulation bin	💵	●
5.13	Use standard containers to move, store, and count inventory	💵 💵	● ●
5.14	Issue parts in full bin increments	💵	●
5.15	Avoid restocking during a picking shift	💵	●
5.16	Optimize inventory storage through periodic location changes	💵 💵	● ●

5.1 Group Single-Line Orders and Pick in Order by Location

It is extremely inefficient for the picking staff to be handed a single-line order by the warehouse manager, walk to the part requiring picking, bring it back, and either ship it to the customer or send it into the production process. There is far too much travel time required. This is a particular problem when a large proportion of customers order just single-line items.

A better approach is to sort all single-line orders in bin location sequence, so a small number of pickers can quickly move through the warehouse and pick all the orders at once. This greatly reduces the total travel time required. Another benefit of this best practice is that it can be implemented without any new programming or reports at all. In its simplest form, one can simply sort the existing pick tickets in order by location. A more advanced variation is to create a new picking report that sorts all single-line picks by location automatically, which crams more picking information onto substantially fewer sheets of paper and requires no one to manually sort individual pick tickets. This approach is obviously most beneficial when there are many single-line picks to be made.

Cost: 🞕   Installation time: 🞋

5.2 Use Single-Order Picks for Emergency Orders

Though wave picking (5.5) and zone picking (5.6) can be highly efficient ways to pick items from the warehouse, they require a certain amount of preplanning and in some cases do not allow for emergency picks. When emergency picks arise, they must be entered into the usual order picking system and emerge from the picking process after the usual time interval, which may be too late for the order recipients.

Unfortunately, the only solution may be to assign one picker the task of picking a single order. Though this approach certainly will result in the most rapid possible order completion, it is also expensive and can cause bottlenecks. Order pickers use much more travel time, while they also may interfere with the working of zone or wave pickers, and may also generate incorrect item quantities if they do not log out picked items from the inventory database. Before implementing this approach, one should appraise the need for more rapid order fulfillment against the confusion and inefficiency that may result. One approach for dealing with emergency orders is to charge a higher price for them, either internally for production jobs or to customers for direct shipments. By doing so, other parties are paying for the resulting warehouse disruption.

Cost: 🞕   Installation time: 🞋

5.3 For Manual Systems, Pick from the Source Document

Most of the suggestions in this chapter for picking improvements require a computerized materials planning system, which some smaller facilities do not have. In their case, the typical approach to picking is to transfer data from the original hand-written customer order to a separate pick sheet, which is used to pick items from the warehouse. This approach presents two problems. First, extra time is required to manually transfer the data to a new sheet. Second and more important, there is a risk of incorrectly transcribing the information, so the warehouse staff either picks the wrong items or the wrong quantities, or must issue a request for clarification back to the order entry staff to fix the problem.

The obvious solution is to pick from the source document. By doing so, there is no risk of transcription errors. There are two risks with this best practice. First, the original order may have been written down so illegibly that the picking staff cannot read it, which will still present a risk of incorrect picking. The more common problem is loss of the order by the picker, which can be easily resolved by picking from a copy of the source document. To make this best practice work more easily, modify the order entry form so there is sufficient room on each order line for the warehouse staff to enter notes regarding the completion of each pick.

A variation on this approach is to print an adhesive bar-coded label for each line item in an order and send these labels to the picking team. Each label contains the inventory location, description, and customer order number. A picker then uses the label as the source picking document, locates the item in inventory, and sticks the label to the picked item. Once shifted to the order consolidation area, barcode scanners identify the bar-coded customer order number stuck to the items and shunt them down a conveyor into separate boxes for delivery.

Cost: 　　　　　*Installation time:*

5.4 Implement Forward Picking

When a company sells small quantities of many items, it tends to suffer from a large number of stock pickers running about the warehouse, covering large distances to fill individual orders, and leaving partial pallets in their wakes. This is not only a very inefficient use of picking staff, but it also requires a massive number of inventory move transactions and a large number of partial pallets for the cycle counting staff to count (a tedious chore).

A possible improvement is to summarize pick lists over a short time period, so that only a small number of passes through the warehouse will remove all required items from stock. Picked items are then shifted to a centralized forward picking location, where they can be broken down into individual orders. By using this approach, only one transaction is required to record the entire set of picking transactions, while the total distance traveled is massively reduced. Further, it is possible to shift full pallets to the forward picking area, where they can be permanently stored if they are regularly used. This practice keeps partial pallets in one area, rather than scattering them throughout the warehouse.

Cost: *Installation time:*

5.5 Use Wave Picking by Grouping to Consolidate Transactions

When the warehouse staff picks customer orders, it typically does so based on the order due date. However, when the company commits to fill a truckload heading for a specific region, the orders picked under this priority system may bear no relationship to the immediate need to fill a truck. This commonly results in either partial truckloads being issued (at a higher shipping cost per unit), or full truckloads being shipped late, after sufficient orders have been picked to fill the trucks. The first approach reduces profitability due to higher freight costs, while the latter approach reduces customer satisfaction, due to late deliveries.

Both problems can be resolved by using wave picking. Under this best practice, the warehouse staff picks groups of orders at the same time, based on common delivery requirements. By doing so, only one inventory relieving transaction is needed for an entire group of orders, which reduces the risk of creating transactional errors. Also, full truckloads can depart sooner.

The main downside to this approach is the need for an order breakdown area near the shipping part of the warehouse, where the consolidated picked orders can be split into individual orders. The order picking software must also be capable of consolidating selected orders into a single pick list.

Cost: 💵 💵   Installation time: 🔴

5.6 Use Zone Picking to Consolidate Total Transactions

When there are many orders to pick in the warehouse, one may see a large number of order pickers scurrying about, each one picking for a single order. This can involve a considerable amount of inefficiency, since each picker may travel throughout the warehouse to pick a single order. In addition, each one must enter an inventory relieving transaction to remove picked items from the inventory database, which introduces a high risk of transaction errors, simply based on the volume of entries being made.

A better approach is to use zone picking. Under this approach, an entire day's picks are consolidated into a single master pick list, which is then sorted by warehouse location. Different pickers are then sent to specific sections of the warehouse with their portions of the master pick list, where they use much less travel time to pick their portions of all picks required for the day. All picked items are then consolidated in a central picking area, where they are broken down to fulfill individual orders. This approach represents a major reduction in travel time by pickers, while also eliminating many inventory transactions. If picking transactions are entered manually at a separate computer terminal (not the most efficient approach, as compared to pick-to-light or real-time bar-coded approaches), one can also assign the best data entry person to adjust inventory balances based on this smaller number of picks, thereby increasing inventory accuracy further. This best practice works best in very large warehouse environments where there are many orders to be filled.

There are several additional benefits to zone picking. One is that pickers can gain great familiarity with the items and locations in their assigned zones, thereby increasing both picking frequency and the accuracy of picks. Further, pickers can be given total responsibility for their areas, so they can slot inventory to increase picking efficiency based on their own picking experience. In addition, they can be kept on duty in their assigned areas, which tends to reduce socializing to some extent. Finally, there are virtually no traffic problems in the picking zones, because only one person is assigned to each zone.

The main downside is the need for an order breakdown area near the shipping part of the warehouse, where the consolidated picked orders are split into individual orders. Also, because people in every picking zone, as well as those staffing the downstream operation, must handle an order before it is shipped, zone picking makes it very difficult to assign responsibility for (or correct) order picking errors.

Another problem is that the picking volume by zone may change, depending on the contents of orders to be picked each day. When this happens, some pickers may find themselves overwhelmed with work, while pickers in other zones are not sufficiently utilized. To avoid this, one can periodically revise zone configurations based on long-term changes in transactions by zone. A more efficient approach to short-term variations in zone volumes is to have a computer system automatically reconfigure zones every day, though this requires a fully integrated (and expensive) warehouse management system.

Cost: *Installation time:*

5.7 Use Zone Picking with Order Forwarding

Some companies find that the cost of maintaining a downstream order breakdown area exceeds the savings obtained from zone picking, because they must have dedicated staff on site to split apart consolidated orders. There can also be a problem with reduced order accuracy, since there is a greater chance that the downstream staff will inadvertently mix orders.

One can use a variation on the zone picking concept to avoid these problems. By starting an order in one zone picking area and then forwarding the partially completed order to the next warehouse zone, one can still gain some benefit from zone picking while keeping orders segregated. This approach avoids the need for any downstream order breakdown area, and also tends to result in higher picking accuracy.

The order forwarding variation works best when a conveyor is available to move partial order bins from zone to zone, so pickers have to move as little as possible. There are also computerized conveyance systems available that will carry a bin past a zone from which it requires no items; such systems avoid the buildup of queues in zones where the pickers would otherwise have to decide on their own if there are no items to be picked.

The chief difficulty with order forwarding is that zone pickers must handle a large quantity of bins, each one containing a separate order. Issuing carts to the pickers containing slots for multiple order bins can mitigate this problem. However, the presence of many bins on one cart still introduces the possibility of placing picked items in the wrong order bin, so picking accuracy still tends to be less accurate.

Cost: 💵 💵   *Installation time:* 🕐 🕐

5.8 Use Voice Picking to Record Low-Volume Picking Transactions

In warehouse situations where the staff is required to pick large numbers of inventory items, there is a significant risk of transactional error, simply due to the massive number of individual item-specific transactions involved. This is a particular problem in picking operations involving hard-to-handle items, since the staff must constantly stop picking to enter transactions, inevitably resulting in missed transactions.

In some situations, a good way to reduce the transaction error rate is the use of voice picking. Under this technology, employees wear a self-contained computer on a belt. The computer communicates by radio frequency with the company computer in real time; it accepts picking information from the main computer and translates this information into English, which it communicates to the worker in English for hands-free picking with no written pick sheet. The worker also talks to the computer via a headset, telling it when items have been picked. The computer converts these spoken words into electronic messages for immediate transfer back to the main computer.

This approach allows employees to record transactions in real time while they pick, and without having to walk to a computer terminal to enter the information. This is a particularly effective solution for people with limited writing skills.

There are a few problems with voice picking. First, very noisy warehouse environments can interfere with communications. Second, batteries on these units can fail, so one should acquire only units with extended-life batteries, or at least keep extra units on hand to replace failed ones. Also, acquire only computers that can operate independently from the main computer if communications are interrupted for a short time. Finally, this best practice works best in a low-volume picking environment. For high-volume scenarios, see the pick-to-light best practice (5.9).

For an example of voice picking hardware and software, see Vocollect's Talkman product at *www.vocollect.com*.

Cost: 🪙 🪙 🪙   *Installation time:* 🕐 🕐

5.9 Use Pick-to-Light to Record High-Volume Picking Transactions

Transaction processing is particularly difficult in situations where stock pickers must quickly pick very high volumes of small-sized SKUs (stock keeping units), especially in broken case situations. Given the need to record transactions coincident to the picking, this environment tends to result in a high incidence of transactional errors. Also, using the traditional approach of picking from a printed pick list, employees must spend time locating SKUs, ensuring that they pick the correct quantity, and entering these changes into the computer system; this is a very inefficient way to use warehouse staff time.

A good alternative for this type of picking is a pick-to-light solution. Under this approach, light sensors are mounted on the front of each bin location in the warehouse. Each sensor unit is linked to the computer system's picking module, and contains a light that illuminates to indicate that picking is required for an order, an LCD (liquid crystal display) readout listing the number of required SKUs, and a button to press to indicate completion of a pick. When a stock picker enters or scans a bar-coded order number into the system, the bin sensors for those bins containing required picks will light up, and their LCDs will show the number of units to pick. When a stock picker has completed picking from a bin, he or she presses the button, and the indicator lights shut off.

This system not only allows pickers to accurately pick without a pick list, but also transmits successful picks back to the inventory database for real-time record updates. Also, because the system itemizes the exact quantity to pick, as well as the bin from which to pick, it is difficult to pick an incorrect quantity or bin, thereby increasing transactional accuracy. More advanced systems also include increment or decrement buttons, so cycle counters can enter inventory quantity adjustments into the inventory database on the spot. It is also possible to summarize a number of orders into a master order and pick just once in larger quantities for this master order, thereby reducing pick time.

Though this is an excellent approach to picking, it is expensive. Besides the cost of indicator panels for each rack location, one must also invest in the integration of all related software into the existing warehouse management system. Given the cost of this best practice, it is most common to see it being used only for the highest-volume SKUs. As prices fall, we may see a larger proportion of inventory being picked using this system. Another issue is changes in picker training and related procedures to mesh with the new system, which one should consider well in advance of system implementation. Any new training and procedures should be tested with a small group of pickers prior to rolling them out to the full picking staff.

For more information about pick-to-light systems, review the websites of Working Machines Corporation (*www.workingmachines.com*) and PCC Systems (*www.lightningpick.com*).

Cost: 💵 💵 💵   *Installation time:* 🕐 🕐

5.10 Use Portable Scales to Pick Small Items

Sometimes an order includes large quantities of very small parts, which require a picker to spend an inordinate amount of time laboriously counting parts during a picking tour. This is particularly inefficient when the parts being counted are very inexpensive; the picker is allocating a large part of his or her picking tour to a relatively insignificant item.

A good solution is a battery-powered portable scale. A picker has only to put one or a few parts on the scale to ascertain the per-unit weight, and then drop a large quantity onto the scale to determine the exact quantity required. This vastly reduces the time required to count parts, thereby increasing the efficiency of the picking staff.

Counting scales are expensive, usually costing between $300 and $1,000 for portable units. They are also subject to damage, especially if not mounted on sturdy carts during picking tours. Further, pickers must be properly trained in their use, since there are several steps involved in calculating the tare weight of any containers used, as well as the weight of individual parts and then the number of parts needed. Without this training, incorrect quantities are likely to be picked, resulting in order line errors that must be fixed at a later date. The best way to fix both problems is to assign counting scales to only a few of the best pickers, and concentrate the very small parts in a specific warehouse location where those pickers are given sole responsibility to do all picking.

Cost: *Installation time:*

5.11 Pick into Multibin Carts

When pickers are asked to pick for multiple orders during a single picking tour, they usually pick into a single container. This merged set of parts is then sent to a centralized downstream picking location where other employees break down the merged set of parts into individual orders. The problem is the extra cost of the downstream picking location, as well as the risk of damage to parts caused by extra handling.

A possible solution is to have pickers use specially designed carts during their picking tours, each one containing a separate bin for each order. Each bin is prominently labeled with a number. When a picker is issued a set of orders to pick, each order line on the pick list has a bin number designated on it into which items are to be placed. When the picker completes a tour, he or she hands off the numbered bins and the completed pick list to another employee who transfers the contents of each bin directly into a shipping container for delivery to the customer. There is no downstream order sorting required, since each order already occupies a separate bin. A more advanced version of this technique is to use shipping containers instead of bins on the picking cart, so a picker is dropping picked items directly into the final container to be sent to the customer. No matter how the bin is configured, try experimenting with the largest possible cart sizes, so that many orders can be picked into containers on the cart during a single picking tour.

The main problem with picking into separate bins is the chance of mixing orders. Picking inaccuracies are definitely higher using this best practice, so it is best used with only the most experienced pickers. Pilot testing this approach will reveal if its total cost is less than using a downstream picking location to sort orders.

Cost: 💵   Installation time: 🕐

5.12 Store Kitted Inventory in an Accumulation Bin

If the warehouse staff accumulates kitted parts on a shelf or the floor of the warehouse, there is a strong possibility that the parts will become mixed with those of adjacent clusters of kitted parts, resulting in confusion on the shop floor and the likely issuance of additional parts from the warehouse to make up the perceived shortfall in each kit. Later, additional transactions will be required to reenter the excess parts issuances back into the warehouse.

These problems can be easily dealt with through the use of accumulation bins. All kitted parts are stored in these bins to ensure that no mixing will occur with nearby kits for other jobs. Bins can be of whatever size is most appropriate for a given kit size—the main issues are that the bin be easily movable to the shop floor and that it have sufficiently high walls to prevent mixing with other kits.

The main issue is ensuring that each accumulation bin be clearly identified as belonging to a specific job. This is not easy, since paper tags can be ripped off bins and lost or mixed with the tags for other kits. One approach is to create a tag storage slot with a Plexiglas cover in the front of each bin, into which a tag can be dropped. Another option is to put order numbers in a durable viewable sleeve and clip the sleeve securely to the bin. Yet another option is to permanently mark a bin number on the side of the accumulation bin, perhaps with paint, and cross-reference the bin number to the order number on a whiteboard mounted next to the accumulation area. The only problem with this last approach is that, though the warehouse staff may know which bin number corresponds to an order number, the manufacturing staff receiving the bin will have no idea what the number means, which calls for a matching whiteboard in the production area, or some similar cross-referencing system.

Cost: 💵   Installation time: 🕐

5.13 Use Standard Containers to Move, Store, and Count Inventory

In many warehouse settings, the ideal container is the pallet. It can arrive at the receiving dock, be efficiently moved to storage with a forklift, and eventually be carried from there to the shop floor. It is also simple to count inventory when stored in pallet sizes, while many racking systems are pre-configured to hold pallets, which readily fills a warehouse's cubic volume. This excellent level of efficiency stops when pallets are broken down into cases or single items. The putaway and picking staffs must now be much more careful in recording quantities moved, while the effort required to count stock becomes much higher.

A very good best practice is the use of standard containers for these partial-pallet situations. By using a standard container size, one can more efficiently move items, which might otherwise require individual piece-by-piece movement. Also, depending on how a container is set up, an inventory counter can glance at a container to determine the total quantity it contains.

Different containers will probably be needed for different types of stock, depending on the cubic volume of each one. A common approach is to fill several standard containers with the same item and pick only from the one in front. By doing so, an inventory counter can easily determine the quantities in all other filled containers and manually count only the one partial container in front. A variation on the standard container is a simple sealed plastic bag, which can be filled with a set quantity, labeled, and stapled shut. An inventory counter can determine its quantity immediately, while the usage signal (a ripped-open bag) indicates that a more careful count is in order.

The use of standard containers can be taken too far. In many situations, it is still easier to move, store, and count a partially used pallet load without going to the sometimes-considerable effort of shifting everything into standard containers. Its best application is for small parts that would otherwise be difficult to handle and count.

Cost: 💵 💵   *Installation time:*   🕐 🕐

5.14 Issue Parts in Full-Bin Increments

The warehouse can be snowed under with high transaction volumes when it incrementally transfers small quantities of parts to the shop floor each day. Every time a transaction is created, there is an increased risk of lowering inventory record accuracy. Also, the warehouse staff must use non-value-added time to create each transaction. Further, materials handlers must make multiple trips from the warehouse to the shop floor, making many small deliveries.

Though not an option in all manufacturing environments, a possible best practice is to issue parts in full-bin increments to the shop floor. By doing so, the warehouse staff never needs to create more than two transactions—one to issue a single large delivery to the shop floor, and possibly one more to return any remainders to stock. The materials handlers, whose work is significantly reduced, also appreciate this approach. Production management is generally pleased with it, since managers are better able to feed their operations with ready parts, but they are sometimes concerned with having more clutter on the shop floor. An alternative is to use smaller bin sizes for the most expensive items.

Cost: 🖩   *Installation time:* ●

5.15 Avoid Restocking during a Picking Shift

Many warehouses operate on a single shift. When they do so, the order picking staff must tour the warehouse in the face of a separate restocking crew that is attempting to replenish bins from which the pickers are attempting to remove items at the same time. This can cause confusion and less efficient picker travel, since they must negotiate aisles being blocked by the restocking crews. Also, it is too easy to record incorrect transactions when items are being removed from and shifted into bins at the same time.

The solution is to separate the picking and restocking shifts. For those companies unable or unwilling to staff an additional shift for the restocking crew, one can still apportion a single shift between the pickers and stockers, or reserve specific aisles for restocking while other aisles are being picked (though this can become an organizational nightmare). The best approach is to invest in multiple shifts, with a single shift solely reserved for restocking activities.

If restocking and picking must be done at the same time, consider using gravity-flow racks. These are racks angled down toward a stock picker, with built-in rollers to facilitate the movement of cases from the back of the rack to the front. Restocking is done from the back of the rack, well away from any pickers, and cartons automatically slide to the front, where pickers are stationed. This configuration allows for simultaneous restocking and picking without any aisle blockages.

Cost: *Installation time:*

5.16 Optimize Inventory Storage through Periodic Location Changes

Though inventory may initially be organized to reduce the travel time of order pickers, this may change over time as different items become more or less popular. This is a particular problem for items whose sales change dramatically on a seasonal basis, or in proportion to their presence in certain catalogs or short-term sales promotions. In such cases, the picking staff may suddenly find itself traveling much further distances to pick items than was the case just the day before.

A labor-intensive solution is to periodically review and revise inventory storage locations based on estimated demand patterns. This is not difficult for seasonal goods, since it is evident which items will soon experience changed levels of demand. Likewise, the imminent release of a new catalog should trigger inventory locational changes based on the contents of the catalog. On a very short-term basis, automated storage and retrieval systems can be assigned the task of completely shifting inventory overnight, so it is properly reconfigured to minimize its travel time the next day.

An advanced warehouse management system can perform this inventory review chore periodically, and can also recommend new inventory locations whenever the warehouse itself is reconfigured with new or revised storage locations. However, warehouse management systems offering this feature are extremely expensive. An alternative is to periodically bring in a consultant who can manually perform the same task; this approach can actually result in a better configuration than what is recommended by a computer since a consultant may use a larger array of configuration criteria than are built into a computer system.

Cost: *Installation time:*

6

Production Issues Impacting Inventory

This chapter addresses those 21 production best practices having a direct impact on inventory. As noted in Exhibit 6.1, the general thrust of these best practices is the simplification of the production process, such as using smaller machines that are more easily maintained, cellular production layouts, conveyors instead of aisles, and shorter setup times. The result of these various improvements is a significant reduction of work-in-process inventory, as well as a reduced need for the raw materials required to support the production process.

Unfortunately, most of the best practices noted in this chapter require a significant investment in either time or money, and usually both. For example, reducing or eliminating aisles requires a very long-term effort to rearrange the work area, as does the use of cellular production, reducing the length of assembly lines, and replacing straight assembly lines with serpentine ones.

Other changes are more organizational in nature, and can be accomplished in less time. These include shifting some easier maintenance tasks to the production staff, eliminating some pay incentive systems, and allowing workers to call suppliers about faulty raw materials. Though these can be implemented more easily, one can also run afoul of union rules or generate employee discontent, which require a considerable time period to overcome.

Other best practices can severely interrupt the flow of production by unbalancing the production process. This is a particular concern when management decides to produce to order rather than to stock, schedule certain parts to be produced only on one machine, reduce container sizes, or schedule smaller production batches. In these cases, it is best to use a pilot

93

Exhibit 6.1 *Summary of Production Best Practices Impacting Inventory*

	Best Practice	Cost	Install Time
6.1	Eliminate incentive pay systems causing excessive production	💵	🕐🕐
6.2	Standardize the number of shifts worked throughout a factory	💵💵	🕐🕐
6.3	Allow production workers to call suppliers about faulty materials	💵	🕐🕐
6.4	Invest in smaller, low-capacity machines rather than high-capacity ones	💵💵💵	🕐🕐🕐
6.5	Purchase machines from a single supplier	💵💵💵	🕐🕐🕐
6.6	Produce the same parts on the same machine every time	💵	🕐🕐
6.7	Perform inspections at the next downstream workstation	💵	🕐🕐🕐
6.8	Improve periodic equipment maintenance	💵💵	🕐🕐
6.9	Shift some equipment maintenance to the production staff	💵💵	🕐🕐
6.10	Preplan major equipment maintenance	💵	🕐🕐
6.11	Replace aisles with conveyors	💵💵💵	🕐🕐🕐
6.12	Schedule smaller production batches	💵	🕐🕐🕐
6.13	Produce to order rather than to stock	💵	🕐🕐🕐
6.14	Reduce container sizes	💵💵	🕐🕐🕐
6.15	Reduce setup times	💵💵	🕐🕐🕐
6.16	Shorten cycle times	💵💵💵	🕐🕐🕐
6.17	Replace straight assembly lines with serpentine lines	💵💵💵	🕐🕐🕐
6.18	Reduce the length of the assembly line	💵💵	🕐🕐
6.19	Use cellular manufacturing	💵💵💵	🕐🕐🕐
6.20	Group machine cells near common inventory storage areas	💵	🕐🕐🕐
6.21	Position local cell storage between workstations and aisles	💵	🕐

process to verify that a best practice can be implemented throughout the facility, or at least a gradual introduction of the concept to improve the production flow over a long period of time.

In short, implementing most of the best practices in this chapter can be difficult. However, the resulting smoother production flow, using short machine setups and minimal cycle times, can contribute to an exceptional reduction in a company's total inventory investment, and is well worth the effort.

6.1 Eliminate Incentive Pay Systems Causing Excessive Production

Some companies have adopted incentive pay systems under which employees are paid a bonus if they produce goods at the maximum possible level. While this certainly leads to high output rates, the practice also leads to three problems. First, employees may ignore quality problems in the drive to manufacture maximum product quantities, resulting in a large scrap or rework expense. If items require rework but there are insufficient rework resources available, this can also lead to a considerable amount of storage space being taken up by faulty products. Second, employees hell-bent on achieving a production bonus may produce in greater quantities than immediately needed, resulting in a large investment in finished goods inventory. This latter problem is generally not a large issue, since a company employing incentive pay systems typically manufactures using very large production runs for which excessive production is impossible. Finally, industrial engineers must be employed to create performance standards against which incentive pay is calibrated, while extra payroll staff is needed to collect detailed time information for all employees subject to the incentive pay system—both groups represent an expensive addition to corporate overhead.

A possible best practice to resolve the issue, depending on the circumstances, is to eliminate incentive pay systems. By doing so, one can shift the focus of employee attention away from the volume produced and toward other issues, such as maximizing throughput from a particular bottleneck operation or increasing product quality. The use of incentive pay systems is particularly inappropriate when cell manufacturing is used, since only one unit is typically manufactured at a time, and production is supposed to cease once immediate needs are fulfilled. Further, the industrial engineers and payroll clerks used to create and track incentive pay standards are no longer needed.

Incentive pay can work well in a high-volume environment, if it is coupled with further incentives requiring employees to also pay attention to the quality of units produced.

Cost: 💰   Installation time: 🕐 🕐

6.2 Standardize the Number of Shifts Worked throughout a Factory

When a company has several subplants operating within a factory, some subplants will operate for additional shifts per day. This may be caused by the requirements of reworking a large amount of inventory, or catching up after extended machine downtime, or perhaps because a subplant includes a major bottleneck operation that must be run around the clock. Whatever the reason may be, the existence of a subplant operating for an extra shift will result in a buffer inventory buildup for the full period of the shift. Not only does this constitute an added investment in inventory, but it also creates a risk that faulty products will be built for an entire shift before the next downstream operation sees the inventory. Further, there is not usually enough storage space available in the production area to store all the inventory created during a shift, so it must be moved into the warehouse and then moved back out again once workers arrive on a subsequent shift to staff the other subplants; this requires extra materials handling labor, and increases the risk of damaging the inventory while it is being moved.

A possible solution is to mandate the same number of shifts worked across all subplants. By doing so, there is neither a buildup of an inventory buffer, nor a need to store the inventory, and the risk of faulty inventory accumulation is eliminated.

The main reason cited for *not* installing this best practice is disparities in the capacity levels of the various subplants, such that production levels are not balanced across the entire facility. This objection is a valid one, and requires a gradual adjustment in equipment capacity levels across the factory before the best practice can be implemented.

Cost: 💰 💰   Installation time: 🕐 🕐

6.3 Allow Production Workers to Call Suppliers about Faulty Materials

There is normally just one person in a company who is allowed to contact suppliers, and that person is usually in the purchasing department. The intent behind this arrangement is to ensure that all information is consistently accumulated and reviewed before being passed to the supplier, on the grounds that the supplier must not be burdened with multiple channels of possibly conflicting communications. The problem with this approach is that, when faulty supplier materials are spotted in the production area, notice of the problem must work its way from there into the purchasing department, and from there to the supplier. Since the purchasing person only has second-hand knowledge of the problem, the exact status of the issue may not be correctly transmitted to the supplier. Further, the supplier representative contacted is probably a salesperson, who then takes the issue to the supplier's production staff, thereby introducing another opportunity to scramble the information. The result is considerable delay in fixing the problem, which may be incorrectly communicated to the supplier.

The solution is to allow the production staff to call their counterparts in the supplier's production department. By doing so, all time delays are eliminated, while the exact nature of the problem is clearly communicated. The result is fewer production delays because high-quality replacement materials will arrive from the supplier more quickly.

This tends to be a difficult best practice to implement, for the purchasing staff has a hard time not being the primary point of contact. This can also be an issue for the supplier, who usually has similar notions about the role of its sales staff.

Cost: *Installation time:*

6.4 Invest in Smaller, Low-Capacity Machines Rather than High-Capacity Ones

Managers like to purchase the latest, largest, and most complex machines. By doing so, they obtain equipment with a higher rate of throughput, typically resulting in a lower cost per unit. However, after having made the considerable investment in this equipment, they also find that any downtime for maintenance results in no production at all, since they could not afford to purchase backup equipment. Also, because of the size and expense of the machine, they are inclined to have long production runs in order to justify the investment, resulting in excess inventory levels. Thus, having the biggest and best equipment does not appear to yield a very flexible manufacturing process.

The solution is to invest in multiple smaller machines. By doing so, there is equipment available to take on immediate production needs while other similar equipment is unavailable due to repairs. Also, because of the general reduction of complexity in lower-capacity machines, it is easy to reconfigure them for different types of production, so they can be used for many short production runs to match their use more closely to demand, thereby avoiding excess inventory. Finally, these less complex machines are easier to maintain and require less skilled maintenance technicians to do so.

However, the use of high-capacity machines still makes sense when a company has enormously long production runs, especially when competition is so intense that reducing the cost per unit to the absolute minimum is mandatory. From a practical perspective, a company will experience varying levels of demand for its product mix, and will need to acquire a range of low- to high-volume equipment to match that demand.

Cost: 💵 💵 💵   *Installation time:* ⬤ ⬤ ⬤

6.5 Purchase Machines from a Single Supplier

A company must stock spare parts for each machine it uses, so there will be no wait time to procure parts at the last minute if a machine breaks down. This can involve quite a large number of parts if the machines are purchased from different suppliers, since there is no chance of commonality of parts between machines. With the larger number of parts to track, the complexity of spare parts inventory grows substantially, increasing the risk of a parts stockout that keeps a machine from running. If this happens repeatedly, the inventory management staff will be more likely to plan for higher levels of inventory in order to work around the problem.

A possible solution is to purchase as many machines as possible from the same supplier. By doing so, a company is more likely to find that many spare parts are used in multiple machines, resulting in an overall decrease in the number of spare parts to track, which can then result in less machine downtime. An added benefit is less maintenance training, since suppliers presumably design all their machines for similar types of maintenance procedures.

Cost: *Installation time:*

6.6 Produce the Same Parts on the Same Machine Every Time

When an item is scheduled for production, the production scheduling staff typically assigns it to whichever machine will be available next. When this happens, a setup person spends a considerable amount of time making minor adjustments to the equipment and making test runs to verify that the items are being produced within predetermined tolerance levels. A common result is a considerable amount of scrap at the beginning of the production run, which in turn forces the materials management staff to keep an excessive amount of raw materials on hand to offset the scrap losses.

The reason for extended test runs is that no two machines are exactly alike, either due to minor tolerance differences or variations in wear and tear. Even if the setup staff keeps extensive notes on each setup, these instructions may not precisely apply to a different machine, resulting in multiple test runs. The solution is to schedule the same part to be run on the same machine as much as possible. Setups can then be fully documented and used repeatedly with minimal test runs required.

The problem is the additional strain on production schedulers, who now have the added constraint of being able to use only certain machines for certain products. The solution is to assign high-quantity parts to a few machines, which will take up all of their capacity, and assign all low-quantity parts to the remaining machines. Since the remaining machines will typically have short production runs, they will be available more frequently for new production requirements. The best setup staff and machine operators can be assigned to the machines running low-quantity parts, since these will require by far the largest number of setups.

Cost: *Installation time:*

6.7 Perform Inspections at the Next Downstream Workstation

The quality assurance function is typically assigned to a specialized team, who are the only ones authorized to conduct quality checks. By segregating this function, only a few inspectors are available to halt production if the production process goes seriously awry, resulting in the possible accumulation of considerable amounts of scrap before a problem is detected. To counteract the amount of scrap being produced, the materials managers will keep more raw materials on hand, increasing the company's inventory investment. Further, if a company tries to reduce scrap by adding more inspectors, it incurs a major addition to its overhead expense.

The solution is to shift as much of the inspection burden as possible to the next downstream workstation. By doing so, inspection is completed as soon after a work step as possible, so that very few additional products will have been made before the error is noticed, resulting in less scrap. Also, the next downstream workstation probably needs to incorporate the newly completed item into a larger subassembly or subject it to further manufacturing steps, so a faulty item will be immediately apparent. Finally, having someone besides the producing employee conduct the review will ensure a more objective examination.

The primary difficulty with this best practice is that it works well only in a cellular manufacturing environment where work-in-process is passed directly from workstation to workstation, with minimal inventory levels building up between them, thereby allowing for immediate downstream testing and feedback loops.

Cost: 💵   *Installation time:* 🕐 🕐 🕐

6.8 Improve Periodic Equipment Maintenance

When a company's production equipment has a continuing habit of breaking down, the materials management staff tends to plan around it by building up reserves of finished goods inventory, so they can still meet customer demands. In addition, a machine's ability to create products within preset tolerances drops in concert with the level of preventive maintenance, so there will be an increasing amount of scrap and rework. As the scrap level rises, materials managers once again plan for more inventory, but this time in the raw materials area. Thus, the net result of poor equipment maintenance is a larger investment in both raw and finished goods inventory.

The solution is to adopt a more aggressive preventive maintenance program. This should involve the creation of and adherence to a long-term maintenance program, as well as an investment in sufficient maintenance staff time to ensure that scheduled work can be completed. The maintenance manager's performance should also be based on his ability to gradually improve both the percentage of operating time of all equipment and the percentage of scrap caused by out-of-specification equipment.

The primary difficulty with this best practice is getting over the initial hurdle of starting up a new maintenance program while at the same time working on machines that have stopped functioning due to the lack of preventive maintenance and require immediate attention. The only solution is budgeting for additional maintenance staff during this startup period, which requires extra funding. Another problem is that the maintenance staff may have no idea of what constitutes preventive maintenance on equipment, so it may be necessary to bring in either consultants or representatives from the equipment manufacturers to assist them in creating preventive maintenance schedules.

Cost: 💵 💵   *Installation time:* 🕐 🕐

6.9 Shift Some Equipment Maintenance to the Production Staff

When a machine in the production area breaks down, all production stops until such time as a maintenance technician becomes available and fixes it. This can seriously throw off the daily production schedule, causing a ripple effect of rescheduled production jobs throughout the facility. The most significant impact is on downstream workstations, which may need the broken machine's output to continue their work. A common result is excess work-in-process in front of each machine in the facility, on the theory that enough inventory must be retained to keep all machines busy in case one of them breaks down. Further, if a machine breakdown is sufficiently critical, a maintenance technician will be pulled off another repair job in order to deal with it, which may result in some other machine being disabled while the more critical repair is being completed.

A partial solution is to train the machine operators to perform continuous preventive maintenance on their equipment. This can include a standard lubrication schedule at the beginning of a worker's shift, or during inactive periods of the day. Also, if simple recurring items cause a breakdown, operators can be shown how to deal with these problems, leaving only major issues for the technicians to deal with.

If a production facility is organized into cells (see best practice 6.19, "Use Cellular Manufacturing"), maintenance staff can even be assigned to specific cells, with local work facilities and local machine parts storage, so they can more quickly address maintenance problems as they arise.

This best practice requires additional operator training, so management must be willing to make this investment. There can also be a problem if there are union-imposed work rules in place, so that only maintenance technicians can fix equipment. In this situation, renegotiation of the work rules is the only solution.

Cost: 💵 💵   *Installation time:* ● ●

6.10 Preplan Major Equipment Maintenance

When the maintenance staff decides to perform major maintenance on machines, it is extremely common to see them dismantle the machine, leaving parts strewn about the production floor, meander through the maintenance task, and find that they must rebuild or order parts, leaving the equipment inoperable for long periods of time. This has a significant impact on the production flow from two perspectives. First, the inventory management staff is probably aware of the maintenance department's penchant for very long maintenance jobs, and so will plan for long production runs in advance of the maintenance, thereby building inventories against a perceived long downtime. Second, if the maintenance period stretches well past the original projection, the company may have to turn away or delay sales orders.

The solution is to thoroughly preplan major maintenance operations. This involves the written itemization of every step in the dismantling, repair, and reassembly process, with estimates of time required for each step and assignments of tasks to specific maintenance personnel. Then, once the maintenance begins, the assigned staff must be locked onto the project until it is completed, so the machine can be brought back online as soon as possible. After several consecutive experiences of completing maintenance within the estimated time period, the inventory management staff will begin to trust the downtime estimate again, and will stop building up excess inventories in advance of the scheduled maintenance dates.

Cost: *Installation time:*

6.11   Replace Aisles with Conveyors

The conventional view of a factory is of a broad, open work area crossed by wide aisles, down which zoom forklifts carrying inventory between the various workstations. The trouble is those aisles, which require heavy lifting equipment to move inventory situated next to a machine on one side of an aisle to the next machine, possibly located just a few feet away on the other side of the aisle. The first machine operator must keep churning out parts until he or she has created a sufficiently full load to make up a pallet, which a forklift operator can then pick up and move to the next machine. This presents several problems. First, inventory builds up between workstations only because of the need to have adequate pallet loads. Second, if the initial workstation operator is making parts that are out of specification, he or she will create an entire pallet load before the next workstation operator notices the problem, resulting in the scrapping of the entire load. Third, the flow of inventory is dependent on the timely arrival of a forklift operator, who may not be available.

For these reasons, one should consider laying out the product area with either narrow aisles or none at all, with conveyors running directly from workstation to workstation. Besides the obvious reduction in work-in-process inventory, this also has a massive impact on the amount of floor space used.

One problem with this approach is the cost of conveyors, which can be reduced by packing workstations as close together as possible. Another issue is that conveyors will break down from time to time. This issue can be dealt with either by using a preventive maintenance program or by using angled conveyors with rollers that require only the force of gravity to move items, rather than a motor system.

Cost: 💵💵💵   *Installation time:* ⬤⬤⬤

6.12 Schedule Smaller Production Batches

Traditional cost accounting dictates that the setup costs associated with a production run can be reduced by spreading the cost over the largest possible number of units—therefore, really large batches give the appearance of yielding the lowest per-unit costs. The trouble is that this logic ignores several key items. First, if there is a quality problem in the manufacturing process, no one may find out until a large part (or all) of the batch has been completed, resulting in a massive amount of scrapped inventory. Second, there is generally no immediate need for all the products completed in such a large batch, so the warehouse must find space for it all. Third, the finished goods inventory may become obsolete while sitting in the warehouse, resulting in a major obsolescence write-off. In short, the downstream inventory cost of a large production run easily exceeds its setup cost.

The solution is to shorten the size of the production batch. Typically, this requires an intensive review of the changeover process at the beginning of each production run to shrink the changeover time. By doing so, the changeover cost becomes so low that it is economical to have batch sizes of as little as one unit. This results in minimal scrap due to quality problems, while there is no longer a need to create massive unit quantities, which in turn shrinks inventory storage and obsolescence costs.

Though an excellent best practice, shrinking batch sizes is not possible in process flow industries. It also requires wholehearted acceptance from the industrial engineering and production staffs, who must implement it.

Cost: 💵   *Installation time:* ⬤⬤⬤

6.13 Produce to Order rather than to Stock

The most common production planning technique is to produce parts in accordance with a demand forecast. Raw materials are ordered, stocked, and converted into finished goods without there being any customer orders directly tied to the production planning process. This approach inevitably results in excess inventory, since some products may never be sold, or will at least sit in the warehouse for a long time before this happens.

A possible solution is to authorize production only in response to a direct customer order. When this approach is used, only enough finished goods are produced to fill the order, leaving no finished goods inventory on hand at all, and therefore keeping a company's inventory investment at the lowest possible level. Making this best practice work requires great attention to machine setup reductions, so that production runs of as little as one unit can be economically produced. Also, a company must do everything possible to reduce total cycle times, since a customer will not usually wait weeks for a product to be manufactured.

This best practice is not applicable in a number of situations. For example, if customers are highly sensitive to delivery times, some finished goods probably will be needed in order to fill spot purchases. Also, if there is a strong order history for a particular product, one can probably schedule production even in the absence of specific orders. Conversely, producing to order is most applicable for low-volume products where the risk of obsolescence is high.

Cost: *Installation time:*

6.14 Reduce Container Sizes

When an employee completes work on an item, he or she typically places it in a container for transport to the next downstream workstation. That container stays next to the workstation until the employee has completely filled it, at which point it is moved to the next workstation. If the container is a large one, a considerable amount of work-in-process inventory can build up before it is time to move the container. If there are a great many workstations in use, each one using the same size container, the total work-in-process created by the size of the container can be considerable. Not only does this represent a significant inventory investment, but there is also a greater risk of scrap losses, since an entire container must be filled with potentially faulty parts before the employee at the next workstation has a chance to review the parts and discover any problems.

Simply reducing the size of the containers can mitigate both problems. For example, if every storage container in the production area is cut in half, this automatically reduces the work-in-process level by one-half. The process can theoretically be continued until each container holds just one item, or the containers are completely eliminated.

The main objection to this best practice is that the containers represent a work buffer between workstations, so there is always enough work to do even if the feeding workstation stops production for some reason. Solving this problem requires either an acceptance that some machines will be underutilized or a great deal of attention to balancing machine capacities throughout the factory.

Cost: *Installation time:*

6.15   Reduce Setup Times

When a machine requires a substantial amount of time to be switched over to a new configuration for the production of a different part, there is a natural tendency to have very long production runs of the same part in order to spread the cost of the changeover across as many parts as possible. The trouble is that not all the parts may be needed right away, so this practice tends to fill the warehouse with excess inventory. Also, if the machine was initially set up incorrectly, a large amount of faulty product may be created before anyone notices the error, resulting in a great deal of rework or scrap.

The solution is to reduce machine setup times to such an extent that it becomes practical to have production runs of as little as one unit. Besides having very small production runs, this best practice also results in greatly reduced scrap, since faulty products will be spotted by the downstream workstation operator at once (assuming a minimal work-in-process buffer between workstations). A large body of knowledge has been accumulated in this area, including the videotaping of a machine changeover session for easier analysis, the use of standardized (and fewer) quick-release fasteners on machine parts, color-coded parts, standardized and prepositioned changeover tools, and so on.

This is an excellent best practice; the only downside is the time required to analyze each machine for changeover alterations. This effort is usually repaid many times over by the results.

Cost: 💵 💵   *Installation time:* 🕓 🕓 🕓

6.16 Shorten Cycle Times

The preceding best practice noted that long machine setup times result in a major investment in work-in-process inventory. The same issue arises for the entire factory when looking at the total time required to complete a product, beginning with the formulation of a production schedule, moving parts to production from the warehouse, wait times between machines, and storage of finished goods prior to delivery to a customer. In many respects, more inventory problems can arise because of a long cycle time than from using long production runs for individual machines. The trouble is that the cycle time may be so long (months, or longer) that completed products that may have appeared to be a good idea at the time of production scheduling are obsolete by the time they reach the finished goods storage area. Thus, long cycle times result in a greater inventory investment, as well as a greater risk of obsolete inventory.

The solution is an ongoing project to reduce cycle times. This involves shrinking supplier lead times, installing production cells where applicable, reducing machine setup times, cutting work-in-process queues, and so on. The end result is the ability to produce on very short notice, which then allows a company either to build strictly to customer orders or at least to build in accordance with a very short-term sales forecast.

This best practice is, in some respects, a compilation of multiple best practices noted in this chapter, and so requires considerable time to accomplish. To focus company attention on it, the production manager should calculate cycle time by using an occasional audit, and track this information on a trend line. Rather than calculate the information for each product manufactured (of which there may be many), it is easier to track this information for a sample of the higher-volume items in order to get a general idea of trend changes.

Cost: 💵 💵 💵   *Installation time:* 🕓 🕓 🕓

6.17 Replace Straight Assembly Lines with Serpentine Lines

The typical assembly line is comprised of a single straight conveyor down which parts flow, with raw materials at one end and a finished product at the other. This classic production method tends to suffer from a high product defect rate, because the assembly line may be so long that people causing incorrect assembly problems at one end of the line are completely out of touch with people at the other end who are discovering the problems. A common result is that quality inspectors are added to the end of the line, who report to management on mistakes found, resulting in investigation a few days later. In the meantime, errors will continue until a manager finds and resolves the problem.

A better solution is the serpentine line, in which the conveyor is compressed into a connecting series of "U" shapes like a snake. By using this approach, assembly workers are much closer together and can communicate far more easily. When a person at one end of this line finds a mistake, it is usually possible to talk to everyone on the line, determine the problem at once, and correct it on the spot. The result is a much lower scrap rate, which in turn results in a lower investment in raw materials.

A common concern with serpentine lines is how to handle product flow around corners, of which there are many in this line configuration. A number of conveyor alternatives exist, though they are more expensive than a simple straight conveyor. Another issue is the reconfiguration of the assembly area to accommodate a serpentine line, which may require a long-term, gradual realignment of equipment in accordance with a master facility plan.

Cost: 🪙 🪙 🪙   *Installation time:* ● ● ●

6.18 Reduce the Length of the Assembly Line

Assembly lines typically contain a fair amount of space between workers, which gives them a spacious feel. Unfortunately, it also leaves a considerable amount of room on the conveyor for extra work-in-process inventory. The amount of excess inventory is the total work-in-process moving between workers on the assembly line that is not currently being modified by the workers. In many cases, this can constitute three-quarters or more of the total inventory moving down the assembly line.

The solution is to shorten the assembly line, which eliminates all work-in-process inventory that would otherwise have been moving between employees. The ideal line length should result in just one unit of work-in-process inventory per assembly worker.

The objection to this best practice is that the extra work-in-process is really a buffer between workers, which is needed in case of worker speed differences, thereby keeping all employees working at maximum speed at all times. Though a valid objection, the industrial engineering staff can be called on to review the work flow and devise work efficiencies to reduce worker speed differences, thereby eliminating the need for work-in-process buffer stock.

Cost: 💷 💷   Installation time: 🎯 🎯

6.19 Use Cellular Manufacturing

A common arrangement of machines on the shop floor is by functional group, where all machines of one type are kept in one place. By doing so, jobs requiring a specific type of processing can all be routed to the same cluster of machines and loaded into whichever one will become available for processing next. The emphasis of this approach is on keeping every machine fully utilized. However, by doing so, there tend to be large batches of work-in-process inventory waiting in front of machines, because this approach calls for the completion of a job at the last workstation before the entire job is moved to the next workstation. The large amount of inventory involved tends to mask the presence of improperly manufactured parts, of which an entire batch may have been created before anyone notices them at the next workstation. It also requires the existence of a sizeable production planning staff, since workflows must be preplanned for all machines in the factory. Further, work-in-process must usually be moved considerable distances across the factory in order to reach the next workstation, which introduces the risk of damage to the parts as well as the added materials handling expense.

These problems with large inventories and scrap can be significantly reduced though the use of cellular manufacturing. Under this technique, a small cluster of machines are set up in close proximity to one another, each one performing a sequential task in completing a specific type or common set of products. Usually, only one or a few employees work in each cell, and walk a single part all the way through the cell before moving on to the next part. By doing so, there is obviously no work-in-process in the cell at all, besides the part on which machining is currently being performed. Also, it becomes quite evident when a part is improperly manufactured, since subsequent machining steps cannot be completed. With no work-in-process to hide scrap, employees can take action at once to fix the problem. Further, by slowing down the fastest machines in the cell to the speed of the slowest machine, there is no way for inventory to build up in front of the slowest machine. In addition, product families (those having similar parts) are typically assigned to the same cells, so the people working in those cells gain considerable experience producing the same items, which tends to improve product quality. Also, cells creating parts for the same finished product are grouped close together, resulting in the minimum amount of inventory movement between cells. In addition, the production planning staff has only to arrange for materials to arrive at the beginning workstation of a cell, rather than planning movements to each machine within the cell, which greatly reduces the amount of inventory planning staff. Finally, cellular manufacturing greatly reduces a product's cycle time, which was just mentioned as another best practice. This approach shortens cycle time by eliminating the wait time from the manufacturing process that arises when jobs must queue in front of machines that have been grouped by function.

There are objections to the cellular manufacturing approach. One is that the full capacity of the fastest machines is not used, since cells move at the speed of the slowest workstation. This is certainly true, but most machines do not operate at anywhere near their maximum capacity anyway, and the cellular approach reduces inventory so much that the capacity issue becomes less important in light of this other benefit. Another problem is that some parts are required so infrequently that it makes little sense to configure a cell for them; if so, some machine groupings by function still can be retained to process these parts. A third issue is that an equipment failure within a cell can stop the entire cell from functioning. When this represents a significant risk, a company can designate another cell as a backup to the primary cell. The backup cell concept is also useful when a cell becomes overloaded, since some jobs can be shifted to the backup at that time. However, when work is offloaded to a different cell, it is better to offload a small number of large-quantity jobs than a large number of small ones, since this will result in the backup cell workers having to get used to machine setups for a smaller number of parts, which results in better efficiency and higher product quality.

Cost: 💵 💵 💵   Installation time: ⏱ ⏱ ⏱

6.20 Group Machine Cells Near Common Inventory Storage Areas

When a company implements cellular manufacturing, it sometimes finds that cells using the same raw materials are positioned a considerable distance apart on the shop floor. When this happens, management has the option to store raw materials in a central warehouse and undergo the materials-handling expense of moving the raw materials to the cells. Alternatively, managers can store the required inventory at each cell; but this involves an investment in twice the inventory, since there are two locations to stock.

The solution is to move the cells as close together as possible, so the inventory can be stored in one location close to both cells. By doing so, both the inventory investment and materials handling expense are minimized.

However, shifting production cells on a crowded production floor is not an easy proposition. The best approach is to adopt a master plan of what the shop floor should look like, with adjacent cells to reduce inventory storage requirements, and gradually work toward completion of the plan as the opportunity presents itself. One should also keep in mind that there is no ideal shop floor layout, given the constantly changing mix of products and the corresponding mix of machine cells required to produce them. Consequently, the master floor plan should be revised regularly to match these changing requirements.

Cost: 💵   Installation time: ⏱ ⏱ ⏱

6.21 Position Local Cell Storage between Workstations and Aisles

When a company installs cellular manufacturing, considerably less of the manufacturing floor space is used, because the machines are jammed much closer together than was previously the case. If this happens in concert with a previous best practice of narrowing the aisles between machines in order to reduce inventory transport distances, a safety issue arises—workers may be stationed immediately adjacent to aisles, and can be injured by movements in the aisles.

The solution is to position localized inventory storage for each cell between the workstations and aisles, thereby providing a safety buffer for the cell workers. If transport equipment in an aisle veers off the aisle, it will strike the buffer inventory rather than the workers. This best practice has the added benefit of positioning both raw materials and finished inventory where it can be most easily dropped off and picked up by the materials handling staff.

Cost: *Installation time:*

7

Inventory Transactions

This chapter addresses those 15 transaction-based best practices having a direct impact on inventory. As noted in Exhibit 7.1, it begins with a simple reduction in the amount of information maintained, continues through several different methods for automatically collecting information, eliminates data entry backlogs, recommends several auditing techniques, and notes several systemic changes for both handling inventory counts and using a warehouse-wide transaction control system.

The first five best practices show an ascending path of automation that can result in a completely paperless system for recording inventory transactions. The most basic improvement is the substitution of barcodes for manual entries, which can be made more efficient through the use of portable radio frequency terminals for real-time transaction updates. The most advanced approach, which is still in its infancy, is the use of radio frequency identification for the seamless and automatic recording of inventory movements. A highly recommended best practice that can be introduced anywhere is the basic approach of eliminating all transactional entry backlogs, so that transactions are recorded closer to the occurrence of the event. There are four best practices noted for improving inventory accuracy, ranging from the 100 percent verification of inventory balances (for high-value items), to the much simpler review of negative book inventory balances. Of the group, the most commonly used is the implementation of cycle counting for long-term improvements in inventory record accuracy. The chapter ends with a discussion of warehouse management systems (WMSs), which are very expensive materials and labor management systems that control all movements within the warehouse. A WMS represents the pinnacle of com-

Exhibit 7.1 *Summary of Inventory Transactions Best Practices*

	Best Practice	Cost	Install Time
7.1	Reduce the number of stored data elements	💵	⬤
7.2	Record inventory transactions with bar codes	💵 💵	⬤ ⬤
7.3	Record inventory transactions with radio frequency communications	💵 💵 💵	⬤ ⬤
7.4	Track inventory with radio frequency identification (RFID)	💵 💵	⬤ ⬤
7.5	Eliminate all paper from inventory transactions	💵 💵	⬤ ⬤ ⬤
7.6	Use the kanban system to pull transactions through the facility	💵	⬤ ⬤ ⬤
7.7	Eliminate all transaction backlogs	💵 💵	⬤
7.8	Verify that receipts are entered in the computer system at once	💵	⬤ ⬤
7.9	Have customers order by part number	💵	⬤
7.10	Audit all inventory transactions	💵	⬤
7.11	Compare recorded inventory activity to on-hand inventories	💵 💵	⬤
7.12	Immediately review all negative inventory balances	💵	⬤
7.13	Replace the physical count process with cycle counts	💵	⬤ ⬤
7.14	Streamline the physical count process	💵	⬤ ⬤
7.15	Install a warehouse management system	💵 💵 💵	⬤ ⬤

puterized warehouse management, and is highly applicable to large, high-volume locations.

With the exception of the radio frequency identification (RFID) and WMS best practices, these transaction-based best practices are not excessively expensive. The ones applicable to the broadest range of warehouse activities are the use of barcodes, radio frequency communications, elimination of transaction backlogs, and use of cycle counting.

7.1 Reduce the Number of Stored Data Elements

The typical company database contains a vast array of fields related to inventory, particularly in the item master file and bill of materials. When entering information into screens that tie to these files, one must tab through many fields before reaching the one requiring an update. This makes it possible to enter information into the wrong field, which can lead to incorrect information output by the system. In addition, when entering a new item, the system commonly requires one to enter information into all the fields; when this happens, it may take a great deal of time to complete the entry of a single record. Further, the company may not use some of the data entered, so the time spent entering the data was a waste of time. Thus, the large number of data elements causes data inaccuracies as well as data entry inefficiencies.

The solution is to limit the number of data elements being stored. This is best achieved through a high-level enterprise resource planning (ERP) or manufacturing resources planning (MRP II) system that allows one to block selected fields. By doing so, one can scroll through a record much more quickly, thereby achieving considerable data entry efficiency.

The concept can be taken a step further if a company is not using some features of its computer systems. For example, if it is not yet calculating the cubic volume taken up by each inventory item, it should consider locking users out of the cubic volume field in the item master file until it is ready to productively use this information. By entering only the information needed to run those system features currently utilized, one can improve data entry efficiency and also avoid dealing with data that may be incorrectly entered into the unused fields.

If a company is already using cellular manufacturing techniques (see Chapter 6, "Production Issues Impacting Inventory"), one can also avoid using the inventory location field. So little inventory is stored in the production areas near cells that there is no need to assign locations to stored items. Instead, cell managers can easily see what is located in the adjacent storage area.

Cost:　　　　　　*Installation time:*

7.2 Record Inventory Transactions with Barcodes

There are many inventory transactions to record in the life of an SKU, such as receipt, storage in a bin, transfer to the shop floor, and so on. Every time these transactions are entered into the computer system, one must manually enter a transaction code, the part number being moved, and typically the location code to which it is being shifted. Each of these data items represents an opportunity for an incorrect entry, which cumulatively results in a significant reduction in the accuracy of inventory records.

Bar coding is a good, time-tested approach for improving the accuracy of inventory transactions. In brief, the warehouse staff creates a bar-coded part number for each item as it enters the warehouse and attaches the barcode to the item. It also creates preset barcode labels for each warehouse location and posts them at each location. Anyone moving stock then scans the part number barcode and the barcode for the location to which it is being shifted, and manually enters a quantity and transaction code to complete the transaction. This information is typically entered on a portable scanner that can be either placed in a cradle to upload information to the central computer system, or used in real-time with a built-in radio to transmit and receive transaction information.

Though this approach can significantly reduce transaction errors, there are a few problems to be aware of. First, if someone creates the wrong barcode label for an item when it first enters the warehouse, then all transactions later using that barcode will also be incorrect—a clear case of technology *increasing* the rate of transaction errors, rather than the reverse. However, one can mitigate this problem by setting the barcode printer to print not only the barcode, but also the product description and part number in English just below the barcode, so one can verify the accuracy of the barcode. Another problem is the cost of this equipment. Though a scanner can easily cost $2,000, and the rugged environment can lead to a relatively short equipment life before replacement, the reduced transaction cost can easily result in a headcount reduction in the warehouse that rapidly pays for the investment. A third problem is the time interval between a scan into a portable scanner and when the stored information is uploaded into the central computer system. If a cycle counter were to run an inventory report after a materials handler had removed an item from stock but before the move had been recorded, she would find an error during her count, and enter a correcting transaction—resulting in another error when the original scan was finally uploaded. The best solution is to use real-time radio frequency scanning (see the following best practice) to upload transactions immediately. Finally, the warehouse staff must be carefully trained in the use of this equipment to ensure that scans are made correctly and properly uploaded. One should schedule not only training for new employees, but also refresher training for the existing staff, as well as formal training in any incremental improvements made to the system over time.

Cost: *Installation time:*

7.3 Record Inventory Transactions with Radio Frequency Communications

Even if a company uses barcodes to accurately record inventory transactions, this still does not address the problem of timeliness. A person could scan a barcode into a portable device but not upload the data to a central database until the end of his shift, resulting in a significant shortfall in database accuracy. If the materials handling staff tries to solve the problem by routing their forklifts past a fixed terminal in order to enter information, they are creating longer putaway or picking routes that contribute to reducing labor efficiency. Further, if a company tries to install a WMS as noted in the final best practice of this chapter, it will be working with transactional data that could be hours old, probably resulting in incorrect putaway or picking instructions to the staff, as well as inaccurate inventories for cycle counters to review.

The solution is radio frequency (RF) communications. This takes the form of a handheld or truck-mounted computer, frequently integrated with a barcode scanner that communicates by radio waves with a central warehouse database. For example, a person picks a part from stock, scans the item's barcode and the location barcode from which it was taken, and enters the quantity withdrawn. The portable unit immediately transmits this information to the central database, along with a time stamp, so that the quantity in the inventory location is adjusted and a picking record is created that can be used for a delivery to either a customer or the production floor. If the database record indicates that there is not enough inventory on hand to record the withdrawal, it can even send a query back to the employee, asking for a recount of the bin's contents. Thus, one can use an RF system to verify transactions, achieve high rates of record accuracy, almost completely eliminate paper-based transactions, and have a more efficient work force.

Mechanically, an RF system begins with a transactional entry being transmitted from a portable unit, which is received by a radio transponder that routes the transaction through a network controller that essentially emulates a hard-wired computer terminal. From there, the information passes along the standard company computer network to the company materials management database. Transaction verifications flow along the same route back to the portable terminal. If there are many portable units in use at one time, the radio transponder will poll the units in a looping sequence until it finds one that wants to deliver a transaction, and then it continues with the polling after receiving the transaction. An alternative approach is for the portable units to transmit transactions only when other units are not transmitting.

A significant problem with RF systems is interference caused by factory equipment. Prior to installing an RF system, one should have the supplier tour all corners of the warehouse, and anywhere else where the portable RF units may be used, to ensure that there are no "dead" zones from which transmissions cannot be made. It is also possible for a large number of portable units to cause a bottleneck on the main company network, simply because of the large volume of transactions they are initiating. This can be corrected by increasing the network throughput at whatever bottleneck is causing the problem.

Cost: 💵 💵 💵   *Installation time:* 🔨 🔨

7.4 Track Inventory with Radio Frequency Identification

A major problem with any manually operated inventory system is the vast number of transactions required to track receipts into the warehouse, moves between bins, issuances to the shop floor, returns from the floor, scrap, and so on. Every time someone creates a transaction, there is a chance of incorrect data being entered, resulting in a cumulative variance that can be quite large by the time a stock item has wended its way through all possible transactions. Incorrect inventory information leads to a host of other problems, such as stockouts, incorrect purchasing quantities, and a seriously inaccurate cost of goods sold.

One way to avoid these transactional errors is to use the new RFID technology. Though only recently formulated (the RFID standards can be found at www.epcglobalinc.org), the technology has already been adopted by Wal-Mart, which should ensure a rapid rollout in at least the retail part of the economy. The basic RFID concept has been around for years—attach a tiny transmitter to each product, which then sends a unique encoded product identification number to a reader device. The cost of these transmitter tags has dropped to about 10 cents, which begins to make it a cost-effective alternative for some applications. Growing use of the technology will likely reduce the cost further.

When a tagged inventory item is passed near a reader device, the reader emits a signal that powers up the tag, allowing it to emit its unique product identification number. In order to read a large number of tags, the reader turns on each tag in sequence, reads it, and turns off the tag, thereby preventing confusion with repetitive reads. The tag information is then logged into the inventory tracking system, indicating an inventory move past the point where the reader was located.

The most likely implementation scenario for RFID is to first roll it out within the warehouse and manufacturing areas of a company, first using it to track entire pallet loads (good for receiving and inventory control transactions), and then implementing it for smaller tracking units, such as cases (good for picking, cycle counts, and shipment transactions) or even individual items (most applicable for work-in-progress inventory or retail applications). This implementation approach allows for a gradually increasing investment in the technology as a company gradually learns about its applicability.

A major advantage of RFID is its ability to provide inventory count information without any manual transaction keypunching. This eliminates the need for manual receiving, inventory move, and issuance transactions. It can also provide real-time information about the precise location of all inventory, which can assist with locating missing inventory, arranging cycle counts, and auditing stock. If issued to suppliers, this information tells them precisely how much inventory is currently on hand, so they can more accurately determine when to deliver more stock to the company.

One problem with RFID is the possibility of radio interference, which can be a major problem in heavy manufacturing environments. As a general rule, if wiring into the warehouse and shop area must already be shielded in order to ensure proper data transmission, then RFID may not work. If this potential exists, then be sure to conduct extensive transmission testing in all areas where inventory may be tracked to ensure that radio interference will not be an issue. Another problem is that certain products, such as steel or fluids, obviously cannot be tagged.

An additional problem is that RFID is simply too new. Few case studies have been completed, so it is difficult to determine what other problems will arise.

Cost: *Installation time:*

7.5   Eliminate All Paper from Inventory Transactions

Every time someone handles a piece of paper listing an inventory transaction, there is a chance of losing the paper, misconstruing its contents, or transcribing it back into the computer system with an error. This problem is especially prevalent in the handling of inventory, since there is a potential for a paper-based transaction at every step in the handling of inventory—receiving, quality assurance, putaway, moves, picking, scrap, shipping, and so on.

The best solution is the complete avoidance of paper documents for all inventory transactions. This can be done through several best practices already noted—bar coding and radio frequency identification—as well as through the pick-to-light and voice picking best practices described in Chapter 5, "Inventory Picking." As an example of how one can use these technologies to avoid paper-based transactions, one can use a bar-coded scanner to record the receipt of an incoming item, scan the barcode again when the item is put away, scan it yet again when picked, and scan it one last time upon either shipment or delivery to the shop floor. As an alternative to bar coding, a pick-to-light system allows one to record picks by pressing buttons on bin displays, while a radio frequency identification system requires no scanning at all—a radio chip attached to each pallet, case, or item transmits its location to receiving stations as it moves about the company premises. All these technologies have the added benefit of requiring much less or no employee labor, so they can concentrate on their primary tasks and have no opportunity to incorrectly record a transaction.

The downside of all these alternatives to paper-based transactions is their cost. Virtually all alternatives require an investment in the real-time updating of inventory records. However, one should compare this added investment to the cost of correcting transactional errors related to the use of paper, which frequently reveals that paper avoidance is a very cost-effective policy.

Cost: 💵 💵   *Installation time:* ⬤ ⬤ ⬤

7.6 Use the Kanban System to Pull Transactions through the Facility

The typical manufacturing system pushes materials through the production facility. Under this "push" system, materials planners calculate the total number of finished units required through a forecasting system, explode this requirement back into individual parts requirements, and send picking information to the warehouse, which pulls the items from storage and sends them to the production area. This approach requires a great deal of planning throughout the production facility. Also, any breakdown in the process will halt production, resulting in large amounts of work-in-process being shunted off to one side until the materials flow problem is fixed. Further, there can be an enormous number of inventory transactions in this system if management thinks it is necessary to track the flow of parts between workstations on the shop floor; whenever there are many transactions, the odds of having incorrect data entry increase, so inventory records are much more likely to be incorrect.

A possible alternative in a job shop environment is to switch to a "pull" system, where parts are requested from a preceding workstation only if they are needed in order to complete a required product. Under this approach, a parts notification, or "kanban," is sent to the preceding workstation, authorizing the completion of a specific number of parts. Once that authorization is filled, work at the preceding workstation stops until it receives another authorization. The kanban can take a number of forms, such as a card or perhaps a tray whose receptacles can be filled up to a predetermined quantity. The approach can also be extended to include suppliers, which eliminates the need for purchase orders. The kanban system almost entirely eliminates the need for transaction data entry, requiring only the accumulation of information about the total number of finished goods produced, which can then be used for shipment and supplier payment transactions. By massively reducing the number of transactions in the system, data entry errors can be greatly reduced, while the production staff is no longer required to record transactions.

The main problem with the kanban system is the difficulty of switching from a push to a pull system. This can cause the near-breakdown of the production process, so one should proceed with great care, using consultants, pilot tests, and extensive training before switching over. The kanban system is also not of much use in process flow environments, where the production system is designed for maximum, continual production. Further, the pull system will result in slower customer service, since items can no longer be shipped direct from stock to customers, but must first be manufactured.

Cost: 💵   *Installation time:* 🕐 🕐 🕐

7.7 Eliminate All Transaction Backlogs

The warehouse staff gets into serious trouble when it develops a permanent backlog of inventory transactions, usually in the areas of receiving, moves between bin locations, picking, and receipts from the shop floor back into the warehouse. When a backlog arises, inventory records are not being updated on time, rendering inaccurate the reports used by cycle counters to verify inventory quantities and locations. If cycle counters use these inaccurate reports, they will undoubtedly find differences between the inventory database and their physical counts, and will make entries into the computer system to eliminate the differences—which will not improve the record accuracy situation once any unentered transactions are included in the inventory database. Thus, a transaction backlog results in permanent inventory record inaccuracy. Further, transaction backlogs tend to create piles of paperwork in which other documents can be lost, resulting in extra search time to locate needed materials.

A crucial best practice is to eliminate these backlogs, usually by allocating extra staff time to do them. Once the piles of paperwork are eliminated, the warehouse manager can focus on increasing levels of training and process improvement to reduce the number of people required to keep the backlog from recurring. Real-time, online data entry using wireless bar-coded scanners is an excellent method for having forklift operators update inventory move transactions on-the-fly, so there is no paperwork for anyone to keypunch at a later date. One can also use real-time entry of receipts at the receiving dock by having a computer terminal stationed there. The main point is to make transaction entries at the time of initial occurrence as easy as possible, so there is no need for the warehouse staff to delay the data entry task.

If the warehouse has a highly variable amount of transaction volume, some backlog may reappear in periods of high activity, though this can be avoided through the careful use of the preplanned hiring of part-time workers to assist the regular staff.

Cost: 💵 💵   *Installation time:* 🔴

7.8 Verify That Receipts Are Entered in the Computer System at Once

There is nothing that throws a wrench into a company's production planning and accounting more than the delayed entry of warehouse receiving information into the computer system. When this happens, the purchasing staff does not know if materials have arrived and they begin a series of frantic calls to suppliers to determine when items are to be shipped. Likewise, the production scheduling staff decides not to produce something because they do not see any receipts in the computer system. Finally, the accounting staff has a very difficult time determining what was really received at the end of the accounting period, resulting in the reporting of inaccurate inventory figures in the financial statements. All this because someone in the warehouse is slow to enter receipts.

The obvious best practice is to require the warehouse staff to make their receiving entries as soon as they receive any parts, but the solution is not quite so simple. The warehouse staff is usually too busy to do it, so this chore waits for a slow period, perhaps at the end of the day. Thus, to make them enter receipts more quickly, one must find a better way to enter the receipts, one so simple and easy that there is no excuse to delay the process. One approach is to require all suppliers to attach a bar-coded label to the outside of all shipments, allowing the receiving staff to scan this sheet directly into the computer system, thereby recording the entry. Another approach is to restructure the receiving data entry screen so that one need only enter the purchase order number on which any receipt is based. The purchase order then comes up on the screen, and the receiver quickly enters the quantity received. This latter approach carries with it the added benefit of forcing suppliers to provide only the purchase order number with their shipments—many suppliers resist having to barcode the detailed delivery information on their shipments. Either technique is an effective way to reduce the time needed to enter receipts, thereby eliminating a host of downstream problems.

Cost: *Installation time:*

7.9 Have Customers Order by Part Number

A significant problem is for customers to place orders based on a general description of the item they want. This is an inherently imprecise ordering method, since the order taker may incorrectly assign a part number to the customer's order that varies from what the customer really wants. The downstream problems are significant—the company ships the wrong item, the customer ships it back and demands a rush order of the correct item or simply stops using the company, and the incorrectly shipped item returns to stock, where it may languish for some time, using up a company's available capital.

One possible solution is to issue price lists and product catalogs (including pictures and product descriptions!) to customers, and let them order from this more precise information. By doing so, there is no longer any interpretation of what the customer wants, thereby eliminating a number of incorrect orders. This approach works well for Internet orders, where customers can browse a product catalog online and place orders themselves. Also, if the customer complains about an incorrect order, the company has some leverage in the situation, since the customer used a specific part number when placing her order.

One downside to this best practice is when there are so many small variations on a part that customers are not certain of which part number they really want, in which case an order taker must become involved in the ordering process anyway. Also, when there is no established base of large customers to whom price lists and catalogs can be sent, and customers do not use the Internet for ordering, it is very difficult to put pricing and part number information in their hands.

Cost: 🖋   *Installation time:* 🌑

7.10 Audit All Inventory Transactions

For any manufacturing organization, there are myriad transactions associated with the receipt of goods, their transfer to locations in the warehouse, and additional movement to the production floor, as well as the return of any excess items to the warehouse. Given the inordinate volume of transactions, some are bound to be done incorrectly. When this happens, the recorded quantities of inventory on hand will be incorrect, resulting in incorrect financial statements. The problem impacts other departments too, since inaccurate inventory volumes impact the purchasing, production, and warehouse departments.

One best practice that targets inventory transaction problems is auditing them. By doing so, one can spot problems, research why they happened, and take actions to keep the transaction errors from occurring again. For example, if an audit uncovers a lack of operator training that results in receiving not being completed in the computer, either a comprehensive or focused training session with that person, along with follow-up reviews, will eliminate the error.

Auditing can be assigned to the internal audit department. However, continual review work may be necessary, for which the audit department may not have sufficient staff; the accounting department is well advised to take on this chore itself if no other approach will work. Once the entity doing the work has been determined, the next step is to find the best way to spot transaction problems among the hundreds or thousands of inventory-related transactions occurring every month. A simple random selection of transactions will eventually discover a reasonable quantity of mistakes to review, but there are ways to improve one's chances of finding them. For example, a transaction resulting in a negative inventory on-hand quantity is certainly worthy of review, as is any transaction taking more out of stock than is actually there. The same exception rules can be applied to transactions with inordinately large quantities. Further, transactions can be compared to the production schedule to see if any of them are scheduled for use in the production process in the near future, and be given a higher probability of an audit if this is the case. Any of these issues are indicative of a problem and should be reviewed first. Though many of the transactions will be valid, the odds of finding an error are greatly enhanced.

The next step in the auditing process is discovering the nature of the problem that caused the transaction error. Since the only two possibilities are systems or people problems, it is wise to assign a team with exceptional systems knowledge and people skills to this task. Since many employees will not admit to an error they have made, the single most important auditing skill is carefully dealing in a nonthreatening manner with the people involved in these transactions. Finally, there must be a follow-up routine established that reviews previously uncovered problems to verify that they have been fixed. Only if *all* of these problems are followed will the incidence of transactional errors decline.

As several departments are involved in the recording of transactions related to inventory, one must be able to deal carefully with the managers of these other departments to ensure that the auditing process does not degrade into a situation where discovered problems are used to attack each other. Thus, interpersonal skills are critical to the success of this best practice.

Cost: 🖙   *Installation time:*   ●

7.11 Compare Recorded Inventory Activity to On-Hand Inventories

Some industries deal with extremely expensive materials. In these situations, it is critical to ensure that recorded inventory levels are completely accurate, since even a small quantity variance can lead to a large impact on profitability. This is a particular concern when dealing with precious metals or gemstones, not to mention a variety of electronic components.

Many of the other best practices noted in this chapter will help to keep inventory accuracy within reasonable limits, such as auditing inventory transactions or cycle counting; but to be absolutely sure that quantities are correct, the best way is to compare all recorded inventory activity to on-hand inventories. This approach varies from auditing because it assumes a 100 percent review of all transactions for selected items. Because it is a highly labor-intensive approach, one must confine it to a minimum number of especially expensive or critical inventory items.

To use this method, one should conduct a daily comparison of on-hand quantities to every transaction associated with them, such as receipts, inventory moves, scrap, production, returns from the production floor, and shipments. Of particular interest during this review process is any transaction not made, or made twice, made in the wrong amount or on the wrong date, or involving the wrong part number or unit of measure. Only by conducting this complete review every day can a company determine where there are problems in the stream of transactions and fix them immediately. One should also try to spot trends in or concentrations of transaction errors, such as the number of receiving or scrap errors, which allows one to target a specific problem and fix it.

This best practice is strongly supported by those other departments relying on accurate inventory levels, such as the warehousing, purchasing, and production departments. However, they support this because they do not have to provide the significant amount of staff time required to ensure its success. Accordingly, one should be careful to use it only with a small minority of the inventory items, monitor it carefully, and eliminate items from the review process as soon as it becomes apparent that there are no transactional errors occurring.

Cost: 💷 💷   *Installation time:* ⬤

7.12 Immediately Review All Negative Inventory Balances

The impact of a variety of transactional problems can result in the computer system reporting a negative inventory balance. Source problems could include the presence of a transaction backlog where offsetting entries have not yet been made, incorrect cycle counts, improper counts at the receiving stage, picks from stock without an update to the inventory records, and so on. Whatever the cause, negative balances are a clear indicator of inadequate warehouse management, and show that the inventory database cannot be reliably used for materials planning, much less inventory valuation.

The solution is to immediately investigate all negative inventory balances. Investigation means not just correcting the book balance to match the on-hand balance, but also reviewing all underlying transactions to find the reason for the negative balance and following through to ensure that the problem does not happen again. One should create a procedure for spotting negative balances right away. Also, include in the daily warehouse activity list a requirement to print an inventory report sorted in ascending order by quantity on hand, so negative balances appear at the top of the report. Also, since cycle counters should have expertise in resolving inventory problems, have them correct and investigate the negative balances as part of their daily cycle counting routines.

Cost:　　　　　　　*Installation time:*

7.13 Replace the Physical Count Process with Cycle Counts

There are a variety of problems associated with a thorough physical count of the inventory, such as production downtime while the count is performed, inaccurate counts, and the incorrect identification of parts. This best practice describes how to use cycle counts to avoid a complete physical count.

One should use cycle counting as the primary way to eliminate the physical counting process. To do so, there is a set of carefully defined steps to follow before inventory reaches an accuracy level sufficiently high to allow one to avoid the physical count. One should read through all of the following steps and make a realistic assessment of a company's ability not only to complete them, but also to maintain the system over a long period. If it is not realistically possible, then do not run the risk of wasting up to a year on this project—there are other best practices in this book that pose a much higher chance of success. The implementation steps follow:

1. *Throw out the trash.* One should first clean up the warehouse before spending a great deal of time counting parts. Accordingly, trash, obsolete parts, and old tools or supplies must be either thrown out or moved to an outlying location.

2. *Identify the remainder.* The first step reduces the amount of inventory items to be reviewed for part numbers. This is now the main task—review all remaining inventory and post a part number on it.

3. *Consolidate inventory.* Once all parts are identified, it is time to cluster them together for easy counting, rather than leaving them in a variety of locations. This takes several iterations before all inventory is completely consolidated, but do not worry about it—the main reason for consolidating at this stage is to make it easier to count and box the inventory in the next step, so a few unconsolidated items will not present much of a problem later on.

4. *Count and box the remainder.* Count all the inventory and then box or bag it. There should be a seal on each container, with the quantity marked on the seal, so that a glance at the container will reveal the complete quantity of the part. This is of vast benefit to cycle counters, who can now count hundreds of items very quickly. Note that it is not necessary at this point to correct all inventory balances in the computer, for the cycle counters will soon take care of this problem when they methodically review the entire warehouse.

5. *Create warehouse locations.* Clearly mark every bin location. The location should include the aisle, rack, and bin number, so there is no question about where an inventory item is located. This step is crucial for cycle counting, since one cannot count a part if one cannot first find it.

6. *Assign inventory to specific locations.* Go into the computer and assign a location code to every inventory item. This may require special programming to put a location field in the computer database.

7. *Create a cycle counting report.* Create a computer report that lists all on-hand inventories, sorted by location code. The cycle counters must have this available as their main tool for reviewing inventory.

8. *Segregate the warehouse.* Install a fence around the warehouse and lock the gate! Now that cycle counting is about to begin, there should be no way for nonwarehouse staff to enter the warehouse in order to remove parts.

9. *Initiate cut-off controls.* All inventory transactions related to a block of parts to be cycle counted must be completed prior to anyone running a cycle count report. Otherwise, the cycle counter will find record discrepancies and correct them, which will be followed by the entry of preceding transactions that will render the inventory records more inaccurate than they were at the start. Consequently, these controls must be in place prior to any cycle counting being conducted.

10. *Initiate cycle counts.* Assign cycle counters a section of the warehouse to count. Issue them the latest cycle counting report. They must carefully count all the items in every bin location and make corrections to the report to ensure that the computer database is correct. The warehouse manager should monitor their progress every day to ensure that they are completing their counts on time. A good cycle counting frequency is to review the entire inventory six times a year; this high volume of counting can drop later, once accuracy levels increase.

11. *Audit inventory accuracy.* Audit the inventory once a week. A small sample of the total inventory is sufficient to determine the total accuracy of the inventory, which should be posted for easy review by the warehouse staff. It may be necessary to post accuracy by aisle, in case some warehouse areas are particularly prone to errors. If so, the best cycle counters should be assigned to the least accurate aisles.

12. *Use a bonus program.* The entire warehouse staff should receive a bonus at the end of each month, based on the audited inventory accuracy. A good measure above which bonuses should be paid is 95 percent accuracy, with any item being defined as accurate if the counted quantity is within 2 percent of the amount listed in the computer (though this may not be a good measure in some industries, such as diamond processing). This is an extremely effective way to maintain the interest of the warehouse staff in the continuing accuracy of the inventory records.

Though cycle counting will certainly allow one to avoid a physical inventory count, it is equally important to investigate why errors are occurring, not just to change inventory balances if they are wrong. If one can get to the bottom of a transaction problem and fix the underlying error, it is possible to greatly increase record accuracy and require less work by the cycle counting staff to keep it that way.

Cost: *Installation time:*

7.14 Streamline the Physical Count Process

Some companies find that they are unable to produce anything for several days while count teams perform a physical count of all on-hand inventories.

When this happens, a corporation loses sales, since it cannot produce anything. In addition, the resulting inventory is not entirely accurate, since the counting process is frequently conducted by people who do not have a thorough knowledge of what they are counting, which results in incorrect counts and misidentified parts. Also, key people are taken away from their other work to conduct the count, resulting in little or no attention to customers for the duration of the count. Finally, the accounting staff usually stops all other work in order to devote themselves to the processing of count tags. Thus, the physical count is a highly disruptive and inaccurate process.

For those organizations that cannot entirely dispense with the physical count, it is still possible to streamline the process so that fewer resources are assigned to it, while keeping the accuracy level relatively high. The improvements follow:

- *Eliminate some inventory from the count with cycle counting.* For situations where a company has just started cycle counting but has not yet brought accuracy levels up to a sufficiently high level, it may still be possible to concentrate the cycle counting effort on a few key areas. By doing so, the accuracy of the inventory in these locations will be so high that there is no need to conduct a physical count.

- *Enter location code on tags.* When counters are entering information on count tags, they should also enter a location code. With this information, it is much easier for the accounting staff to later locate where a tag was used to record information, rather than wandering through the warehouse in a frustrated search for the information. This approach is even better than the common practice of tracing blocks of tags that are assigned to teams counting specific locations; though this brings a review person to the general vicinity of an inventory item, it does not precisely identify the location, which leads to lost time while someone searches for the part.

- *Enter tags directly into the computer.* It is much more efficient to directly enter tag information into the computer system, rather than entering it into an electronic spreadsheet for manual comparison to a computer-generated inventory report. This approach allows the computer to automatically issue a comparison of the counted quantities to the quantities already stored in the computer, so that one can quickly determine where there may be counting errors. Most good computer software packages contain this feature; if not, one must evaluate the cost of programming the feature into the system.

- *Identify all items in advance.* A team should review the warehouse well in advance of the physical count to spot all items that lack identifying part numbers. By researching these items and correctly marking them in advance, the counting teams do not have to address this task while also trying to count inventory, thereby shortening the counting process.

- *Allow only warehouse staff to count.* Warehouse employees have an excellent knowledge of all parts stored in the warehouse and so are the most qualified to identify and count inventory in the most efficient manner possible. If other, less knowledgeable people are brought into the counting process, it is much more likely that there will be counting problems, resulting in wasted time at the end of the physical count, when extra counting teams must be dispatched to research potential miscounts.

- *Conduct only one count.* Do not count something more than once! Though some companies conduct a double count of all inventory items and then compare the two counts to spot errors, it is much easier and faster to complete a single count and compare this to the book balances already stored in the computer system. Conducting a double count adds to the time and effort needed to complete the counting process.

- *Precount the inventory.* A team should begin counting the inventory days or weeks in advance of the formal physical inventory count. This group's job is to gather inventory into single locations, count it, seal it into containers, and mark the correct quantity on the containers. By doing so, it is much easier for the physical count teams to complete their work in an efficient and accurate manner. Though this may seem like a considerable amount of advance work (it is), it results in a much shorter interval for the physical count, allowing a company to be shut down only for the briefest possible time.

When these suggestions are implemented together or individually, a company will experience significant reductions in the effort needed to complete a physical inventory, while increasing the accuracy of the resulting information.

Cost: *Installation time:*

7.15 Install a Warehouse Management System

A typical warehouse's staff receives picking information each morning from a central computer operation that controls all material requirements planning for the company. The staff then reviews the inventory locations in which the items to be picked were stored as of the previous day, picks items from them, and records the picks at a local computer terminal when they have a free moment, which may be several hours later. Meanwhile, the receiving staff roams the warehouse aisles, looking for a place to store newly arrived inventory. When they find a spot, they write down this information and record it in a computer terminal when they too have some free time. Because of the delays in processing information, the picking staff may not find all the items they need in the locations printed on the picking report, while the receiving staff may not put away a received item in a location that minimizes the travel time of the receiving staff. In the worst-case scenario, the receiving staff may put away something immediately needed by the pickers, but the information may not be available through the materials tracking system until information is updated hours later, resulting in as much as a one-day delay before the pickers even know where to look.

A good solution to this problem is a warehouse management system. This computer system uses real-time processing of information through the use of wireless radio frequency terminals to maintain a totally current database of inventory locations and requirements. It has the added benefit of telling the receiving staff where to put away newly received items in those open bin locations that will optimize both travel time by the picking staff and overall cubic storage space, while the picking staff receives real-time information about correct locations and quantities in the locations closest to their current positions. Further, cycle counters can work with the freshest possible inventory location and quantity information, and even enter correction transactions on the spot. In addition, the WMS can direct staff to move the most urgently needed items out of the staging area, so there is no time lost in either filling orders or sending raw materials to the production area. It can also maximize the use of cross-docking by telling materials handlers to move the items to specific outbound docks as soon as the inbound delivery arrives. The system can even warn the receiving staff of special inspection requirements for incoming deliveries, while noting any special outbound packaging requirements for upcoming shipments. Thus, a WMS can significantly improve the efficiency of the warehouse staff, leading to reduced costs and cycle times.

However, a WMS is not a cost-effective solution for a small warehouse. Only if there are several thousand possible inventory locations and over a dozen warehouse staff does this capital-intensive solution present an attractive cost-benefit tradeoff. Further, it should be installed only with real-time information, so a radio frequency communications system tied to portable terminals is mandatory.

Cost: 💵 💵 💵   *Installation time:* 🕐 🕐

8

Inventory Planning and Management

This chapter addresses those 29 planning and management best practices having a direct impact on inventory. As noted in Exhibit 8.1, these best practices start with the product design phase and proceed through sales forecasting, usage modeling, production substitution and service levels provided, distribution systems, the treatment of obsolete inventory, and the outsourcing of selected functions. In short, this chapter covers the full range of activities, from product design through distribution, in which planning and management efforts can reduce a company's inventory investment.

The first block of recommendations involves the use of much greater control over and involvement in the product development process, so the minimum number of new inventory items will be required for new products while existing items will be depleted before product changes go into effect. All these best practices are recommended without reservation.

The second block of best practices covers inventory planning. Implementation of these items will be much more selective, since they are not applicable in all situations. Forecasting demand by product family will work only if there is a great deal of parts commonality and sales patterns across products, while delaying the order penetration point relies to a great extent on product design, the use of subassemblies, and the range of possible final product options. Similarly, using variable safety stocks, eliminating expediting, and developing a product substitution system will work only under specific circumstances. However, centralized inventory planning, the use of a material requirements planning system for modeling, and periodically reviewing the customer service level are applicable in most situations.

The next major block of best practices involves distribution systems. A distribution requirements planning system is an excellent choice if a company has multiple distribution locations, as is the distribution of slow-mov-

Exhibit 8.1 *Summary of Inventory Planning and Management Best Practices*

	Best Practice	Cost	Install Time
8.1	Include materials managers in the new product design process	💵	🕐
8.2	Reduce the number of product options	💵	🕐🕐
8.3	Reduce the number of products	💵	🕐🕐
8.4	Design products with lower tolerances	💵	🕐🕐🕐
8.5	Require formal review and approval of engineering change orders	💵	🕐
8.6	Forecast demand by product families	💵	🕐
8.7	Centralize responsibility for inventory planning	💵	🕐🕐
8.8	Delay the order penetration point as long as possible	💵	🕐🕐🕐
8.9	Use a materials requirement planning system to model alternative lot sizes, safety stocks, and lead times	💵💵💵	🕐🕐
8.10	Use variable safety stocks for fluctuating demand	💵	🕐
8.11	Eliminate expediting	💵	🕐🕐
8.12	Develop a product substitution system	💵	🕐🕐
8.13	Question the level of customer service provided	💵	🕐
8.14	Focus inventory reduction efforts on high-usage items	💵	🕐🕐
8.15	Create a visual review system for noninventoried parts	💵	🕐🕐
8.16	Eliminate departmental stocks	💵	🕐
8.17	Install a distribution requirements planning system	💵💵💵	🕐🕐🕐
8.18	Distribute slow-moving items from regional warehouses	💵💵💵	🕐🕐🕐
8.19	Use overnight delivery from a single location for selected items	💵	🕐
8.20	Use fair shares analysis to allocate inventory to warehouses	💵💵💵	🕐🕐🕐

Exhibit 8.1 *(Continued)*

	Best Practice	Cost	Install Time
8.21	Periodically rationalize the warehouse network	💵💵💵	⏱⏱⏱
8.22	Create a materials review board	💵	⏱
8.23	Identify obsolete inventory via physical inventory tags	💵	⏱
8.24	Reserve otherwise obsolete inventory with "service/repair" designation	💵	⏱
8.25	Avoid product obsolescence with shelf life control	💵💵	⏱⏱
8.26	Create an obsolete inventory budget for disposals	💵	⏱
8.27	Batch excess inventory for sale to salvage contractors	💵	⏱
8.28	Sell excess items through the service department	💵	⏱
8.29	Outsource selected warehousing functions	💵💵	⏱⏱

ing items from a centralized location and distribution using fair shares analysis. Periodically rationalizing the warehouse network is a mandatory best practice when there are many warehouses in the company distribution system.

Finally, a large block of best practices deals with the selection and disposition of obsolete inventory. Though the use of a materials review board is generally a good idea, companies with very low inventory levels will find this to be an exercise in excessive bureaucracy. Also, a company that has eliminated physical inventory counts in favor of cycle counting will find spotting obsolete items by their old physical inventory tags to be impossible. However, reserving some obsolete items for future servicing needs, selling old items through the service department, and batching items for sale to salvage contractors are best practices that will find broader applicability.

The most highly recommended planning and management best practices that generally yield a high cost-effectiveness ratio are reducing the number of both products and product options, reducing product design tolerances, implementing tight controls over engineering change orders, eliminating expediting, and periodically questioning the level of customer service provided. Note that these best practices are largely positioned at the beginning of the product design, manufacture, and sales cycle; thus, implementing best practices before a product design has been finalized tends to have the largest positive impact on inventory issues.

8.1 Include Materials Managers in the New Product Design Process

New product design teams usually include nothing but design engineers, who are superb at creating cutting-edge products. However, they are not so good at creating products that are easily manufactured, are highly reliable, or use preexisting parts. If a new product is difficult to manufacture, there will probably be more scrap than usual, which calls for the retention of extra inventory to counterbalance the extra material losses. Poor reliability requires the storage of extra service parts, while the inclusion of totally new components in a design calls for additional SKUs in the warehouse. A further problem is that once these problems become apparent, engineering change orders must be implemented, which can require complex switches from old to new components that leave excess parts in stock.

The solution is to broaden the membership of the new product design teams to include materials managers and industrial engineers. The materials managers can assist with the identification of commonly used parts, or those more easily obtained than others, while industrial engineers can modify the design to increase its ease of manufacturability. The result is a substantial reduction in required inventory levels.

The only problem with this best practice is the time required of these additional people on the design teams, since they are being pulled away from their regular tasks to participate in the design process. However, the cost savings from reduced inventory levels should easily counterbalance any loss in their productivity.

Cost: 🖙   *Installation time:* 🌢

8.2 Reduce the Number of Product Options

Design engineers like to offer a wide range of product options from which customers can choose. The assumption is that customers will perceive a company to have a high degree of customer service by offering products in a multitude of variations. The trouble with this approach is the considerable expansion in the number of subassemblies and items that must be kept in stock to deal with the full range of possible variations in product configurations. In many cases, specific configurations are ordered so rarely that inventory must be stored for long periods prior to use; the odds of eventual obsolescence due to nonuse are also high.

The solution is to offer customers a greatly reduced set of product options. One can then reduce the number of inventory items kept in stock to those used on a small number of basic offerings. This approach does not mean that customers are offered only a bare-bones product—on the contrary, a fully loaded product is acceptable, but the number of variations from that fully loaded model must be kept low in order to avoid retaining inventory for rarely ordered features. Customer satisfaction levels will still remain high as long as they can choose from a clustered set of features offering them the choice of minimal extras at a low price, many features at a high price, and just one or two variations between these two extremes.

Cost: *Installation time:*

8.3 Reduce the Number of Products

The sales department loves to shower customers with a broad range of products to fit every possible need. A company can certainly maximize its sales by doing so. The problem is that it is not maximizing its profits. With an enormous range of product offerings comes a massive investment in finished goods inventory, since many of the products will sell only occasionally but still must be stocked against the possibility of an order. Further, raw materials and subassemblies must be stocked in case more products are needed. In addition, the rates of obsolescence will be higher with more products, since some products will almost certainly be overproduced and will languish in the warehouse for years.

The solution is a periodic planned review of the entire range of product offerings, with the intent of eliminating the slow-moving items. The accounting staff must be heavily involved in this effort, reporting on sales trends, inventory investment, and direct profits by product. The sales department will resist the reduction on the grounds that sales will be lost, so the company should involve senior management in the process in order to enforce the decision to eliminate products.

The primary downside to this best practice is the initial reduction in earnings caused by inventory write-offs when it is first implemented, since a number of products may require pruning.

Cost: 🖅   Installation time: 🌑 🌑

8.4 Design Products with Lower Tolerances

Engineers love to design superior products, incorporating the tightest possible part tolerances that will achieve uncommonly high product performance. When they do this, the purchasing department must obtain components falling within the designed tolerance limit or the production department must create them. When this happens, the purchasing staff must pay a higher price for the high-tolerance items. Alternatively, the production department will generate more scrap as it struggles to manufacture parts falling within extremely tight tolerance limits, since it is statistically more difficult to produce all items within a small tolerance range. This results in the purchase of more raw materials to offset the increased scrap level.

The solution is to design products whose functions still meet customer expectations, but which do so with the lowest possible tolerances. By doing so, the purchasing staff can specify the lower tolerance levels when buying parts, resulting in lower purchase prices, while the production department can accept manufactured parts falling within a larger tolerance range. The resulting lower scrap levels means that the materials management staff can plan for a smaller investment in raw materials inventory.

This best practice requires a long time to implement, since it is usually difficult to alter tolerances for existing products; instead, one has to wait for a full range of new products to be designed, gradually flushing out the old, higher-tolerance products.

Cost: 🖅   Installation time: 🌑 🌑 🌑

8.5 Require Formal Review and Approval of Engineering Change Orders

Best practice 8.1 enumerated all the problems that can arise when an engineering design team creates a new product with no input from other parts of the company. When such products are created, engineers are likely to react to the numerous resulting problems by issuing a stream of engineering change orders to modify the product after it has already gone into production. Whenever it does so, there is a chance that the product cost will change substantially, while the production department may have more difficulty manufacturing the revised version. Of particular concern is the amount of inventory marooned in the warehouse when it is replaced by a new component being used as part of the change order.

A solution is to formally involve the cost accounting, production, industrial engineering, and materials management departments in the approval of each engineering change order. This will probably require a formal review meeting by all parties, and a sign-off by each one of the proposed change order. By doing so, everyone has a chance to verify the acceptability of the proposed change. The materials managers can go a step further and specify the date on which the change will take place, thereby allowing them to reduce the on-hand quantity of any components about to be replaced as part of the change order.

The main problem with this approach is the bureaucracy added by having so many additional people involved in the change order process. Thus, change orders are likely to be completed much more slowly than was previously the case. To keep completion dates from getting out of hand, consider imposing a standard timetable on the process, so that everyone must complete their investigations of a proposed change order within a set number of days, or else their approval will be automatically assumed.

Cost: 　　　　　　　　*Installation time:*

8.6 Forecast Demand by Product Families

A variety of techniques can be used to forecast product demand. No matter which one is used, companies tend to maintain individual forecasts for each product, which requires a considerable amount of time to update on a recurring basis. Further, individual forecasts are not that accurate, since consumers can vary their purchases between similar products in a manner that can throw off forecasts to a considerable extent. The result is a constant swing between finished goods stockouts or excess inventory.

A possible solution is to restrict demand forecasting to the product family level. This approach greatly reduces the amount of forecasting work required, since it commonly reduces the number of items requiring a forecast by a factor of up to 10. Further, there is less variability in demand across an entire product family, so forecasts tend to be more accurate.

The key issue with this best practice is ensuring that only parts with common components are included in each product family. If so, the materials management staff can purchase components or schedule the production of subassemblies that can be used in any product across the product family, which is the main point behind forecasting at the product family level. However, if a product not sharing common parts is included in a product family, the higher-level demand forecast is of no use in calculating how many units are to be produced.

Cost: *Installation time:*

8.7 Centralize Responsibility for Inventory Planning

The use of inventory to fulfill a variety of company goals is rife with inherent conflicts of interest. The sales staff wants to see high inventory levels in order to maximize order fulfillment rates, the finance staff wants to reduce inventory to minimize the working capital investment, the manufacturing staff wants large raw materials stocks to feed its production activities, the purchasing staff wants to buy materials in large quantities, and the warehouse manager wants to reduce inventory to keep his warehouse from exploding with excess goods. To say the least, these conflicting needs result in a constant tug-of-war over the proper level of inventory to be maintained.

A good solution is to vest full control over inventory with a materials manager. This person must have the authority to combine demand requirements with corporate stock-keeping policies to arrive at appropriate stocking levels. The key point is ensuring that the company holds to those stocking levels by purchasing only enough to reach them, which means that the materials manager must supervise the purchasing department. In addition, the materials manager should supervise the warehouse in order to have control over inventory in this location, as well as the materials handling staff that feeds materials to the production floor.

The primary difficulty is making the materials manager position sufficiently senior in the corporate hierarchy that no one can override his or her decisions. One approach is to place the position under a senior management position that is *not* the vice president of sales (who has a natural tendency to inflate stock levels), while another is to make the materials manager a vice president–level position reporting directly to the company president.

Cost: 🖋   Installation time: 🕐 🕐

8.8 Delay the Order Penetration Point as Long as Possible

When products are configured for specific customers, a company must tag them as belonging to that customer and then set them aside in inventory for delivery to only those customers. If a customer delays, halts, or cancels an order, the company is stuck with this inventory, being forced to either dismantle it, sell it off for a reduced price, or scrap it. No matter which form of disposition is used, the company loses money. Even if a company only builds to stock, it may offer so many product variations that it must retain an enormous variety of finished goods, some of which may never be purchased. When this happens, the same disposition problems (and related lost profits) arise.

The solution is to maintain inventories at the highest possible subassembly level for as long as possible and then add the last few product features when a customer order arrives. This is known as delaying the order penetration point into the completion process of a product until the last possible moment. By doing so, a company can store far fewer product variations. By reducing the number of SKUs in its warehouse, a company can save storage space as well as its investment in inventory, while also reducing its risk of generating a large amount of obsolete inventory. The engineering staff can assist with this best practice by designing as many products as possible to be based on a common set of subassemblies that can be easily reconfigured into as many products as possible. Further, the engineering staff can redesign existing products to follow this concept, or gradually phase them out with newer designs that accomplish this purpose.

Cost: 💵   *Installation time:* 🕐 🕐 🕐

8.9 Use a Material Requirements Planning System to Model Alternative Lot Sizes, Safety Stocks, and Lead Times

A manufacturing organization of any size typically deals with thousands of planning factors, such as lot sizes, safety stock levels, and lead times, as part of its daily materials management function. Changes to these planning factors arrive from a variety of sources, and are used to update the existing data fields for each item. The result is constant fluctuations in the dates on which materials are needed, and the quantities required. The materials management staff is typically in a reactive mode, trying to deal with these constant planning changes.

While constant changes to planning factors will not go away, there is no reason why the materials management staff cannot deal with the issue in a proactive manner by determining which planning factors it wants to change, and modeling the results through a material requirements planning (MRP) system. For example, if a supplier wants to alter minimum purchase quantities to a larger size, they can model this change and see if the inventory impact is great enough to require sourcing through a more amenable supplier. Similarly, they can try to achieve a higher level of inventory turnover by using modeling to determine which planning factors will have the greatest impact on lowering inventory levels.

The key issue with modeling is having an MRP system on which to perform it. If a company is not already using an MRP system, this is hardly the reason to obtain one, given the cost of implementing such a system. Thus, this best practice is useful only if an MRP system is already in place.

Cost: 💵 💵 💵   *Installation time:* 🕐 🕐

8.10 Use Variable Safety Stocks for Fluctuating Demand

Most materials planning systems include a feature that calculates an adequate safety stock level based on parts usage levels and supplier lead times.

If a company experiences a steady level of demand, this approach will yield reliable safety stocks. However, what if demand fluctuates to a high degree, as is the case for seasonal sales? When this occurs, safety stocks calculated during a low-demand period will result in repeated stockouts, while safety stocks calculated during a high-demand period will result in an excessive inventory investment. Even the midway approach of using a safety stock level based on the average level of demand satisfies no one—still some stockouts during high-usage periods, and still too much inventory during low-usage periods.

The solution is to obtain materials planning software that allows for variable safety stocks. These systems automatically reset safety stock levels as forecasted demand levels change, so the conflicting objectives of minimal stockouts and minimal inventory levels are both balanced. If the existing system does not contain this feature, the software development staff may be able to program it into the existing system.

A low-budget approach is to schedule a quarterly review of safety stocks, focusing on those impacting the largest dollar value of inventory, and manually adjust safety stocks at that time. Since the materials management staff rarely has time for such a review, be sure to examine only the highest-investment safety stocks, so the review results in a significant impact on inventory investment and stockout levels in exchange for the minimum amount of staff review time.

Cost: *Installation time:*

8.11   Eliminate Expediting

There are times when an order absolutely, positively, has to be shipped by a certain date, but the order is well down in the work queue or there are not enough parts on hand to construct it. No matter, just assign an expediter to walk the order through the shop. The trouble is the rippling waves of confusion this activity breeds. Inventory already allocated for other uses suddenly disappears into the maw of expedited jobs, causing stock shortages for any number of other jobs, not to mention the additional machine changeovers required to restore machines to their prior operational status. Further, hordes of expediters are needed to watch over the orders being rushed through the production process. Finally, all these interruptions cause total production volume to drop precipitously.

Though quite obvious, breaking the expediting habit can be a surprisingly difficult best practice. It will result in some customers not receiving orders as fast as possible, especially early on when the production planners are trying to settle down a production process muddled by previously expedited orders. Also, even one expedited order can cause unwanted ripple effects throughout the organization, so one must go "cold turkey" when implementing this best practice. One solution is to reserve some excess capacity in the production schedule for last-minute orders, though this may still require the sudden, unplanned loss of inventory intended for other uses. The best alternative is to drive purchasing lead times down as much as possible in order to make valid, short-term ship dates available to customers, thereby allowing for reasonably fast ship times.

Cost: *Installation time:* 🍶 🍶

8.12 Develop a Product Substitution System

A company may put a customer order on backlog status if it does not have the precise item ordered on hand. This increases customer frustration due to the longer order cycle time, which can lead to the loss of the customer if orders are repeatedly placed on backlog status.

One solution is to offer customers the option of taking a substitute product that may have essentially the same characteristics as the ordered item and be reasonably acceptable to the customer. The company also benefits by using up stocks of the substitute inventory.

This best practice is useful only in a minority of situations, since customers usually can be appeased only if a substitute is an extremely close match for the item ordered. It can also be taken to extremes if the customer service staff pressures customers into taking substitutes, if only because the incidence of returned items will increase. To make a substitution system work smoothly, the order entry system should note the availability of related items on the computer screen alongside the quantity available, so the order entry staff can knowledgeably offer them to customers. This also calls for the linkage of products in the item master file, so the computer system will know which items to recommend as possible substitutes.

Cost: *Installation time:* 🍶 🍶

8.13 Question the Level of Customer Service Provided

One avenue for company growth is to follow the strategy of providing the highest possible level of customer support. This typically entails the use of very high inventory levels, so that every part is in stock when needed by a customer. If there is even one stockout, management calls for a review of inventory levels so that this will not happen again, resulting in an even higher level of inventory investment. Over time, a company finds itself burdened with very large amounts of obsolete inventory, since it acquired excessive amounts of stock for which customer demand was not very high.

Though a difficult exercise, a solution is to question the level of inventory needed to meet management's perceived level of customer service. By initiating this discussion along with an analysis of how much extra inventory is needed to provide the highest levels of service, the management team can see the cost of its service policy. If excellent customer service is the company's hallmark, it is entirely possible that this discussion will result in no changes in inventory policy. However, management at least will be aware of the cost of its service policy, which may result in a policy change at some point in the future.

The presentation of this best practice to management should be approached with a considerable degree of caution. In those cases where customer service drives all company decisions, such questioning may be looked on as undermining the company's reason for existence, with unhappy consequences for the person bringing up the topic.

Cost:　　　　　*Installation time:*

8.14 Focus Inventory Reduction Efforts on High-Usage Items

When the directive is handed down to reduce the total company investment in inventory, the materials management staffers tend to throw up their hands in dismay and tackle the directive for all the thousands of items in stock. The result is a pitiful effort on a per-unit basis, since the materials management staff can devote only a minor amount of time to this goal. Due to the broad scope of its efforts, the company's inventory investment may not decline at all.

A solution is to focus their attention only on the reduction of high-usage items. There are several reasons for doing so. First, by definition, slow-moving items are not going anywhere soon, so the materials management staff would have to wait a long time before the natural ongoing usage of these items will bring about any sort of reduction. Conversely, the turnover speed of high-usage items will cause a rapid inventory reduction in short order. Second, high-usage items represent a small portion of the total items in stock, so the staff can focus on reducing the quantity of far fewer items, resulting in both more attention to fewer items and plenty of leftover time for the staff to complete other tasks.

Cost: 💵   *Installation time:* 🕭 🕭

8.15 Create a Visual Review System for Noninventoried Parts

When inventory is tracked through a computerized inventory database, the system can easily match on-hand quantities plus on-order quantities to recommend purchases to the purchasing staff. This is not the case for parts untracked through the inventory database, which typically includes any items stored outside the warehouse and near the shop floor, such as fittings and fasteners. Though these items are low-cost, stockouts can still have a significant adverse impact on production, necessitating the use of a reordering system that will be guaranteed to keep a sufficient quantity of items on hand.

This best practice comes in two pieces. First, a purchasing manager should talk to both the production and engineering managers, perhaps once a month, to determine if some items should be removed from noninventoried stocks kept near the shop floor, on the grounds that they are no longer being used. Without this review, floor stocks can grow to an impressive and thoroughly unnecessary size. The group should also review the amount of stock kept on hand, since the production plan may require a change in parts quantity based on an altered sales forecast. Further, the discussion could occasionally address the need for shifting additional items from the warehouse to floor stocks, in the interest of reducing inventory moves from the warehouse.

The second part of this best practice is to set up a visual review system, enabling one to easily scan the floor stock to determine what items require reordering. One approach is to store each part in two bins—once the first bin is empty, this triggers a purchasing transaction by an inspector to refill the bin. While the newly ordered parts are in transit, the production staff continues to use parts from the second bin, which represents a safety stock. This approach is somewhat bulky, since it requires two bins, and also people may take parts from either bin before the first bin is empty, thereby depleting the safety stock. An alternative is to use a single larger bin that incorporates a fill line. When the on-hand quantity drops below the fill line, an inspector orders additional inventory. No matter which approach is used, one can ensure that there are sufficient parts on hand to meet short-term production needs.

This best practice succeeds only if followed regularly, so one should include it in the job description of a specific purchasing person, add it to the daily purchasing calendar of activities, create a procedure for it, and review the assigned purchasing person's job performance based on its successful ongoing completion. One must take all these steps to ensure that visual reviews are being conducted on a regular basis.

Cost: *Installation time:*

8.16   Eliminate Departmental Stocks

When production managers receive more inventory than they immediately need, they have a tendency to squirrel it away on or near the shop floor, so they have a nearby safety or buffer stock available in case they run out of material. This practice results in a number of problems; first, it uses additional floor space to store the departmental stocks, which may also clutter the shop floor, interfere with the materials handling process, and keep production facilities from expanding. Second, the warehouse staff has no idea if any parts were issued in excess quantities, since none are ever returned, so no one corrects the underlying bills of material, which in turn results in yet more excess parts issuances in the future. Further, the purchasing staff will not be aware of the extra stocks, and so will order even more of them in anticipation of future manufacturing needs, which represents an overinvestment in inventory.

For these reasons, one should attempt to eliminate all departmental stocks by moving them back into the warehouse. This is simplest in a clean shop floor environment where excess stocks are easy to spot, and less so in labyrinthine environments. The main problem is resistance by production management, which may well require an authoritative command from upper management before they will cooperate. Consequently, the proper implementation and continuing enforcement of this best practice requires a certain sensitivity to the politics of the situation.

Cost: 🖆　　　　　　*Installation time:* 🌢

8.17 Install a Distribution Requirements Planning System

When a company has a multitiered delivery system incorporating regional warehouses, and possibly retail stores, it can have problems planning when and which items are needed in its various warehouses and stores. In an unorganized system, each store asks for items from its regional warehouse when stocks become low; the warehouse, in turn, requisitions goods from the main warehouse when incoming orders from stores bring its internal stocks down to a preset reorder level. The result is that the main warehouse has no idea of when items will be needed, or which ones.

The information to rectify this problem is internal to the company if it owns the warehouse and the stores. By installing a distribution requirements planning (DRP) system, one can have the stores input their demand forecasts into a central database, which is then netted against available inventory at the warehouse level to arrive at not only the amount of inventory required from a central facility, but also the latest possible date on which it can be released to the warehouse in order to fill store demand, thereby keeping overall stocks as low as possible. A DRP system gives materials planners excellent visibility into downstream demand by item, allowing them to create an orderly flow of goods from central to regional warehouses, and from there to individual stores. An added benefit of a DRP system is its ability to cluster deliveries into a shipping schedule that reduces transport costs while still meeting the delivery needs of downstream locations.

The trouble with the information produced by a DRP is its reliance on the accuracy of demand forecasts at the store or regional warehouse level. If these forecasts are substantially inaccurate, so too will be the DRP output. Also, a DRP system is a substantial software package requiring considerable installation time, frequently assisted by consultants; the cost of completed systems can easily exceed seven figures.

Cost: 💵 💵 💵   *Installation time:* ⏱ ⏱ ⏱

8.18 Distribute Slow-Moving Items from Regional Warehouses

In a retail sales situation, slow-moving items comprise a significant part of any inventory. If every retail location in a large chain stocks significant quantities of an item, then a company is holding a massive amount of safety stock across all its locations for that item. The likely result is both a significant investment in slow-moving inventory and a high probability of product obsolescence at some point in the future, resulting in a writedown in the inventory valuation.

A good best practice to mitigate this problem is to keep smaller stocks of slow-moving items in the retail locations, and to replenish those stocks more frequently from a single holding location at a regional warehouse. By doing so, the total amount of inventory in the system can be significantly reduced, thereby shrinking the risk of excessive inventory investment and product obsolescence.

There are three problems here. First, the retail locations must have sufficient inventory control systems in place that they can reorder items from a regional warehouse as soon as their on-hand stocks are depleted. Second, the warehouses must have short enough delivery times to quickly replenish the retail locations, thereby avoiding stockouts at the retail level. Third, the inventory control systems for the company as a whole must be able to promptly recognize which items are becoming slow moving and reposition inventory back to the regional warehouses, as well as reduce replenishment, as soon as this problem becomes evident.

Cost: 💵 💵 💵   *Installation time:* ⏱ ⏱ ⏱

8.19 Use Overnight Delivery from a Single Location for Selected Items

It makes a great deal of sense to store most types of inventory in distribution warehouses strategically located in a company's primary markets or near major customers. By doing so, one can more easily ship products to customers on short notice. However, this approach does not work well for the minority of products having uncertain demand levels. It is impossible for materials planners to estimate how much of these items to stock in each distribution warehouse, so they face the alternatives of frequent stockouts or the expense of an excessive inventory investment (especially for those items having a high unit cost).

An inexpensive best practice that resolves this issue is to retain high-value items with uncertain demand levels in a central warehouse, and use overnight delivery services to ship them to customers when needed. By doing so, materials planners can store a large quantity of the items in only one location, rather than several. The cost of overnight delivery services is usually minor in comparison to the saved inventory investment. However, this best practice works less well for bulkier items, since express delivery expenses rise dramatically with the size of the shipment. Consequently, one should conduct a cost-benefit analysis to determine the maximum item size beyond which it is impractical to ship items from a central location.

It may also be necessary to alter the customer order system, so that orders placed for items retained in the central storage facility are automatically flagged and forwarded to that location for immediate shipment.

Cost: *Installation time:*

8.20 Use Fair Shares Analysis to Allocate Inventory to Warehouses

What happens when a central supply point receives orders from multiple warehouses for the same item, but there is not enough quantity on hand to fill all the orders? A common result is that the orders are received in a first-come, first-served fashion. When this approach is used, the first downstream warehouse can turn around and supply customers with the full amount of their orders, and have some left over to replenish stock. However, there may not be enough inventory left for any other warehouses, so their customers will not be served at all, resulting in reduced company sales.

The solution is fair shares analysis. Under this approach, available inventory is first allocated to actual customer orders, followed by allocations to those warehouses whose projected demand indicates that they are most likely to receive additional customer orders in the near future, followed by replenishment of safety stock levels. Any remaining inventory is allocated to warehouses based on their historical inventory usage. Note that the sequence in which an order was received from a warehouse is not factored into this analysis at all. By using fair shares analysis, a company services all actual customer orders first and makes remaining stock available in those areas from which new orders are most likely to originate, thereby maximizing company sales.

The primary difficulty with fair shares analysis is that information at the individual warehouse level for on-hand inventory balances, safety stock levels, customer orders, and projected demand must be consolidated in one place, which requires an expensive centralized inventory tracking and forecasting system. A less expensive alternative is to upload data from the warehouse management systems of individual warehouses into a central monitoring database, which eliminates the need for similar systems at all warehouses, but still calls for the creation of software interfaces between the various systems.

Cost: 💵 💵 💵   *Installation time:* 🔔 🔔 🔔

8.21 Periodically Rationalize the Warehouse Network

When the time required to process and ship a customer order was long, companies used to ensure fast delivery times by locating large numbers of warehouses as close to customer sites as possible. This resulted in an excess investment in finished goods and spare parts inventories, since items were duplicated in many locations. It also introduced the cost of moving inventory between locations, as materials planners shifted items between warehouses to match supply to demand. A further expense was the cost of maintaining separate staffs in each of the various warehouses. An excessive number of warehouses is an even greater problem for companies using an acquisition strategy, since they end up owning multiple warehouse chains whose areas of coverage may overlap.

The solution is a periodic rationalization of a company's entire warehouse network. This involves measuring the average cycle time for customer orders from each location in comparison to a target level, and modeling the situation to see if the target service level can be achieved with a smaller number of regional warehouses. This goal is particularly appropriate for companies trying to cost-justify the use of advanced materials-movement systems within their warehouses, since these investments can result in such significant cycle time reductions that entire warehouses can be closed down and centralized as a result, providing massive cost savings and a far smaller investment in inventory.

This is obviously a very long-term strategy. Given the massive effort involved in closing warehouses, including reshuffling their contents among the remaining warehouses and determining which customers will be served by the remaining distribution centers, this best practice requires a long-term network rationalization plan, a large implementation team, and continuing plan revisions to accommodate changes in the mix of products, customers, and additional warehouses acquired as part of corporate mergers and acquisitions. Warehouse rationalization planning should include a study of the operating cost and expandability of remaining warehouses, warehouse union problems, freight rates and transportation issues from surviving locations, required changes to automated picking systems, customer delivery requirements, cross-docking needs, and forecasted changes in ordering patterns.

Cost: 💵 💵 💵   *Installation time:* 🔋 🔋 🔋

8.22 Create a Materials Review Board

Though it is certainly encouraging to see a manager attack the obsolete inventory problem in the warehouse, a common problem is to see some items disposed of that were actually needed, possibly for short-term production requirements, but also for long-term service parts or substitutes for other items. In these cases, the aggressive manager who is only trying to help will likely be castigated for causing problems that the logistics staff must fix.

A good solution is to form a materials review board (MRB). The MRB is composed of representatives from every department having any interaction with inventory issues—accounting, engineering, logistics, and production. For example, the engineering staff may need to retain some items that they are planning to incorporate into a new design, while the logistics staff may know that it is impossible to obtain a rare part, and so prefer to hold onto the few items left in stock for service parts use.

It can be difficult to bring this disparate group together for obsolete inventory reviews, so one normally has to put a senior member of management in charge to force meetings to occur, while also scheduling a series of regular inventory review meetings well in advance. Meeting minutes should be written and disseminated to all members of the group, identifying which inventory items have been mutually declared obsolete. If this approach still results in accusations that items have been improperly disposed of, then the group can also resort to a sign-off form that must be completed by each MRB member before any disposition can occur. However, obtaining a series of sign-offs can easily cause lengthy delays or the loss of the sign-off form, and is therefore not recommended.

The MRB is less frequently used in companies having minimal inventory levels, which is especially common in just-in-time environments.

Cost: *Installation time:*

8.23   Identify Obsolete Inventory via Physical Inventory Tags

Companies with no computerized inventory database can have a hard time determining which inventory items are not being used, and so must rely on guesswork to determine if any items have become obsolete. This is also a problem for companies using computerized databases from which reports cannot be easily generated.

In either case, an easy solution is to leave the physical inventory count tags on all inventory items following completion of the count. The tags taped to any items used during the subsequent year will be thrown away at the time of use, leaving only the oldest unused items still tagged by the end of the year. One can then tour the warehouse and investigate each of these items further to see if an obsolescence reserve should be created for them.

The main problem with this best practice is that tags can fall off or be ripped off inventory items, especially if there is a high level of traffic in nearby bins. Though extra taping will reduce this issue, it is likely that some tag loss will occur over time.

Cost: *Installation time:*

8.24 Reserve Otherwise Obsolete Inventory with "Service/Repair" Designation

When inventory is designated obsolete, the entire on-hand balance is typically disposed of, usually at some loss to the company. However, it is possible that some parts should be kept on hand for a number of years, to be sold or given away as warranty replacements. This will reduce the amount of obsolescence expense, and also keeps the company from having to procure or remanufacture parts at a later date in order to meet service/repair obligations.

The amount of inventory to be held in this service/repair category can be roughly calculated based on the company's experience with similar products, or with the current product if it has been sold for a sufficiently long period. Any additional inventory on hand exceeding the total amount of anticipated service/repair parts can then be disposed of.

Of particular interest is the time period over which management anticipates storing parts in the service/repair category. There should be some period over which the company has historically found that there is some requirement for parts, such as 5 or 10 years. Once this predetermined period has ended, a flag in the product master file should trigger a message indicating that the remaining parts can be disposed of. Prior to doing this, management should review recent transactional experience to see whether the service/repair period should be extended or if it is now safe to eliminate the remaining stock.

Cost: *Installation time:*

8.25 Avoid Product Obsolescence with Shelf-Life Control

Some products have limited shelf lives and must be thrown out if not used by a certain date. This certainly applies to all food products and can even be an issue with such other items as gaskets and seals, which will dry out over time. In a large warehouse with thousands of SKUs and only a small number of these limited-life products, it can be difficult to specially track them and ensure that they are used before their expiration dates.

A mix of changes must be implemented to ensure proper shelf-life control. First, the computer system needs to have a record of the ending shelf-life date for each item in the warehouse. This calls for a special field in the inventory record that is not present in many standard inventory systems, so one must either obtain standard software containing this feature or have the existing database altered to make this feature available. The receiving staff must be warned by the computer system of the arrival of a limited-shelf-life item, so a flag also must be available in the item master file for this purpose. With both of these software changes in hand, one can use the computer system to warn of impending product obsolescence for specific items.

A simpler variation is to still have a flag in the item master file warn of the arrival of limited-shelf-life items, but to then have the warehouse staff manually track the obsolescence problem from that point onward. This means clearly tagging each item with its shelf-life date, so anyone picking inventory can clearly see which items must be picked first. Though a much less expensive solution, it relies on both the receiving staff and stock pickers to ensure that the oldest items are used first.

A third variation is to use a gravity-flow rack. This is a racking system set at a slight downward angle to the picker and containing rollers. Cartons of arriving items are loaded into the back of the rack, where they queue up behind cartons containing older items. Pickers then take the oldest items from the front of the rack. Because of this load-in-back, pick-in-front configuration, inventory is always used in a first-in, first-out manner, ensuring that the oldest items are always used first. This is an excellent way to control item shelf life, since there is no conscious need to pick one item over another in order to use the oldest one first. Similar racking systems are available for pallet-sized loads. However, it does not absolutely ensure that items will be used prior to their shelf-life dates—if an item is pretty far back in a gravity-flow rack, or if demand is minimal, then it still will not be used in time.

Cost: 💵 💵   *Installation time:* 🕐 🕐

8.26 Create an Obsolete Inventory Budget for Disposals

Senior management can be a collective group of pack rats; often senior managers simply do not want to get rid of inventory that is clearly obsolete and is taking up space in the warehouse. This is a particular problem when company policy requires the warehouse manager to obtain advance approval of all inventory disposals. The result is an ever-increasing pile of unused inventory jamming every corner of the warehouse, eventually requiring additional storage space and racking systems.

A simple best practice is to create an obsolete inventory reserve as part of the annual budget, and allow the warehouse manager to dispose of as many items as he or she wants within that budget without further approval, as long as the items have already been declared obsolete by the Materials Review Board (see Best Practice 8.22, "Create a Materials Review Board"). Under this approach, one can typically count on the warehouse manager to throw out the maximum possible amount of stock on the first day when the new budget takes effect.

The only problem with this approach is that the warehouse manager is most likely to eliminate the bulkiest items first in order to clear out the largest possible amount of storage space, so items occupying a small cubic volume may languish for some time.

Cost: 💵   *Installation time:* 🕐

8.27 Batch Excess Inventory for Sale to Salvage Contractors

The worst way to sell off excess inventory to salvage contractors is to allow them to pick over the items for sale, only selecting those items they are certain to make a profit on. With this method, the bulk of the excess inventory will still be parked in the warehouse when the contractors are gone.

Instead, divide the inventory into batches, each one containing some items of value, which a salvage contractor must purchase in total in order to obtain that subset of items he really wants. Then have the contractors bid on each batch. Though the total amount of funds realized may not be much higher than would have been the case if the contractors had cherry-picked the inventory, they will take on the burden of taking the inventory away from the company's premises, thereby allowing the company to avoid disposal expenses.

Cost: 💵   *Installation time:* 🕐

8.28 Sell Excess Items through the Service Department

When a company discovers that it has too much stock on hand, the accounting staff usually sets aside an obsolete inventory reserve only slightly smaller than the total original book value of the items, on the theory that the items will be disposed of at a significant loss through the usual approaches of discounted sales, scrapping, or donations for a tax write-off.

In some situations, one can recover nearly the entire cost of excess items by asking the service department to sell them to existing customers as replacement parts. This approach is especially useful when the excess items are for specialized parts that customers are unlikely to obtain elsewhere, since these sales can be presented to customers as valuable replacements that may not be available for much longer.

Conversely, this best practice is least useful for commodity items or those subject to rapid obsolescence or having a short shelf life.

Cost: 💵   *Installation time:* 🕐

8.29 Outsource Selected Warehousing Functions

Sometimes a company does not have the monetary resources to create a first-class warehousing area, nor to staff it with carefully chosen, experienced personnel. This can also occur when a company ramps up its sales so fast that there is no time to create a warehousing function. The result is usually cramped warehouse space, inaccurate inventory records, damaged or obsolete goods, and very poor customer service.

A possible solution is the selective use of third-party warehousing operations. The most common application of this best practice is the simple rental of overflow storage space, but it can extend into such additional services as warehousing for questionable new markets from which a company may choose to withdraw on short notice, repackaging services, creating point-of-sale displays, freight consolidation with deliveries by other companies to garner full-truckload shipping rates, the addition of barcodes for retail customers, import/export shipments, and even the complete outsourcing of the entire warehousing function.

One should consider the outsourcing option carefully, for it is clearly more expensive than creating the same operations in-house, given the need for suppliers to obtain a reasonable profit. It is most useful in situations where a company requires warehousing services on extremely short notice, has significant in-house warehousing problems requiring immediate solution, does not wish to allocate funds to this area, or considers warehousing activities to be outside its set of core capabilities.

Cost: *Installation time:*

9

Warehouse Layout

This chapter addresses those 18 warehouse layout best practices having a direct impact on inventory. As noted in Exhibit 9.1, this includes inventory storage by zones, maximization of vertical storage space, proper placement and size of aisle space, and the selective use of automation for putaway, picking, and transport, as well as alterations to some warehouse space and even the complete elimination of the warehouse.

Most of the best practices listed in this chapter require reconfiguration of the warehouse area, and so are generally assigned a fairly lengthy installation period. The sole exception is expanding the receiving area, which requires the less time-consuming dismantling of any storage racks intruding on that area.

One block of four best practices addresses warehouse automation—the use of automated storage and retrieval systems, automated guided vehicle systems, and conveyors. The fourth best practice in the cluster is intended to mitigate excessive enthusiasm for automation, since automated systems are extremely expensive and require careful cost-benefit analysis to ensure that they are a valid investment.

Two best practices can be used only in specific circumstances. One is the locked warehouse, which is best used in a traditional factory configuration of kitted inventory and functional work cells but is of little use when inventory is delivered straight to the production areas. The other recommendation is the complete elimination of the warehouse, which is viable only when inventory turns are extremely high and just-in-time concepts have been fully implemented.

Exhibit 9.1 *Summary of Warehouse Layout Best Practices*

	Best Practice	Cost	Install Time
9.1	Include other issues than cost in a warehouse acquisition decision	💵	🕐
9.2	Generally organize the warehouse in a "U"-shaped process flow	💵 💵	🕐 🕐 🕐
9.3	Organize the warehouse by storage zones	💵 💵	🕐 🕐
9.4	Maximize vertical storage space	💵 💵	🕐 🕐
9.5	Tailor vertical storage space to manual picking needs	💵 💵	🕐 🕐
9.6	Enclose building supports in racks	💵	🕐
9.7	Use narrow aisles in manual putaway and picking zones	💵 💵	🕐 🕐
9.8	Avoid aisles adjacent to outside walls	💵	🕐 🕐
9.9	Use automated storage and retrieval systems	💵 💵 💵	🕐 🕐
9.10	Use automated guided vehicle systems	💵 💵 💵	🕐 🕐
9.11	Use conveyors to reduce employee travel	💵 💵	🕐 🕐
9.12	Avoid an excessive level of warehouse automation	💵	🕐
9.13	Eliminate the quality review area	💵	🕐 🕐
9.14	Enlarge the receiving area	💵	🕐 🕐
9.15	Design just-in-time docks for the largest anticipated trucks	💵 💵	🕐 🕐
9.16	Lock down the warehouse area	💵 💵	🕐 🕐
9.17	Plan for maximized warehouse space utilization	💵	🕐
9.18	Eliminate the warehouse	💵	🕐 🕐 🕐

9.1 Include Other Issues than Cost in a Warehouse Acquisition Decision

The finance department typically has a great deal of influence over the decision to acquire warehouse space—in short, always acquire at the lowest cost per square foot. Many warehouse managers subscribe to this view as well, especially if this cost forms part of their annual evaluation. However, the least expensive warehouse may actually cost substantially more once other factors are brought into consideration. Several additional points to consider when evaluating additional warehouse space are:

- *Proportion of usable storage space.* Measure the amount of building space that can actually be used for inventory storage. Many buildings have irregular sizes that do not allow for the use of evenly spaced aisles, and also include side rooms and staging areas in which inventory cannot be conveniently stored.

- *Floor quality.* If substantial racking systems are contemplated, then the floor must have the capability to support the weight, which calls for substantial pad thickness. Also, racking systems require an extremely level floor. Of lesser importance but certainly contributing to warehouse maintenance is a recently renewed floor seal, which reduces the amount of moisture and particulates.

- *Column spacing.* Support columns should be evenly spaced, so that racking systems can be configured consistently throughout the warehouse. This also allows one to configure aisles with no stray columns impeding the flow of materials.

- *Unobstructed height.* Usable cubic volume is just as important as the amount of square feet. If there are serious overhead obstructions interfering with the addition of more rack space, it will be necessary to acquire far more square feet of storage on which to locate the displaced inventory. Consequently, take note of all hanging lighting fixtures that cannot be moved, as well as sprinkler systems, beams, and ductwork.

A good way to create a defensible financial review of a potential warehouse acquisition is to lay out a best-case floor plan as allowed for by the building shape, including optimal rack heights based on any obstructions, and determine a cost per bin or cubic foot, rather than a cost per square foot.

Cost: 🖢   Installation time: ⬤

9.2 Generally Organize the Warehouse in a "U"-Shaped Process Flow

A warehouse can be organized in a variety of ways to maximize the flow of goods into it, with some items being cross-docked directly to outbound transport, and other items going to a variety of racking and bin systems, as noted in Chapter 4, "Inventory Storage." However, sometimes the warehouse planner loses sight of the general flow of materials through the facility, resulting in inefficient flow patterns, irrespective of how well the underlying storage systems are organized or laid out.

The solution is to *generally* organize the warehouse in a "U"-shaped process flow, where the receiving dock is located on one side of a building, from which materials are moved straight back through a putaway staging area to primary and reserve storage, and then back toward the front of the building through picking and shipping areas to the shipping docks, which should be located next to the receiving docks for the most efficient cross-docking travel. The premise behind using the "U" flow is that material movements will not cross over each other, which would otherwise create movement bottlenecks throughout the warehouse. This approach is also efficient for future facility expansion, since three sides of the building can be opened for add-on square footage.

This best practice is noted only as a general principle, since specific warehouse needs may call for decidedly different flow patterns. It is best to call on the services of a warehouse facility planner to construct the most efficient layout possible, and to also retain that person's services at regular intervals to see if incremental changes in item requirements call for a floor plan change as well.

Cost: 💵 💵   *Installation time:* 🕐 🕐 🕐

9.3 Organize the Warehouse by Storage Zones

If a warehouse evolves over time without significant up-front planning, there is a strong tendency for items to be stored without any thought given to their storage requirements, for example, bulky, small, perishable, refrigerated, or flammable items. The result is a hodgepodge environment in which it is difficult to put away or pick inventory, and where obsolescence rates are higher than would normally be the case.

The solution is to organize the warehouse by storage zones. This means identifying all items in advance with special handling and storage requirements, and then building the warehouse storage configuration around those requirements. Further, one must include in this calculation the cubic volume of each type of inventory likely to be kept on hand, so the appropriate storage volumes are assigned. As an example, a warehouse can include a bin-shelving or modular storage drawer area in which to store the smallest items, a double-deep racking system to store large quantities of pallet loads, and a carousel area for the picking of small-volume, high-usage items.

There is no downside to this best practice. The proper organization of a warehouse into storage zones is absolutely fundamental to the efficient storage and movement of inventory. It is best to perform this best practice during the planning stages of a new warehouse, though it can be done later, despite the obvious inefficiency of reconfiguring an existing layout.

Cost: *Installation time:*

9.4 Maximize Vertical Storage Space

Many warehouses have considerable vertical space available, frequently in the range of 30 feet, before encountering such obstructions as sprinkler systems and support beams. Nonetheless, a common mindset is to extend storage only a modest distance above a person's height, typically in the range of a dozen feet or so. When there is not enough space left in the warehouse using such storage systems, a company will waste money adding storage space in other locations.

One should investigate the possibility of increasing a warehouse's vertical storage capability in one of two ways. First, see if it is possible to stack multiple layers of the same SKU on top of each other (known as "stackability"). This may require the insertion of a slip sheet made of plastic, wood, or cardboard between SKU layers to provide some rigidity to a stack. One should carefully test the stackability of each SKU on a controlled basis to determine the maximum number of layers that can be stacked while still providing maximum security to the warehouse staff. If this approach works, be sure to include the stackability factor of each SKU in the item master file, in case management wishes to install a computerized system for maximizing the storage of SKUs.

A second alternative is to extend racks skyward. This can be expensive, but may also be significantly cheaper than the alternative of renting additional space elsewhere. However, existing racks may be too flimsy to stand the strain of additional racks, so one may have to consider the cost not of just a few incremental racks, but of the entire warehouse rack system. One should also evaluate the ability of the warehouse floor to bear the weight of additional storage, since some building pads may be too thin.

When maximizing vertical storage space, try to store items requiring significant manual putaway and picking in low-height areas, since employees can reach higher storage bins only with portable ladders, though a second-story mezzanine could also be constructed. This policy will typically require one to store items with high storage requirements in areas with higher vertical storage capabilities, thereby maximizing storage per square foot.

Cost: *Installation time:*

9.5 Tailor Vertical Storage Space to Manual Picking Needs

Though maximizing the cubic availability of space is important, as noted in the preceding best practice, one must also account for the needs of manual stock-picking operations. It does little good to store goods near the rafters when the warehouse picking staff must constantly use forklift or ladder equipment to laboriously retrieve the stock. When this happens, pick times become painfully slow, leading to a much lower order-fulfillment speed.

A reasonable alternative is to organize the warehouse so that those items most frequently picked manually are stored within easy reach of a person standing on the warehouse floor. This imposes a vertical restriction on the storage of such items at about seven feet. This does not mean that racking can extend only to seven feet, just that the small subset of frequently picked items should be located in this floor-level region. Slow-moving or very large SKUs can still be stacked much higher than this seven-foot limitation.

Cost: *Installation time:*

9.6 Enclose Building Supports in Racks

Larger warehouses require a considerable number of support columns to support the roof. If racks are laid out without regard to column positioning, there is a good chance that the columns will interfere with aisle traffic, causing bottlenecks in the orderly flow of materials through the warehouse.

The obvious best practice is to enclose all building supports within the storage racks. When this is done, aisles are kept clear for traffic. The only problem is that the presence of columns can make it difficult to set up racking systems, possibly requiring breaks in the racks. An alternative is to position racks adjacent to support columns, so the columns are located at the far sides of aisles, representing only a minimal hindrance to traffic.

Cost: 🪙   Installation time: 🌑

9.7 Use Narrow Aisles in Manual Putaway and Picking Zones

The typical warehouse is laid out on the assumption that all aisles are of exactly the same width, which is usually sufficiently wide for a forklift to put away or extract items from racks. Though this makes for consistently wide aisles, there is a potential loss of storage space in those areas where the items stored are all so small that forklifts are not needed. The result is excessively wide aisles that could have been used for more storage.

The solution is to plan for narrower aisles in the minority of situations where manual putaways and picking are the norm. This best practice also can be used when automated storage and retrieval systems are installed, since these systems require far less operating width than a forklift.

If some kind of lift truck is still intended for use in a narrow-aisle environment, there tends to be considerable damage to both the truck and the inventory when the truck operator inevitably drifts out of the centerline of the aisle. To eliminate this problem, narrow aisles can be equipped with either a rail or wire tracking system. Trucks traveling down these aisles will automatically correct their direction of travel to stay within a fraction of an inch of the aisle centerline.

The main problem with narrow aisles is making sure that the aisles are still large enough for kitting carts to negotiate. If a company adopts a variety of batch picking techniques, pickers will likely need pick carts of some heft to accommodate portable scales and bins, so be sure to plan some additional aisle width for the carts.

Cost: 💵 💵   *Installation time:* 🕐 🕐

9.8 Avoid Aisles Adjacent to Outside Walls

Any warehouse aisle constitutes space that would otherwise have been used for storage. By including perimeter aisles in a warehouse layout, a warehouse has aisles that serve storage space located on only one side of the aisle, which cuts the effectiveness of these aisles in half.

The solution is to shift perimeter aisles sufficiently inward to include storage space on the outside of the aisles. By doing so, every aisle can be used to access storage on both sides, which reduces the proportion of aisle space to storage space and increases the useful storage capacity of the warehouse.

This concept does not work near dock doors, and so is least effective when dock doors appear on all sides of the warehouse facility. However, in most cases, there are sufficiently few doors to allow for storage space along most warehouse walls.

Cost: 💵   *Installation time:* 🕐 🕐

9.9 Use Automated Storage and Retrieval Systems

In limited situations, warehouse managers find themselves in extremely high-cost environments, with expensive building rent, high-cost labor, and large numbers of inventory move transactions. Normally, this would require a warehouse layout with wide aisles and many forklift operators, resulting in a very expensive storage cost per SKU. This situation arises in high-rent, high-wage-rate areas, typically close to major cities.

A possible solution is the use of automated storage and retrieval systems (AS/RSs). These are extremely expensive, fully automated systems running on rails that take a pallet from a drop-off point at the end of any aisle and move it to an open bin. More advanced systems will also pick up a requested pallet from another bin on the way back to the drop-off point. An AS/RS system also allows for the use of much narrower aisles, usually five feet, so more storage space can be packed into a warehouse. Obviously, all materials-handling labor in the aisles is completely eliminated. An AS/RS system is usually able to carry heavier loads than many forklift models, and can also store pallets in higher rack locations than any forklift. Further, it has excellent record accuracy and eliminates product damage that otherwise would be caused by improper forklift handling. This best practice is particularly useful in a refrigerated warehouse, where the cost of refrigeration mandates the smallest possible cubic storage space for the largest amount of inventory.

A variation on the warehouse use of an AS/RS system is to use it for the delivery of inventory directly to cellular operations within the production facility. This constitutes just-in-time delivery if the production workflow is sufficiently integrated with the material management computer system to trigger an AS/RS delivery when needed. However, this approach requires the addition of expensive conveyor systems to the production area.

A variation on the AS/RS system is to locate a picker on the machine, who rides with it to various locations. Under this approach, the picker typically picks an entire order before returning to the drop-off point.

However, these advantages can be heavily offset by the high fixed cost of an AS/RS system. For more information about AS/RS systems, see the websites for HK Systems (www.hksystems.com), Westfalia Technologies (www.westfaliausa.com), and Shelf Plus (www.shelfplus.com).

Cost: 💵 💵 💵   *Installation time:* 🕒 🕒

9.10 Use Automated Guided Vehicle Systems

When a company uses lift trucks to move items within the warehouse and out to the production area, the speed and timeliness of inventory moves becomes a function of the number of lift truck operators, their experience level, and congestion at key choke points in the building through which the lift trucks must travel. Further, in order to achieve the maximum level of lift truck efficiency, only full pallet loads are normally moved, so work-in-process inventory levels tend to increase to full pallet load sizes before a lift truck operator will appear and move the load to the next downstream workstation. Both issues tend to increase the inventory investment in the production area.

One solution for selected situations is the use of automated guided vehicle systems (AGVSs). These vehicles usually run over guide wires embedded in the floor, though more advanced models can range throughout a facility by using laser scanners and onboard positioning systems. The vehicles can even be programmed to automatically accept loads from automated storage and retrieval systems and drop them off at delivery stations located on spurs alongside the main track, thereby eliminating the need for lift truck operators for some activities. The vehicles can automatically recharge themselves by backing onto a recharging spur and then automatically reentering the conveyance system once they are recharged.

Because AGVS systems run along preset routes, there is little chance of congestion unless someone blocks the route. Also, an AGVS can deliver parts to a workstation in very small unit quantities and take them away in the same manner, so a company's work-in-process inventory investment can be substantially reduced. Further, additional AGVS vehicles can be added as capacity demands increase, so the capital investment in this system can be spread over a considerable period of time. Another advantage is the ability of AGVS systems to operate in environments that are intolerable to human materials handlers, such as refrigerated warehouses. Finally, depending on the level of automation used, one can precisely track the location of specific inventory items as they move through a facility on an AGVS system.

There are three main objections to an AGVS system. One is its substantial up-front capital cost. Second, one must create a simulation of traffic patterns in advance to avoid bottlenecks, or else a system may be designed that does not maximize the theoretical carrying capacity of the system. Third, one can eliminate the need for an AGVS over time by consolidating space in a production facility; if it can be made small enough, less expensive gravity conveyors can handle much of the AGVS workload.

Cost: 💵 💵 💵   *Installation time:* 🕐 🕐

9.11 Use Conveyors to Reduce Employee Travel

The picking function involves a great deal of travel time, as employees search for the correct locations from which to pick items and then take them back to a central shipping location for further processing. The proportion of their time spent traveling can easily exceed their picking time by a wide margin, especially when the warehouse is a large one.

It can be cost-effective in some situations to selectively install conveyors to move items within a warehouse. Since conveyors are moderately expensive, one should be careful to install them only when travel times per person are high, and when item movement volumes are sufficient. They are particularly effective when employees would otherwise have to manually move heavy loads, since a conveyor can be positioned at waist-height for an easy move from a storage location to the conveyor surface. They can also be used as an alternative to forklifts in situations where forklifts are being used for the movement of relatively small, lightweight items.

One problem with conveyors is their use when not cost-effective. Also, they can significantly interfere with flow lines in a warehouse, so the industrial engineering staff must carefully lay out not only their configurations, but also how other material flow patterns will move around the conveyors. They also require periodic maintenance, which must be planned for periods when material movement is not occurring in the warehouse, such as weekends or the second or third shift. Finally, the use of conveyors tends to lock in a specific warehouse configuration, since any subsequent reshuffling of racks and conveyors becomes extremely difficult and time-consuming.

Cost: 💵 💵   *Installation time:* 🕑 🕑

9.12 Avoid an Excessive Level of Warehouse Automation

Several of the preceding best practices involved the installation of computerized or mechanical systems that eliminate the need for employees in certain locations or functions within the warehouse. Though these best practices can bring about substantial improvements in a warehouse, they should be installed only after considering the following issues:

- *Investment.* Some warehouse automation equipment, such as forklifts, vertical carousels (see Chapter 4, "Inventory Storage"), and automated storage and retrieval systems, are expensive. Though companies may be tempted to install such systems in order to impress visitors, they may find that some investments do not save a sufficient amount in other expenses or provide enough other benefits to be worth their cost. Thus, one should carefully analyze the initial investment decision to ensure that each proposed new system has a significant payback without having major attendant risks.

- *Increase in fixed costs.* Mechanical equipment requires ongoing maintenance. The warehouse manager must determine how this maintenance and resulting equipment downtime will be scheduled into ongoing warehouse activities, as well as the cost of the maintenance and who will complete it.

- *Maintenance downtime.* If a complex system requires continual maintenance, it can prove to be more of a hindrance than help. For example, if a conveyor is installed down the center of a busy aisle and then fails, there may not be sufficient room left in the aisle for other types of equipment to move items in or out, reducing a company to manually shifting items until the equipment problem has been fixed.

- *Reconfiguration problems.* An expensive automated system tends to be very difficult to reposition once it has been installed; good examples are automated storage and retrieval systems and some conveyors. Consequently, a warehouse manager may find it nearly impossible to alter the general warehouse layout if there is too much automation equipment cluttering it.

- *Training.* The staff must know how to operate any new equipment installed in the warehouse, which should include refresher training. If not, the finest automation solutions in the world will not function at an optimum level, reducing the efficiency levels that a company would otherwise have gained from the new equipment.

- *Changes in warehouse staff skill set.* It is possible that some warehouse staff cannot or will not understand the training required for new warehouse automation equipment. If so, the warehouse manager will need to replace them with more skilled employees or face the same problems resulting from training shortfalls.

The bottom line on warehouse automation is that one should first implement more basic improvements to enhance warehouse performance, such as proper storage layout and inventory slotting, ABC inventory storage, and storage systems matching inventory picking and cubic volume requirements. Only after these basic improvements have been made, which typically yield the bulk of all warehouse efficiency improvements, should one consider the addition of expensive automated systems that are likely to result in efficiency improvements of a lower order of magnitude.

Cost:　　　　　　*Installation time:*

9.13 Eliminate the Quality Review Area

In many companies, the quality of goods received is sufficiently suspect that all received items are stored in a separate quality review area, after which they are released to the main warehouse area for storage. This approach causes several problems. First, the movement of inventory to the shop floor is delayed by the quality control bottleneck. Second, it requires valuable personnel to conduct a quality review of all incoming inventory. Third, space must be set-aside in the warehouse for a review area. Fourth, it requires two additional inventory transactions—one to move inventory into the review area, and another to move it from there to warehouse storage. Since the possibility of creating a record inaccuracy increases with every transaction made, these extra transactions are likely to reduce record accuracy.

A moderately difficult best practice that resolves all these problems is to completely eliminate the quality review area, with all attendant transactions and staff time. Instead, all receipts are moved directly to stock. The problem, of course, is that an alternative must be found to ensure that quality levels are maintained. This typically requires the creation of a supplier quality program by the engineering department, whereby supplier quality levels are certified at the supplier site. This program can take a considerable amount of time to set up, and may call for so much engineering staff time, especially for smaller companies, that company management perceives no cost advantage to the approach. Also, suppliers delivering peripheral items may not be worth the effort of running through a certification program. A common result of these issues is a reduction of the quality review area as the deliveries of major suppliers are received directly into stock, while smaller deliveries still undergo a quality review.

Cost: ✎   *Installation time:* ● ●

9.14 Enlarge the Receiving Area

Much of this book has been oriented toward the reduction of on-hand inventory and the packing of more inventory into less space, with the objective of reducing the company investment in square footage. That concept does not work well in the receiving area, since a considerable amount of buffer space is needed to temporarily store items removed from incoming trailers, repackage it, and cross-dock it to other outbound trucks. If the warehouse layout includes an insufficient receiving area, this can result in so much congestion that inventory is damaged, shipments are mixed, and orders are lost.

The solution depends on the ability of the company to schedule the arrival time of inbound trucks and put away items as soon as they arrive. If it can do so, then the receiving area in front of each dock needs to be only slightly larger than the contents of an inbound truck. However, if deliveries arrive on an unscheduled basis, the receiving area must be sufficiently large to store all inventory received during the maximum receiving part of the day. Thus, floor planning for receiving is driven to a considerable extent by a company's control over delivery arrival times.

Cost: ✎   *Installation time:* ● ●

9.15 Design Just-in-Time Docks for the Largest Anticipated Trucks

A company can construct a state-of-the-art production facility with small dock doors on all sides that allow suppliers to feed parts directly into production process from all directions. However, what if suppliers do not arrive with a sufficiently small side-load trailer for these deliveries? They must instead find the dock door with the largest dock approach and make their delivery at that point, irrespective of where the inventory is supposed to be delivered in the facility. This requires longer travel times within the factory from the dock to the intended point of receipt, which is not only an inefficient use of materials handlers, but also may delay delivery times to the production area and introduces the risk of inventory damage during the lengthened delivery distance.

The solution is to verify with suppliers the maximum truck size to be used for just-in-time deliveries, and create dock approaches sufficiently large to accommodate them.

An opposing view is to create smaller dock approaches in order to reduce the cost of land used, and to require suppliers to acquire delivery vehicles of the size needed to access the resulting facilities. However, if a company has little control over its suppliers, this can be an exceedingly difficult transition. Instead, it is sometimes necessary to leave full-size truck access areas near a limited number of dock doors in the warehouse area to accommodate those few suppliers who still deliver using large trailers.

Cost: 💵 💵   *Installation time:* 🕰 🕰

9.16 Lock Down the Warehouse Area

The single most important cause of inventory inaccuracy is parts "walking out of the warehouse." This means that the physical layout of the warehouse allows anyone to wander in and take any parts they need for the production process. When this happens, there is no record that any item was taken from stock, so no one knows what is left on the shelf, or even if there is *anything* left, which renders any automated reordering system useless. From the accountant's perspective, the physical inventory count will probably be significantly different from what the accounting records show, resulting in a large negative inventory variance at the end of the year.

Segregating the warehouse can eliminate all of these problems. This is done by installing a fence around the entire storage area and locking the gate when there are no warehouse personnel on hand. In addition, there must be ironclad rules about who has a key to this gate. If too many keys are handed out, anyone will still be able to enter the warehouse after hours. To prevent this, there should be no more than one key given to the production personnel, and then only to the most responsible person, who will faithfully mark down anything taken from the warehouse. If possible, even this should be avoided by prepositioning any needed parts outside of the warehouse for use by the production staff when the warehouse staff is not available. Further, the warehouse staff must be carefully instructed as to why no one else is allowed in the warehouse; in addition, they should receive additional training in how to process inventory transactions, and then be given a bonus plan based on reaching high inventory accuracy levels. Only by taking all of these steps will there be a good chance that nonwarehouse personnel can be kept out of the warehouse and that the warehouse personnel are committed to a high level of inventory accuracy.

This best practice is usually opposed by the production department, which claims either that it will be too time-consuming to wait for the warehouse staff to pick parts from the shelf or that they will not receive any parts at all if the warehouse staff is not available. The best way to allay these fears is to have all the systems in place and fully functional before locking down the warehouse. By doing so, the production staff will find that there are no problems with the new system and will have no complaints left to make.

Cost: 💵 💵   *Installation time:* 🕐 🕐

9.17 Plan for Maximized Warehouse Space Utilization

The efficiency of warehouse operations tends to degrade rapidly once at least 80 percent of its storage space is filled. The degradation occurs because the putaway staff must travel further to find open bins in which to deposit inventory; further, because there are few open bins, fast-moving items may be stored in a distant corner of the warehouse, requiring excessive travel times by pickers. In addition, because slow-moving and fast-moving items are jammed into any remaining available space, the warehouse staff must spend more time shifting loads into optimum locations, which not only uses up valuable staff time, but also requires more inventory move transactions and increases the chance of damaging inventory.

The solution is not only to constantly monitor the warehouse space utilization percentage, but also to project significant changes in the percentage in the near term, based on planned changes in receiving or production volumes. While short-term advance planning will not yield enough notice to build out new warehouse space, one can at least plan for the rental of overflow stock locations while more permanent arrangements can be made.

Cost: 💸　　　　　Installation time: ⬤

9.18 Eliminate the Warehouse

The warehouse is the source of many accounting transactions. This department records entries for the receipt, movement, and issuance of parts to and from stock. If any of these transactions are incorrect, the inventory quantities used to derive the cost of goods sold, as well as of on-hand inventory, will be incorrect. In addition, there is probably a fair amount of obsolete inventory somewhere in the warehouse, which the accounting staff must identify and cost out. These are major issues that can seriously impact the accuracy of financial statements.

A very difficult best practice to implement is the complete elimination of the inventory, which in turn means the elimination of the warehouse. Several world-class companies have achieved this best practice by switching to just-in-time receiving and production, which allows them to bypass the storage of all parts in a warehouse. By doing so, a company can avoid all of the transactions needed to log something in and out of the warehouse, not to mention avoiding all the staffing, space, insurance, and inventory obsolescence and damage costs that go along with having a warehouse. From the perspective of the accounting staff, this is the ultimate best practice in inventory accounting, since there is no inventory to account for besides relatively minor amounts of work-in-process.

Unfortunately, this is a goal that very few companies achieve, for a variety of reasons. First, just-in-time receiving and production are very difficult concepts to fully implement, given the difficulty of changing both internal processes and the delivery systems of suppliers. Further, there may be some parts shipped from long distances or that are difficult to obtain, and that *must* be kept in some sort of warehousing facility. Finally, the existing amount of inventory may take years to reduce to zero, unless a company is willing to take write-downs to eliminate some stock or return it to suppliers at a loss. Nonetheless, if a company can convert even some of its systems to just-in-time, it is possible to send received parts directly to the production facility without spending any time in the warehouse; this reduces the number of inventory transactions that might be made in error, resulting in an overall increase in the level of transaction accuracy.

Cost: *Installation time:*

10

Cost Accounting

This chapter addresses those 18 cost accounting best practices having a direct impact on inventory. As noted in Exhibit 10.1, the first items listed involve the elimination of cost accounting practices, such as work-in-process (WIP) tracking, scrap reporting, and purchase price variances. If the elimination of cost accounting systems is not a viable option, then one can proceed to the alteration of cost accounting systems to enforce positive changes, such as assigning overhead costs based on square footage used in an effort to make managers reduce storage space. Lower in priority, and further down the best practices list, is the creation of new costing systems, such as activity-based costing and target costing, in order to either make management more aware of the cost of inventory (as is the case with activity-based costing) or ensure that new products are designed in accordance with strict cost targets (as is the case for target costing). Last on the list are a number of unrelated costing best practices, such as locking out access to the critical unit-of-measure field, establishing cost trend reviews, and revising cost accounting reports to address such issues as faster information feedback, more use of direct costing, and reporting only by exception. The precise mix of best practices adopted will vary widely, based on a company's existing production systems and the views of management regarding the need for altered costing information.

10.1 Eliminate Purchase Price Variance Tracking

When a company purchases materials from multiple suppliers using short-term or spot pricing, purchase prices can vary wildly from the standard or

179

Exhibit 10.1 *Summary of Cost Accounting Best Practices*

	Best Practice	Cost	Install Time
10.1	Eliminate purchase price variance tracking	💵	🕐🕐🕐
10.2	Eliminate the tracking of work-in-process inventory	💵	🕐🕐
10.3	Eliminate scrap reporting in the production area	💵	🕐🕐🕐
10.4	Charge the entire inventory to expense	💵	🕐🕐
10.5	Have the cost system separate value-added and nonvalue-added activities	💵	🕐🕐
10.6	Assign overhead based on square footage used	💵	🕐🕐🕐
10.7	Do not credit internal departments with sales when production is completed	💵	🕐🕐
10.8	Report on landed cost instead of supplier price	💵	🕐🕐
10.9	Report on the total cost of product ownership	💵	🕐🕐
10.10	Implement activity-based costing	💵💵	🕐🕐🕐
10.11	Assign overhead personnel to specific subplants	💵	🕐🕐
10.12	Implement target costing	💵💵	🕐🕐
10.13	Limit access to unit-of-measure changes	💵	🕐
10.14	Review cost trends	💵	🕐🕐
10.15	Review material scrap levels	💵	🕐🕐
10.16	Revise traditional cost accounting reports	💵	🕐🕐
10.17	Audit labor routings	💵	🕐🕐
10.18	Follow a schedule of inventory obsolescence reviews	💵	🕐🕐

historical purchase price. When this happens, the accounting staff tracks the purchase price variance from a standard price, which management uses to castigate or reward the purchasing staff for their performance. Given the massive number of purchasing transactions in a typical company, the accounting department can spend a great deal of time tracking this variance, while the analysis of it can be a waste of time—it focuses attention on historical performance rather than on upcoming issues.

The solution is complex—use a single supplier for each item or commodity purchased, which allows the purchasing staff to negotiate annual pricing agreements with the reduced number of suppliers. Once the purchase price is fixed, there is no longer any need for a purchase price variance.

The difficulty in implementing this best practice has nothing to do with eliminating the variance—that is a byproduct of the more difficult issue of sole sourcing purchases, which can take a considerable amount of time.

Cost: *Installation time:* ● ● ●

10.2 Eliminate Tracking of Work-in-Process Inventory

One of the most complex and error-ridden tasks for the cost accountant is the tracking and accumulation of costs for work-in-process inventory. Because inventory can pass through many workstations, picking up machining and labor costs as it progresses through the production facility, there can be a multitude of transactions to accumulate and charge to inventory. Also, because inventory-tracking systems are typically at their worst in the production area (as opposed to the controlled environment in the warehouse), it is common to see inventory records disappear. Materials themselves can also disappear, since scrap can occur throughout the production process. The end result is a labor-intensive accounting mess that frequently yields inaccurate costing results.

The solution requires the conversion of the production process to cellular manufacturing and the elimination of WIP queues in the production area. Once this has been accomplished, WIP levels will have been driven so low that there is no point in tracking WIP at all. Instead, the cost accounting staff will continue to record items as being in raw materials inventory until they are assembled into final products, after which they are transferred directly into the finished goods inventory.

The problem is certainly not with the elimination of WIP inventory—the cost accounting staff will adopt this practice with enthusiasm. The issue is the massive alteration in production practices leading to the minimization of WIP inventory.

Cost: 🖋   Installation time: ● ●

10.3 Eliminate Scrap Reporting in the Production Area

Production workers must perform a carefully orchestrated routine throughout the day, picking up an incoming product, performing a specific set of tasks on it, and handing it off to the next worker. When a product has a flaw requiring rework or scrap, the workers are usually required by the cost accounting system to stop what they are doing, log in the scrap on a form, and then return to what they were doing. This pause creates a buildup of WIP inventory in front of the worker, since upstream employees have continued to create products in the meantime. The person filling out the scrap report has to work hard to catch up and may not be able to do so, causing a semi-permanent cluster of WIP inventory next to him. Further, the scrap forms are not usually summarized for several days, at which point the production management team descends on the production line to see what can be done to fix a problem that occurred so far in the past that no one remembers it. In short, scrap reporting in the production area is disruptive and has no meaningful impact on the reduction of scrap levels.

A better approach is to let the employees correct scrap problems on the spot and not bother them with scrap reporting requirements. By doing so, scrap issues are fixed at once, thereby reducing the total amount of scrap produced and rendering the scrap reporting system unnecessary.

Several steps must take place before this best practice can be implemented. First, nearly all of the work-in-process must be eliminated from the production area. By doing so, large piles of scrap cannot build up before someone spots the problem. Second, the production staff must be empowered to stop production and fix the problem, or to at least call in a supervisor before production is allowed to resume—this also keeps scrap from building up. Third, it is helpful to rearrange the production process so that employees are close together, so they can easily communicate problems and resolutions among themselves.

Cost: 🖋   Installation time: ● ● ●

10.4 Charge the Entire Inventory to Expense

The cost accounting function allocates a great deal of time to the tracking of inventory expenses—purchases costs, variances, overhead allocations, backflushing, and so on. All these activities are essentially involved with the delay of expense recognition, which is clearly a nonvalue-added activity. A company incurs a considerable expense related to the cost accounting staff simply to put off into the future the recognition of expense associated with inventory that it has already acquired.

A possible solution applicable only in a minority of situations is to charge the entire inventory to expense. By doing so, the primary cost accounting activity vanishes, resulting in a reduced cost accounting staff. Also, a number of inventory tracking systems probably can be dispensed with, since they are used only to accumulate costs related to inventory.

The trouble is that some companies have so much inventory that charging it all to expense would result in a massive one-time loss. It would be a brave management team that would be willing to take the step in such a situation! Also, generally accepted accounting principles (GAAP) state that inventory must be maintained as an asset if there is no offsetting sale in the current period (the matching principle). However, if inventory levels can be driven very low through the application of other best practices noted in this book, the inventory investment can become insignificant in comparison to sales, which gives a company a very good case for writing off whatever inventory is left. If auditors insist on maintaining an inventory costing system, a possible solution is to argue in favor of expensing selected portions of the inventory that have low value, which frequently comprises the bulk of the inventory.

Cost: 💵   *Installation time:* ● ●

10.5 Have the Cost System Separate Value-Added and Nonvalue-Added Activities

Cost accountants tend to dump all kinds of costs onto inventory—not just the usual materials and labor costs, but also allocated costs for warehouse storage, insurance costs, the labor of production planners, and so on. Do these costs really contribute to a product's value? No; in most cases, the accounting staff is simply layering on as much additional cost as possible in order to increase the value of inventory, thereby driving down the cost of goods sold and increasing profits. Though profits may appear higher, it becomes extremely difficult to determine those costs actually adding to the value of a product, or conversely those nonvalue-added costs on which management should focus their attention.

The solution is to revise the reports issued by the costing system, so that value-added and nonvalue-added costs are clearly separated. By doing so, management can easily determine a product's direct cost, which is useful for incremental pricing decisions, while also gaining an understanding of the size of nonvalue-added expenses, so they can focus the most attention on the reduction of the largest cost areas.

Issuing revised costing reports may sound easy, but it is difficult to impose on a packaged costing system that may be capable of presenting only a limited number of cost reports. One solution is to layer a third-party reporting package, such as Crystal Reports, onto the system in order to gain some reporting flexibility. It is also necessary to separate costing data into value-added and nonvalue-added components, which requires more data accumulation labor or equipment than was previously the case.

Cost: *Installation time:*

10.6 Assign Overhead Based on Square Footage Used

A problem with the production process is that it tends to fill every last corner of the area assigned to it. The industrial engineers like to leave lots of space around installed equipment, while the forklift operators want aisles wide enough for them to comfortably pass each other, and the production staff wants to keep as much inventory stacked up in front of machines as possible, so they never run out of parts to feed their machines. This tendency causes four problems. First, the space taken could have been more profitably used for some other application, or subleased. Second, it is more difficult for employees to communicate across the longer distances in a large production area. Third, there is more space over which WIP inventory must be moved between machines. Fourth and most important, inventory on the production floor tends to expand to fill all available space, resulting in a major inventory investment in this area.

A rather subtle solution to this problem is to allocate overhead costs to the production area based on the square footage of space used. By doing so, production management will realize that they can cut their allocated overhead expense and appear more profitable if they condense the production area into a smaller space. This action will cut inventory transport distances between machines, squeeze out inventory being stored in the production area, and improve communications between employees. It tends to be an extremely long, ongoing best practice.

This approach will not work if the department profitability is not of great concern to the production manager; by tying it to his or her compensation through a bonus plan, there is a much greater chance that square footage reduction will ascend on the manager's priority list.

Another issue is that, as square footage used declines, the overhead still must be allocated somewhere. If the overhead pool is simply allocated over the smaller square footage base, there will be no impact on the production department's allocation, so one should give consideration to shifting the expenses elsewhere, perhaps through the use of a different allocation base, in order to reward the production department for its efforts.

Cost: *Installation time:*

10.7 Do Not Credit Internal Departments with Sales When Production Is Completed

In situations where a company likes to treat its internal departments as profit centers, a common practice is to credit them for some portion of the sale price of a product as soon as any processing related to it has been completed. By doing so, a production department has achieved a "sale" to the next downstream department. This approach gives an incentive to each department to complete its share of the production process as soon as possible, thereby increasing its internal "sales" and profitability. The trouble is that departments also have an incentive to complete production even if that production is not needed, thereby burying downstream departments with more work than they can use. Thus, crediting internal departments with sales tends to result in excess inventory.

One can eliminate the crediting of internal departments with sales, thereby eliminating the incentive to create too much inventory. This also eliminates an accounting task that is decidedly nonvalue-added. Other incentive systems can be installed in its place that force the organization to achieve companywide optimization of results, rather than at the department level.

Stopping this practice can be difficult if the company bonus plan is closely linked to it, so one should coordinate any changes with the management team and human resources department to ensure that replacement systems mesh as closely as possible with existing compensation systems.

Cost: *Installation time:*

10.8 Report on Landed Cost Instead of Supplier Price

When the purchasing department focuses exclusively on reducing the purchase price charged by suppliers, it is not seeing the entire expense associated with bringing a product to the company. There is also the transportation cost associated with the purchase, as well as the lot sizes in which items are shipped (and associated storage requirements), damage incurred while in transit, the potential for foreign exchange losses, and shipping insurance. For example, the purchasing department may use an overseas supplier in an attempt to reduce the per-unit cost of an item. However, by doing so, it must order in much larger lot sizes and several weeks earlier than was previously necessary. It must also pay for shipping insurance, as well as the services of an international shipping broker. The net result is no change in the total cost of the product once it arrives at the company's receiving dock.

The solution is for the accounting department to focus the company's attention on the landed cost of purchased items rather than the supplier price. By doing so, the purchasing department gains a better understanding of the total cost of bringing items to the company, and avoids incorrect purchasing decisions that might otherwise increase company expenses.

The downside is the extra work required by the accounting department. Rather than simply recording the amount listed on the supplier invoice as the total product cost, the accounting staff must accumulate expenses from several other sources, such as foreign exchange costs from the finance department, shipping insurance and loss claims from the materials management department, and order lot sizes from the purchasing department. Given the extra accounting effort required, one should concentrate recurring landed cost reporting efforts on only the largest-dollar-item purchases, with spot checks of other items.

Cost: 　　　　　　　　*Installation time:*

10.9 Report on the Total Cost of Product Ownership

Management rarely has a complete picture of the entire cost of a product. Though they usually have a bill of materials that compiles all the obvious costs—materials, labor, and perhaps overhead—they usually have no idea of the other hidden costs required to procure parts, and store, transport, and maintain products in the field. These extra costs can make a seemingly profitable product a major drain on resources. For example, a company's dishwasher product is designed with inadequate packaging, so it is frequently scratched on receipt by the customer and must be replaced by a field service technician. This added cost does not appear in the bill of materials, so management has no idea that its initial profit margins are being completely offset by an inadequate packaging problem.

The solution is to report on the total cost of product ownership. When fully addressed, this includes the cost of qualifying new suppliers for the delivery of parts specific to a product, the contracting process with the new suppliers, order placement, delivery costs, parts inspection, paperwork related to rejected parts, handling customer calls related to defective products, field replacements, keeping replacement parts on hand, and disposing of excess inventory. By periodically assembling this information in a report, management can see where significant costs are being accumulated, and can act to reduce them. In some cases, the added costs may be so high that management may elect to drop a product, though they must be careful to differentiate between overhead and incremental costs on the report. Otherwise, they may drop a product against which a great deal of immovable overhead costs have been charged, and still have the overhead after the product is gone.

The considerable problem with this best practice is the amount of cost accountant labor required to assemble the total cost of ownership. The best way to reduce this labor is to report on the total cost of ownership only after an activity-based costing (ABC) system has been installed. By doing so, the cost accountant can much more easily assemble the required information from the ABC system.

Cost: 🖻   Installation time: 🌑 🌑

10.10 Implement Activity-Based Costing

Inventory can sit in the warehouse for years, apparently there for a free ride. However, this is not the case. Inventory accumulates costs every day because it takes up storage space, requires insurance coverage, gradually becomes obsolete, and requires labor to move, among other costs. Without some way to reliably assign these costs to specific inventory items, a company has no way of knowing which inventory items are costing it more money than it makes from them.

A good method for determining the cost per item is ABC. Under this methodology, you assign costs to specific activities, such as receiving, storage, inventory moves, picking, and delivery. You then determine how many of each transaction type are consumed by each inventory item, and multiply the cost per activity by the usage per item, thereby yielding the cost consumed by each inventory item. By doing this on an annualized basis and then comparing the cost to the gross margin earned on each inventory item per year, you can determine which inventory items are not earning their keep, and can remove them from stock. This can result in a drastic reduction in inventory, since a common finding is that a very high proportion of the total inventory is not profitable—frequently half of it.

Though a very fine tool for improving the profitability of inventory items, there are also some problems with ABC. The main issue is the difficulty of setting it up. Few accounting systems are designed to track costs by activity, so new cost collection systems must be designed for the warehouse. These systems can be highly detailed ones that track costs every day, though a simpler approach is to conduct a costing survey once a year to update activity costs. The same problem applies to transaction volumes by inventory item—if the transaction tracking system used by the warehouse is already computerized, one can create new reports to summarize this information. However, if a manual card-based tracking system is in place, it is very time-consuming to obtain this information.

Another problem is that many warehouses do not stock just finished goods, for which an ABC analysis is most helpful. Instead, a pure manufacturing operation may have mostly raw materials in stock. Though an ABC analysis can still reveal those items accumulating excessive costs, it is more difficult to do anything with the information. One can roll ABC information into product bills of material to determine the "true" cost of the parent items, which may result in pricing changes or the cancellation of some products that are proven to be no longer profitable. Though certainly useful, this can be a very time-consuming process for the cost accountant to implement.

Cost: *Installation time:*

10.11 Assign Overhead Personnel to Specific Subplants

One of the largest headaches for the cost accounting staff is determining what overhead costs are assigned to which products. Not only are these assignments subject to considerable personal interpretation, but they can strongly impact the way management views the profitability of various products. For example, if a product is assigned overhead costs that are not related to its manufacture, storage, or use in any way, its costs will appear artificially high, and management may even stop manufacturing it on the false grounds that it is not profitable.

A possible solution is to divide the production area into subplants, each one assigned the task of manufacturing a subset of all company products. One can then assign most of the overhead personnel, such as buyers, shop supervisors, and materials handlers, to specific subplants. By doing so, the cost accounting staff can much more easily allocate overhead costs to specific products. This approach meshes nicely with the ABC concept previously discussed, since costs are more closely identified with specific products.

The trouble is the considerable effort required to reshuffle the production layout into subplants. Further, if subplants are too small, it may not be possible to assign staff full time to just one subplant, forcing them to service

several subplants at once, and reducing the efficiency of costing allocations.

Cost: 🖭   *Installation time:* 🌑 🌑

10.12 Implement Target Costing

A cost accounting staff can create the best costing reports in the world, constantly update this information, and hound the production, engineering, and
purchasing staff incessantly to improve the situation, and yet find little
change in product costs. The reason is that most product costs are locked in
when the product is designed. For example, a poor microwave oven design
will lead to production inefficiencies because the product was not designed
for ease of manufacturability. Similarly, if the oven was not designed to be
sufficiently sturdy, there will be a number of customer returns, resulting in
added engineering and manufacturing costs to fix the problem. Further, the
oven may contain nonstandard parts that are both difficult and expensive to
obtain and that may not allow for the use of existing parts that are used with
other products. Thus, cost accounting is focused on the wrong target—product costs during production, instead of product costs during the design stage.

The best practice addressing this issue is called target costing. Under this
concept, the existing market is reviewed and a target price determined at
which a certain set of product specifications would probably sell quite well.
A design team is then assigned the task of creating a product with those
specifications and a maximum cost. The maximum cost figure allows a
company to sell for the previously determined price while still making an
acceptable profit. If it is impossible to manufacture the product for the maximum assigned cost, the project is abandoned. This approach is in contrast
to the more traditional method of designing a product, determining how
much it costs when the product is finished, and then adding on a profit percentage to arrive at a selling price.

The obvious advantage of target costing is a company's total control
over product costs before any product reaches the shop floor. It is easy to
determine which products should be produced and which ones abandoned,
thereby keeping losing or marginally profitable products out of a company's product mix. From the accounting department's perspective, its
costing work shifts away from tracking production costs and into tracking

costs during the design phase. This means that a cost accountant should be reassigned from the first activity to the latter so there is a daily review of the range of costs into which target costs are likely to fall. By shifting the direction of the accounting department's costing analysis, one can report on the activities having the greatest impact on product costs.

Cost: 💾 💾   *Installation time:* ● ● ●

10.13 Limit Access to Unit-of-Measure Changes

The unit-of-measure field, an apparently innocuous field in the computer system, can have a major impact on the accuracy of product costs. When the quantity in a bill of materials or inventory record is created, it has a unit of measure listed next to it. For example, one inch of tape on a bill of materials will have a quantity of one, and a unit of measure of an inch. However, if the unit of measure is changed to a roll without a corresponding reduction in the amount of tape listed in the quantity field, the amount of tape picked for production will increase from one inch to an entire roll. The same problem applies to the inventory, where a change in the unit-of-measure field without a corresponding change in the quantity field will result in a potentially massive change in the amount of inventory on the books. This seemingly minor issue can result in a major change in the cost of goods sold.

The best practice resolving this issue is the limitation of access to the unit-of-measure field in the computer system, preferably to one person or position. By doing so, all changes must be reviewed by one person, who presumably will be trained well enough to realize the relationship between units of measure and quantities. If access by multiple people cannot be avoided, then a less-reliable variation is to require approval by a manager before making a change. However, as someone can make a change without approval, this system is too easy to bypass. A third variation is to carefully review changes in the unit-of-measure fields after the fact, perhaps with an occasional internal audit, but this approach finds problems only after they have already occurred; the best solution is always to keep the problem from occurring in the first place.

An excellent alternative is to set up the computer system so that multiple units of measure are allowed. To use the previous example, the roll of tape can be listed as both one roll and 1,760 inches in the same inventory or bill of materials record; this approach eliminates anyone's need to change the unit-of-measure field, since all possible variations are already described. Unfortunately, only the more advanced accounting and manufacturing software packages contain this feature; it is not normally available unless a company is willing to invest in some complicated and expensive programming.

Cost: 🖊   *Installation time:* 🔋

10.14 Review Cost Trends

The typical cost accounting report shows the current cost of each product, perhaps in relation to a standard cost put in place when the product was first created. Though this report does give management a snapshot of how existing costs relate to standards, there is no way to see if the cost was gradually increased or decreased from the preset standard cost, if the actual cost was close to the standard cost, or if there have been sudden changes in costs that are probably related either to step-costs in the overhead category (such as adding a new facility) or to material cost changes. Given the lack of information, management has no way of knowing if the current costing situation reflects deterioration in costs or an improvement.

The best practice eliminating this problem is to switch to reporting based on cost trends. An example is shown in Exhibit 10.2. As noted there, the re-

Exhibit 10.2 *Cost Trend Report: Sample*							
Product Description	**Base Cost**	**Actual Cost 3/31/04**	**Actual Cost 6/30/04**	**Actual Cost 9/30/04**	**Target Cost**	**Variance from Target**	**Target Date**
Pail	$4.00	$4.12	$4.15	$4.29	$3.98	8%	3/31/05
Bucket	3.92	3.92	3.90	3.88	3.75	3%	3/31/05
Trowel	1.57	1.65	1.72	1.67	1.57	6%	3/31/05
Spade	8.07	9.48	10.93	10.93	8.07	35%	6/30/05
Shovel	8.08	9.49	10.94	10.94	8.08	35%	6/30/05
Hose	15.01	14.98	14.95	14.90	14.90	0%	6/30/05
Sprinkler	23.19	28.01	28.77	27.75	23.00	21%	6/30/05

port starts with a base cost established with actual cost date when the product was first released to production. Then the series of columns in the middle of the report show the historical total cost of each product, based on any time period that is most appropriate (quarterly costs are shown in the exhibit). Then the projected target cost that the company is striving for is noted on the right side of the report, with a final column noting the percentage difference in cost between the most recent cost and the target cost, along with the date by which the company is expecting to achieve the target cost. This format allows management to easily determine where costing problems are developing, or if there are potential problems with reaching a targeted cost by the due date. This approach gives management a much more potent tool to use in tracking product costs.

Supplemental information can enhance the information shown on the cost trend chart. For example, it can include a column showing either unit or dollar volume for each item, allowing management to quickly determine where they should invest the bulk of their time in fixing problems—on those products having a large dollar impact on total revenues, as opposed to those that may have large cost variances but have only a negligible profitability impact. It may also be useful to include the price and margin in the chart, though this can be difficult to determine if pricing varies significantly by customer, perhaps due to variations in the volumes sold to each one. Another reporting possibility is to issue a subsidiary-level report breaking down product costs into multiple components, so management can determine which costs are deviating from expected values. If this option is used, there should be matching target costs for each component, so management can compare actual to expected costs in all categories and see where there are problems.

Finally, if there are many variations on a standard product design, the report may become too lengthy and unwieldy to be easily readable. For example, this can happen when the same product is issued in 10 different colors, resulting in a report with 10 line items—one for each product variation. In this instance, it is useful to cluster product groups together into a single line item for each group, resulting in a much shorter and more readable report. All or some of these reporting variations can give management a better idea of the cost trends to which their products are subject.

Cost: *Installation time:* ● ●

10.15 Review Material Scrap Levels

There are a number of ways to tell if a production process is not operating as efficiently as it could. For example, labor hours are higher than expected, materials usage exceeds the standard, or delivery times are chronically late. However, the accounting department does not do well in reporting on late deliveries, since this does not involve the database of financial information that the accounting staff normally accesses. Also, the direct labor pool tends to be relatively fixed in the short term, and so is surprisingly difficult to reduce. Thus, accounting reports showing excessive labor may not result in an immediate impact on this area. However, reporting on material scrap rates is well worth the effort; a high scrap rate is the primary indicator of a host of potential problems in the production process. For example, scrap can be caused by poor operator training, bad machine maintenance, an excessive level of WIP inventory, and design flaws. By using material scrap as the prime indicator of problems in the production process, management can further refine the reason for it, target those problems, and eliminate them.

The problem for the accounting department is how to issue a valid material scrap rate report. If the report is inaccurate, management will not believe the numbers and will not use the information to improve the production process. It is vital to derive the most accurate information possible from the evidence at hand. There are a variety of scrap reporting methods available, as noted in the following points:

- *Weigh the scrap.* The simplest method for determining the amount of scrap is to put it in a pile and weigh it. This is a practical approach if a company can recycle the bulk of its scrap and therefore keeps it in recycling bins. One can then weigh the bins and multiply the weight by the average cost of the scrap to determine a total scrap cost.

- *Summarize receipts from scrap purchasers.* An even easier approach is to let the scrap purchaser weigh the scrap bin and use this information to derive the total cost of the scrap.

- *Compare standard to actual materials usage.* The approach resulting in the most detailed information about exactly which materials have been scrapped is a comparison of standard materials quantities to actual usage. This requires accurate bills of materials, production records, and inventory counts; without them, a comparison of these records will not result in an accurate determination of scrap costs.

- *Create a floor reporting system.* This is the approach used the most by those companies with poor production records. If they cannot use the preceding option due to the existence of inaccurate bills of materials, production records, or inventory records, they must require the production staff to manually track the scrap they are generating. This approach tends to underreport scrap, since production personnel do not like to report on the inefficiencies of their own department. Also, the scrap reporting by the manufacturing personnel can be voluminous and may require extra staff to summarize and analyze. Thus, this approach is prone to inaccuracy and high reporting costs.

Of the previous scrap reporting methods, some are not accurate enough to provide more than a rough guess at the exact items that were scrapped; these include weighing the scrap or perusing the receipts from scrap purchasers. The other two reporting systems reveal the most useful information because they detail the exact items scrapped. Of the two, comparing actual to standard usage is the easiest to implement, since it requires no additional reporting by the manufacturing personnel; however, the standards must be accurate, or the basis of comparison will not function properly. If the standards (e.g., bills of materials, production records, and inventory records) are not accurate, one is faced with the problem of either correcting the underlying information or implementing the final reporting option, which is creating a shop floor reporting system for tracking actual material scrap rates. The exact reporting method used will depend on the level of reporting detail needed, as well as the accuracy of a company's production database.

Cost: 🪙   *Installation time:* 🥁 🥁

10.16 Revise Traditional Cost Accounting Reports

Though other best practices advocated in this chapter involve doing away with or replacing the existing set of cost accounting reports, there are instances in which they can be sufficiently modified still to be of great use. This section deals with a number of small changes that can greatly enhance these reports. Though it would be best to install all of these upgrades, even using just one or two would bring about an incremental improvement in costing information. The changes are:

- *Assemble products into reporting groups.* Too often, a cost report presents a list of hundreds of products, sorted by product number. Though there may be plenty of valid information in such a report, there is no easy way for a busy executive to determine where it is. Instead, it should be grouped into relevant categories, such as clustering all product variations into a single summary number or clustering product sales by customer. These clusters should always contain subtotals so managers can take in the total cost impact of each group at a glance.

- *Give rapid feedback.* There is no point in compiling a perfect cost analysis if it is done months after a product is assembled. Instead, a good cost report should be issued as soon as possible after a product is completed, allowing management to make changes to improve costs the next time the product is made. The best case of all is when a cost report is issued to management while a product is still being made (and preferably near the beginning of a production run) so immediate alterations will result in a rapid cost reduction.

- *Report only on exceptions.* Some companies have such enormously long cost reports that there is no way to glance through them and spot the problem situations. To resolve this issue, reports should be issued that show only exceptions. For example, a report may show only those products with negative cost variances of at least 10 percent. By doing so, a voluminous report can be reduced to a short memo revealing those items requiring immediate attention.

- *Report on costs by customer.* All too many cost reports focus only on product costs, not the total costs of dealing with each customer. By widening the focus of a traditional cost report to include this extra information, one can reveal some startling information, especially if a customer that was previously thought to be highly profitable is eating up an outsized proportion of a company's resources in such areas as purchasing, warehousing, and order entry.

- *Use direct costing.* Many costing reports show product margins only after overhead is included in the total costing mix. However, if the overhead allocation is not valid, management has no way of knowing what margins really are and usually ends up ignoring the cost reports entirely. An easy way to avoid this problem is to insert an extra pair of columns in the cost report, in which are inserted the dollar margin after direct costs (i.e., price minus labor and materials) and the direct cost margin percentage. Though this variation leaves no room for any overhead cost at all, it does result in a good analysis of direct costs.

These best practices focus on assembling information into a format that is easy to read, is relevant, does not require the reader to wade through vast amounts of data, and presents information as rapidly as possible. By installing them, one can make the existing cost reports much more relevant to the decisions management must make every day.

Cost: 💵   Installation time: 🕑 🕑

10.17 Audit Labor Routings

The labor a company charges to each of its products is derived from a labor routing, which is an engineering estimate of the labor hours required to produce a product. Unfortunately, an inaccuracy in the labor routing information has a major impact on a company's profitability for two reasons. First, the labor hours assigned to a product will be incorrect, resulting in an inaccurate product cost. By itself, this is not a major problem, because the labor cost is not a large component of the total product cost. However, the second reason is the real issue—since the labor rate is frequently used as the primary basis on which overhead is allocated to products, a shift in the labor rate can result in a massive change in the allocated overhead rate, which may be much larger than the underlying labor cost. Thus, an inaccurate labor routing can have a major impact on the reported cost of a product.

The best practice that addresses this problem is auditing labor routings. By doing so, one can gradually review all labor records and verify their accuracy, thereby avoiding any miscasting of products. To do so, one must enlist the help of the engineering manager, who should assign a staff person to review this information on a regular basis and make changes as needed. The accounting department can assist in the effort by comparing the labor routings of similar products to see if there are any discrepancies and bring them to the attention of the engineering department for resolution. Also, it can review computer records (if they exist) to see when labor routings have been changed and verify the alterations with the engineering staff. Finally, the accounting staff can work with the production planning department to see if the assumed production-run quantities noted in the labor routings match actual production quantities. This last item is a critical one, for the assumed per-unit labor quantity will go down as the run length increases, due to the improved learning curve that comes with longer production runs, as well as the large number of production units over which the labor setup time can be spread. Some unscrupulous businesspeople will assume very short production runs in order to increase the assumed labor rates in their labor routings, resulting in the capitalization of much higher labor and overhead costs in the inventory records. Thus, a continual review and comparison of labor routing records by the accounting staff is a necessary component of this auditing process.

Cost: *Installation time:*

10.18 Follow a Schedule of Inventory Obsolescence Reviews

A great many companies find that the proportion of their inventory that is obsolete is much higher than they believed. This is a major problem at the end of the fiscal year, when this type of inventory is supposed to be investigated and written off, usually in conjunction with the auditor's review or the physical inventory (or both). If this write-off has not occurred in previous years, the cumulative amount can be startling. This may result in the departure of the materials manager and/or the controller, on the grounds that they should have known about the problem.

The best practice resolving this problem is adopting and sticking to a schedule of regular obsolete-inventory reviews. This is an unpopular task with many employees because they must pore over usage reports and wander through the warehouse to see what inventory is not needed and then follow up on disposal problems. However, these people do not realize the major benefits of having a periodic obsolete-inventory review. One is that it opens up space in the warehouse for other purposes. Also, spotting obsolete inventory as early as possible allows a company to realize the best salvage value for it, which will inevitably decline over time (unless a company is dealing in antiques!). Further, a close review of the reason why an inventory item is in stock and obsolete may lead to discoveries concerning how parts are ordered and used; changing these practices may lead to a reduction in obsolete inventory in the future. Thus, there are a number of excellent reasons for maintaining an ongoing obsolete-inventory review system.

The composition of the obsolete-inventory review committee is very important. There should be an accountant who can summarize the costs of obsolescence, while an engineering representative is in the best position to determine if a part can be used elsewhere. Also, someone from the purchasing department can tell if there is any resale value. Consequently, a cross-departmental committee is needed to properly review obsolete inventory.

The main contribution of the accounting department to this review is a periodic report itemizing those parts most likely to be obsolete. This information can take the following forms:

- *Last usage date.* Many computer systems record the last date on which a specific part number was removed from the warehouse for production or sale. If so, it is an easy matter to use a report writer to extract and sort this information, resulting in a report listing all inventory, starting with those products with the oldest "last used" date.

- *No "where used" in the system.* If a computer system includes a bill of materials, there is a strong likelihood that it also generates a "where used" report, listing all the bills of materials for which an inventory item is used. If there is no "where used" listed on the report, it is likely that a part is no longer needed. This report is most effective if bills of materials are removed from the computer system as soon as products are withdrawn from the market; this more clearly reveals those inventory items that are no longer needed. This approach can also be used to determine which inventory *is going to be* obsolete, based on the anticipated withdrawal of existing products from the market.

- *Comparison to previous-year physical inventory tags.* Many companies still conduct a physical inventory at the end of their fiscal years. When this is done, a tag is usually taped to each inventory item. Later, a member of the accounts staff can walk through the warehouse and mark down all inventory items with an inventory tag still attached to them. This is a simple visual approach for finding old inventory.

- *Acknowledged obsolete inventory still in the system.* Even the best inventory review committee will sometimes let obsolete inventory fall through the cracks and remain in both the warehouse and the inventory database. The accounting staff should keep track of acknowledged obsolete inventory and continue to notify management of those items that have not yet been removed.

Any or all of these reports can be used to gain knowledge of likely candidates for obsolete-inventory status. This information is the mandatory first step in the process of keeping the inventory up-to-date.

Cost: 💸   *Installation time:* 🕐 🕐

11

Bills of Materials

This chapter addresses those nine bill of materials best practices having a direct impact on inventory. As noted in Exhibit 11.1, these best practices cover three general areas—ensuring the accuracy of the bills of materials or the products based on them, using the bills to locate or identify obsolete parts, and using them to standardize parts.

The best practices noted here are generally inexpensive to implement, but can take a long time to install. The standardization of parts is a particularly lengthy project, while a bill of materials audit can be a major undertaking if all the bills are to be reviewed. Despite the time involved, these are worthwhile improvements, since they can have a significant positive impact on the total number of parts used, the amount of inventory returned to the warehouse, obsolete-inventory levels, and the smooth running of the production process.

11.1 Audit Bills of Materials

Some companies use backflushing as the means of recording changes to inventory. Under this methodology, inventory is taken from the warehouse without any associated picking transactions put into the computer. Then, when production is completed, the total amount of production by item is entered into the computer, and the software automatically removes the associated inventory amounts from the warehouse records, using bills of materials as the basis for doing so. Though this is a simple method for keeping warehouse paperwork to a minimum, an incorrect bill of materials will quickly alter the on-hand inventory balances to such an extent that inventory accuracy will plummet. In addition, the accounting department uses the bills of materials to determine the cost of any finished goods; an in-

Exhibit 11.1   *Summary of Bill of Materials Best Practices*

	Best Practice	Cost	Install Time
11.1	Audit bills of material		
11.2	Conduct a configuration audit		
11.3	Modify the bills of materials based on actual scrap levels		
11.4	Modify the bills of materials for temporary substitutions		
11.5	Eliminate redundant part numbers		
11.6	Standardize parts		
11.7	Review inventory returned to the warehouse		
11.8	Use bills of materials to find inventory made obsolete by product withdrawals		
11.9	Identify inactive inventory in the product master file		

accurate bill will also impact the accuracy of this costing. Thus, the accuracy of a company's bills of materials impacts not only the records for inventory quantities, but also their cost.

The best practice that keeps the bills of materials errors to a minimum is an ongoing audit of them. This practice keeps inventory quantities from becoming too inaccurate in a backflushing environment, while making the costing of finished goods more precise. To do so, a person who is knowledgeable about the contents of bills of materials must be assigned to a regular review of them. Any problems must be corrected at once. To be the most effective, it is best to concentrate the efforts of the reviewer on those bills used the most or that are expected to be included in upcoming production runs. By focusing on those bills receiving the most usage, a company can be sure of maintaining a high degree of bill accuracy for the bulk of its products.

Measuring the accuracy of a bill of materials includes several steps. One is to ensure that all correct part quantities are listed. Another is to verify that parts should be included in the product at all. Yet another is that the correct subassemblies roll up into the final product. If any of these items are incorrect, a bill of materials should be listed as incorrect in total. For a large bill with many components, this means that it will almost certainly be listed as incorrect when it is first reviewed, with rapid improvement as corrections are made. It is not uncommon for a company to record an initial overall bill of materials accuracy of zero. One should shoot for a target accuracy level of 98 percent. At this level, any errors will have a minimal impact on accuracy, cost of the inventory, and cost of goods sold.

The only difficulty in implementing this approach is that it requires the cooperation of the engineering manager, who must assign a staff person to the reviewing process. This assistance is critical, since engineers are the ones with the best knowledge of bills of materials.

Cost: *Installation time:*

11.2 Conduct a Configuration Audit

Companies can run into warranty trouble when their engineering departments design a product correction, but the engineering change never makes its way into the production process. This is also a problem when the engineering changes make it partway through the company to the purchasing department, which orders new components to match the change, but not to the production floor, which assembles products based on the old configuration. This problem leaves the warehouse manager caught in the middle, storing inventory for the new configuration that is not used by the production staff, while running out of components for the old configuration that is still being assembled. The problem is exacerbated if bills of materials are not updated for the changes, so that pick lists are incorrect—in short, mass confusion.

The solution is an ongoing configuration audit, preferably right after an engineering change or a new product is released. Under a configuration audit, an engineer or internal auditor familiar with the product pulls a completed product from the manufacturing line, disassembles it, and compares it to all engineering documents related to the product, including all authorized updates. If the product accurately reflects the current design, then no further action is required. If not, one must verify the accuracy of the bill of materials, pick lists presumably derived from the bill, outstanding purchase orders, and production work instructions.

This is a necessary best practice that reveals any weaknesses in the procedures used by a company to roll out new products and manufacture modifications to existing ones.

Cost: ✎   Installation time: ⬤ ⬤

11.3 Modify the Bills of Materials Based on Actual Scrap Levels

The typical company relies heavily on its bills of materials to determine the cost of its products. They can be used not only as a reference tool to quickly look up a cost, but also as the primary means of calculating the remaining on-hand inventory balance if backflushing is used. Under the backflushing concept, a company simply enters the amount of its production for the day, and the computer automatically clears this inventory from stock based on the amount of materials that should have been used, as noted in the bills of materials. Though this approach is remarkably easy to use given the reduced volume of paperwork, it can quickly lead to very inaccurate inventory balances if the underlying bills of materials are incorrect. This is a particularly difficult problem if the true scrap level is not reflected in the bills of materials. If this is the case, the amount of materials listed in each bill will be too small, resulting in an inadequate amount being backflushed out of inventory, leaving inventory balances too high.

The best practice that resolves this situation is to ensure that the correct scrap levels are included in each bill of materials. By doing so, the quantity of materials backflushed out of inventory will be much more accurate, resulting in a more accurate inventory and cost of goods sold, and fewer (if any) material stockouts to interfere with production.

To add scrap rates to the bills of materials, there must be a scrap reporting system already in place, noting the precise quantities of scrap occurring whenever a product is produced. With this information in hand, one can easily update scrap rates with a great deal of precision. Also, access to the information in the bills of materials must be severely restricted to ensure that no one but an authorized user is allowed to change the scrap rates in bills; without this security point, there is no way to ensure that the most accurate scrap rates are indeed in the computer system. In addition, there must be constant attention to the scrap rates, for they will change over time as production practices and machinery change. Without this continual process review, the existing scrap rates in the bills of materials will gradually depart from actual rates. Finally, there should be a provision in the computer system for automatically changing large blocks of scrap rates in many bills of materials; given the time needed to alter individual scrap line items in all existing bills, this is an extremely helpful labor-saving device. If all of these issues are addressed, the accuracy of the bills of materials should rise markedly, along with the accuracy of the inventory and cost of goods sold.

Cost: *Installation time:*

11.4 Modify the Bills of Materials for Temporary Substitutions

When a company has some excess items in stock that could be used in an existing product, the materials management staff is sometimes unwilling to use the part, because they perceive it to be so difficult to modify the bill of materials and all related parts ordering systems. The result is excess parts sitting in the warehouse.

The solution is to create a simplified system for modifying the bill of materials for temporary substitutions. To do so, there must first be a written authorization from the engineering department, specifying exactly which component is to be removed from an existing bill of materials, which one is to replace it, the quantities involved, and the dates during which this change will be in effect. The materials management staff needs to be involved in the date range, since they must schedule a production run that will use up the replacement part. Finally, the person in charge of bill of materials changes must make the swap in the bill of materials file. Of particular concern here is that the person also reset a reorder flag for the replacement part in the item master file, so that the material requirements system does not automatically reorder the part just because it now appears to be an active part.

These steps can be reduced if the bill of materials database already contains a feature allowing for the short-term swapping of parts. If this is available, the swapping procedure will be somewhat shorter.

Given the number of steps involved, temporary substitutions are not worthwhile when the swapping procedure being contemplated is for components having a small total value, since the work required to do so will off-set the savings from eliminating inventory. The cost accounting staff should develop a standard transaction cost for temporary substitutions, and use this as the cut-off point below which inventory will not be substituted.

Cost: *Installation time:*

11.5   Eliminate Redundant Part Numbers

When a company consolidates multiple locations in an effort to streamline its engineering and purchasing functions, a common problem is the discovery of duplicate part numbers, since each location has assigned a different part number to the same part. Part duplication is also common when many new products are being launched at the same time, since multiple engineers are needed at the same time for design work, and they may not be aware of part designations being made by their counterparts. It also occurs when a company switches to a new supplier, since the person assigning part numbers may not be aware of existing designations. Whatever the reason may be, redundant part numbers typically result in a considerable increase in the amount of on-hand inventory.

The key task in eliminating redundant part numbers is finding these parts. There are several methods for doing so. One is to simply ask the warehouse staff's cycle counters, who have the best knowledge of what parts are currently on hand. Though this approach will highlight some duplicates, it will not spot everything—cycle counters are frequently assigned to specific warehouse aisles, and so have no knowledge of what lies elsewhere in the warehouse. Also, they frequently count sealed containers, and have no idea of their contents.

Another possibility is to audit a sample of the inventory, deliberately looking for duplicate parts. This will eventually spot some duplicates, but is more effective when the warehouse is organized by part type, so one can conduct 100 percent audits of selected bins and aisles.

Yet another approach is to assign meanings to part numbers, so that certain letters or numbers in each part number refer to a type of part. By using this approach, one can review certain ranges of part numbers for duplicates. Though this approach initially appears attractive, it can quickly become unwieldy if a company must renumber all the parts of an acquired company in order to match its internal numbering system. Also, unless very carefully laid out, a part numbering scheme can run out of space for new parts. Further, one must run the part numbering task through a single person (or small group) who is responsible for assigning "smart" part numbers, which can become a bottleneck. Thus, despite its initial attractiveness, this approach is not heavily used.

Whichever of the preceding approaches is used, there are several additional implementation steps to follow once duplicate parts are found. One must assign a single part number to all parts found in the warehouse with other part numbers, alter the related quantity information in the inventory database, designate the old part numbers in the item master file as inactive, adjust any outstanding purchase orders using the old part numbers, modify bills of materials to include only the single remaining part number, and also alter any engineering drawings to reflect the changed number. Thus, a great many steps are required to ensure that more inventory using the duplicate part numbers is not inadvertently ordered as replacements.

Cost: *Installation time:*

11.6 Standardize Parts

Though one can certainly use the steps just noted in the "Eliminate Redundant Part Numbers" best practice to reduce the number of items in the inventory, this still does not eliminate those very slightly different parts designed to be used in different products. The engineering department has probably created a series of products without regard to the components used in preceding designs, so fittings, fasteners, and other items are used in slightly varying sizes across a range of products. The result is an ever-growing list of components, each one varying just enough from other items to require separate stocking.

A long-term solution is to standardize parts across multiple products, thereby greatly reducing the number of items in stock. The key ingredient in this best practice is to require approval of all new components by the engineering manager, whose performance is judged partially on his or her ability to keep the number of parts at a minimum. By requiring engineers to go through a tough review before being allowed to use new parts, they will be much more inclined to design existing stocks into new designs. A useful tool in the identification of commonly used parts is the matrix bill of materials; this format displays the components of similar products in a side-by-side format, so that visual comparisons can be more easily made.

The concept can be taken further by reviewing the on-hand components list and winnowing out those for which there is clear duplication in similar components. By reducing the approved parts list in this manner, the number of components used in new products can be gradually reduced. Further, the engineering manager can gradually eliminate the use of redundant parts in existing products by using engineering change notices to eliminate some components from use. This last step is the most difficult, since one must alter work instructions and the bill of materials, as well as dispose of excess parts. The easier approach by far is to limit engineers to a specific parts list and design parts standardization into new products.

Cost: 🖮   *Installation time:* ● ● ●

11.7 Review Inventory Returned to the Warehouse

Most organizations producing any sort of tangible product will be familiar with this scenario: The warehouse staff uses a computer-generated picking list to pick a number of items from the shelf for use in an upcoming manufacturing order, delivers these items to the production facility, and then finds after the job is completed that a number of items are returned, even though the pick list it used was intended to completely use up all items picked. Any returns of this type indicate that the bills of materials used to compile the pick lists are incorrect. When this happens, the bills of materials are using too high a quantity of materials; if these bills are also used to calculate the amount of items to be purchased, this results in an excessive number of purchases being made. From an accounting perspective, an inaccurate bill of materials leads to inaccurate product costs, leading to an inaccurate finished goods valuation.

The best way to avoid this issue is to create a procedure for closely examining the parts returned to the warehouse in order to determine exactly which line items in the bills of materials are inaccurate. This may require the assistance of the engineer who is responsible for each bill, since this person has the most knowledge of what is supposed to be contained in each product. By making changes to the bills, one can improve the accuracy of purchases, eliminate the labor of the warehouse staff in logging parts back into the warehouse, and be assured of accurate finished goods costs.

The only problem with installing this procedure is the active cooperation of the warehouse manager, who will most likely try to avoid the hassle of investigating product returns and just put items back on the shelf with no further investigation. However, explaining that a proper amount of up-front investigation will lead to a smaller number of part returns in the future may sway this person to be of more assistance.

This best practice can also be used in reverse, so one can investigate inadequate parts issuances to the production floor. In this situation, the quantities listed on the bills of materials are too low, resulting in parts shortages that will probably lead to incomplete production runs, on the grounds that the production staff runs out of parts before completing the scheduled quantity of products.

Cost: 　　　　　Installation time:

11.8 Use Bills of Materials to Find Inventory Made Obsolete by Product Withdrawals

When the marketing department investigates the possibility of withdrawing a product from sale, it frequently does so without determining how much inventory of both the finished product and its component parts remains on hand. At most, the marketing staff concerns itself only with clearing out excess finished goods, since this can be readily identified. Those unique parts used only in the manufacture of the withdrawn product will then be left to gather dust in the warehouse, and will eventually be sold off as scrap only after a substantial amount of time has passed.

A better approach is to have the engineering department use the product's bill of materials to create a list of component parts unique to that product. This typically requires a custom program and a fair amount of processing time, since the bill's components must be compared to the contents of all other active bills, including their subassemblies, to determine which parts are not used in the manufacture of any other products. Once determined, this information can be used to calculate the product withdrawal date, since it may make sense to continue manufacturing the product a bit longer in order to use up expensive stock. Engineers can also use the list to incorporate excess parts into the design of new products, if this makes sense. Worst case, the list at least brings excess parts to the attention of the purchasing department, which can work on returning them to suppliers for credit or disposing of the parts in some other manner, thereby creating shelf space in the warehouse as soon as possible for more heavily used items.

Many materials planning software packages include a "where used" report, which fulfills this need to some extent. The report lists every product whose bill of materials calls for the use of a specific component. The report may require a fair amount of investigation before one can determine which items have truly been made obsolete, since one must compare each item listed on a retired product's bill of materials to the items shown on the "where used" report to verify which items are not being used elsewhere and can be therefore designated as obsolete.

Cost: *Installation time:*

11.9   Identify Inactive Inventory in the Product Master File

There are few things more frustrating than for someone to disposition obsolete inventory, only to find that more inventory is then ordered, requiring additional effort to disposition once again. This typically happens when the company's automatic reordering system notices that the inventory balance for this item has dropped to zero, and sends a message to the purchasing department, asking for a new purchase to bring the inventory balance up to some predetermined minimum.

The obvious best practice is to reset the product's activity flag in the product master file to "obsolete," "inactive," or some similar code. This not only tells the system to stop buying more inventory, but also makes it impossible for the purchasing staff to create a purchase order through the computer system. The main problem is getting the person responsible for rendering inventory obsolete to remember to reset the flag. This can be accomplished by noting the deactivation step in bold on the written inventory deactivation procedure. However, if the person doing this work ignores the procedure, it may be necessary to include a pop-up reminder in the inventory software code that appears whenever an inventory balance is set to zero. Another alternative is to modify the software to automatically alter the product master file whenever an obsolescence code is used as part of a transaction to write down inventory.

Cost: *Installation time:*

12

Inventory Policies and Procedures

This chapter contains a mix of best practices related to policies and procedures and example formats for 11 of the most commonly used inventory procedures. The four best practices shown in Exhibit 12.1 form a cohesive cluster of activities—first create a policies and procedures manual for inventory-related activities, and then use several approaches to train the staff in its use. It is no accident that the cost of all the best practices is low, while the installation time is significant—these are labor-intensive activities requiring ongoing reinforcement.

The 11 sample procedures are designed to be templates for conversion into a company's own procedures manual, and address the most common inventory-related activities:

1. Drop ship inventory.
2. Receive inventory.
3. Track inbound consignment inventory.
4. Kit inventory.
5. Cycle count inventory.
6. Perform physical inventory count.
7. Calculate period-end inventory.
8. Calculate lower of cost or market value.
9. Reorder supplies with a visual review system.
10. Receive sales returns.
11. Review inventory for obsolescence.

Several of the procedures include sample reports, which can also be used as report formats for a company's internal inventory transactions.

213

Exhibit 12.1 *Summary of Inventory Policies and Procedures Best Practices*

Best Practice	Cost	Install Time
12.1 Create a policies and procedures manual		
12.2 Train the warehouse and accounting staffs in inventory procedures		
12.3 Cross train for mission-critical activities		
12.4 Train using training teams		

12.1 Create a Policies and Procedures Manual

An unorganized warehouse department is inefficient, suffers from a high transaction error rate, and does not complete its assigned tasks on time. One of the best ways to create a disciplined warehouse team is to create and maintain a policies and procedures manual.

This manual should list the main policies under which the warehouse department operates, such as those listed in Exhibit 12.2. These policies deal with key materials handling issues, and are usually limited to just a few pages. Anything longer probably indicates an excessive degree of control or some confusion in the difference between a policy and a procedure.

A policy is one that sets a boundary for an activity (e.g., defining an obsolete inventory item as one having been withdrawn from production). A procedure, however, defines the precise activities taking place within the boundaries of the policies created. A procedure is usually sufficient to use as a guideline for an employee who needs to understand how a process works. When combined with the proper level of training, the policies and procedures manual is an effective way not only to increase control over inventory, but also to increase the efficiency with which it is handled.

Though there are few excuses for not having such a manual, there are some pitfalls to consider when constructing it, as well as for maintaining and enforcing it. They are as follows:

- *Not enough detail.* A procedure that does not cover activity steps in a sufficient degree of detail is not of much use to someone using it for the first time; it is important to list specific forms used, computer screens ac-

Exhibit 12.2 *Sample Policies Page*

- *ABC classification.* The warehouse manager shall review the ABC classification of all items in stock at least once a year, and rearrange inventory storage within the warehouse based upon this revised classification.

- *Bill of materials.* Only the engineering department shall make changes to the bill of materials database.

- *Delivery.* The company shall deliver completed customer orders no later than two days following receipt of those orders.

- *Drop shipping.* The company shall endeavor to have suppliers drop ship items directly to customers whenever possible.

- *Engineering changes.* The engineering department shall only implement an engineering change order after the proposed change has been formally reviewed and approved by the cost accounting, production, and manufacturing departments.

- *Hedge inventory.* The company shall not invest in hedge inventories for such events as possible strikes or supplier disputes without prior approval by senior management.

- *Obsolescence.* Inventory parts shall be designated obsolete once the products of which they are components have been withdrawn from production and there is no recent evidence of service or repair requirements.

- *Putaway.* Inventory items shall be putaway immediately after receipt.

- *Supplies reordering.* Supplies not tracked through the inventory system shall be visually reviewed at least daily for reordering purposes.

cessed, and fields on those screens in which information is entered, as well as the other positions either supplying information for the procedure or to which it sends information. It may also be helpful to include a flowchart, which is more understandable than text for some people.

- *Not reinforced.* A procedures manual does not do much good if it is immediately parked on a remote shelf. Instead, one must make it an integral part of all training programs and include it in periodic discussions regarding the updating and improvement of key processes. Only through constant attention will the manual be used to the fullest extent.

- *Not updated.* Even the best manual will become obsolete over time, as changing circumstances alter procedures to the point where the manual no longer describes conditions as they currently exist. When this happens, no one bothers to use the manual. Accordingly, it is necessary to update the manual whenever changes are made to the underlying systems.

- *Too many procedures.* A common problem is for the procedures manual never to be released because it is never "finished"—someone wants to include every conceivable procedure. It is better to issue the manual promptly with just the key procedures covering the bulk of all inventory transaction volume, and address lesser procedures at a later date. This approach gets the key information to those employees who need it the most, and does so quickly.

Cost: *Installation time:*

12.2 Train the Warehouse and Accounting Staffs in Inventory Procedures

The underlying problem behind the bulk of all inventory record errors is a lack of knowledge among warehouse workers of how to process a variety of inventory transactions. As a result, cycle counting teams waste time investigating errors, the materials planning staff must order parts on short notice that are caused by unexplained materials shortfalls, the company incurs express delivery charges to bring in parts on short notice, and the accounting staff must record unexplained losses related to inventory adjustments.

Many of these problems can be mitigated by creating a procedures manual for all inventory transactions, and constantly training both the warehouse and accounting staffs in their use. It is not enough to simply create a handsome procedures manual and issue it to the staff. On the contrary, all employees involved with these transactions should go through regular refresher training, while new employees should be trained several times early in their employment and certified by an experienced co-worker in their knowledge of the procedures. Further, any procedural change calls for a complete retraining of the entire staff on that topic. Only by enforcing the corporate commitment to training in inventory procedures can a company reduce its incidence of inventory transaction errors.

Cost: *Installation time:*

12.3 Cross-Train for Mission-Critical Activities

There are a number of crucial inventory-related activities that will cause a significant amount of disturbance within a company if they are not completed on time, every time. Examples of these activities include receiving, creating bills of lading, picking, and investigating transaction errors discovered during cycle counts. In these cases and others, the greatest risk is that only one person knows how to process transactions. If that person leaves the company, or is incapacitated for any reason, there can be a serious system failure that will quickly bring large portions of the company to a halt.

The best way to avoid this dependency on a single person is to implement cross training, using other accounting and materials handling personnel. By doing so, there is far less risk that mission-critical activities will not be performed in a reliable manner. To do so, one should create a schedule of key activities for which there is a listing of required training elements. One should identify those personnel most qualified to act as backups, put them through the training regimen, and ensure that they receive continual retraining so they can easily step into the needed jobs. A small pay hike for those employees receiving cross training will ensure their enthusiastic participation in this system. The key factor to remember is that training alone does not make for a good backup person—only continual hands-on practice under the direct tutelage of the person who is currently responsible for the work will ensure that this best practice will succeed.

The only people who regularly oppose this best practice are those currently in charge of mission-critical functions, because they feel more valuable if they are the only ones who can complete a task. Overcoming this problem requires great tact and diplomacy. Sometimes they continue to be hostile to the concept and must be removed to other positions while their replacements figure out the system with no support at all. These are difficult alternatives, but must be followed through if there is to be an adequate level of cross training in key functional areas.

Cost:　　　　　*Installation time:*

12.4 Train Using Training Teams

A key problem for managers is how to determine the correct amount and type of training to require of their employees. Sending them to degree programs is too expensive and provides relevant training only for a small proportion of the time spent being trained. Shorter programs are more targeted, but are still expensive and may not directly relate to work requirements. For these reasons, many managers do not allow any training, or only under very restricted circumstances. By doing so, they are limiting the skill sets of their employees and not allowing them to fulfill personal career advancement goals, which may result in increased employee turnover.

A solution to this problem is the use of internal training teams. The basic process is to conduct a periodic survey of employees and job functions to determine what types of training programs are needed. A consultant or manager-level employee then creates the general course syllabus for each training program (consultants can be useful here, since managers may not have sufficient available time to work on syllabi). Each syllabus is then handed over to a group of in-house staff, which becomes responsible for creating the details of each course and teaching it. A manager is typically assigned to each course to oversee its development and act as a mentor.

The primary advantage of this approach is that training can be precisely tailored to a company's needs, throwing out all irrelevant topics that might otherwise be taught during a university-sponsored class. Because of their extreme specificity, these classes are also usually quite short, allowing employees to fit them either into daytime schedules or into abbreviated evening training sessions. Examples of training topics under this approach could be cycle counting techniques, proper warehouse layout techniques, and training on the company's receiving software. Also, by bringing together trainers from all parts of the accounting organization, from administrative assistants to the CFO, the level of communication will likely improve. Finally, because all training classes are created and taught in-house, the incremental cost of classes is reduced.

Cost: *Installation time:* 🎯 🎯

SAMPLE PROCEDURES

Procedure 1: Drop Ship Inventory

The following procedure describes the steps required to drop ship inventory from a supplier to a customer location, with no physical handling at the company location.

Policy/Procedure Statement		Retrieval Number	INV-01
[Company Name]		Page:	1 of 1
		Issue Date	10/28/05
	Subject: Drop Ship Inventory		

1. PURPOSE AND SCOPE

This procedure is used by the order entry, logistics, and accounting staffs to ensure that products are shipped directly to customers from suppliers, and that the company properly invoices customers for these deliveries.

2. RESPONSIBILITIES

Accounting Staff
Logistics Staff
Order Entry Staff

3.   PROCEDURES

3.1 **Relay Customer Order for Drop Shipment (Order Entry/Logistics Staff)**

1. If a customer order arrives through an automated Web order entry system, the order entry system automatically flags an item as a drop shipment from a supplier to the customer, and sends an electronic data interchange or e-mail message to the supplier, containing all relevant shipment information. The order entry system or staff then verifies a return receipt message from the supplier.

2. If a customer order is entered manually by the order entry staff, they enter it in the order entry database in the usual manner. The logistics staff planning in-house production and delivery identifies the ordered item as a drop shipment, and notifies the supplier of all shipment information; either by fax, e-mail, or electronic data interchange. The logistics staff then verifies a return receipt message from the supplier.

3.2 **Invoice Customer for Drop Shipment (Accounting/Order Entry Staff)**

1. Upon shipment of the order, the supplier sends to the company accounting department a shipping notification, identifying the customer, date of shipment, and items and quantities shipped.

2. The accounting staff prepares two copies of an invoice and sends one to the customer.
3. The accounting staff makes two copies of the shipping notification, attaches one copy to the retained invoice, and files it in the customer file.
4. The accounting staff stores the second copy of the shipping notification until the supplier bills the company for the shipped goods, at which point the accounts payable staff attaches the notification to the supplier invoice as proof of delivery and processes the invoice for payment.
5. The accounting staff sends the remaining copy of the shipping notification to the order entry staff, which logs the shipment into the order entry system, thereby completing the order in the system. If the supplier's delivery only partially fills an order, the order entry staff contacts the supplier to discuss the delivery date for any backlogged items.

3.3 **Verify Drop Shipment Delivery (Accounting/Order Entry Staff)**

1. The accounting staff periodically investigates all supplier invoices for which no shipping notification has been received. This involves contacting the supplier for a copy of the shipping notification and then billing the customer based on the information in the shipping notification.
2. The order entry staff periodically investigates all customer orders for which no supplier shipping notification has been received. This involves sending a summary list of all unfilled orders from the order entry system to the supplier, verifying receipt of the list, and discussing shipment status.

Procedure 2: Receive Inventory

The following procedure describes the steps required to receive incoming inventory into the warehouse, inspect it, and update related databases.

Policy/Procedure Statement	Retrieval Number	INV-02
[Company Name]	Page:	1 of 1
	Issue Date	10/28/05

Subject: Receive Inventory

1. PURPOSE AND SCOPE

This procedure is used by the receiving staff to ensure that incoming goods are properly inspected and logged into the accounting database.

2. RESPONSIBILITIES

Receiving Staff

3. PROCEDURES

3.1 **Review and Accept Inbound Shipment (Receiving Staff)**

3.1-1. When a shipment arrives, find in the shipping documentation the authorizing purchase order number and locate either a paper-based or electronic copy of the purchase order.

3.1-2. Compare the product quantity and quality to the specifications noted in the purchase order. If there are significant discrepancies, reject the shipment.

3.1-3. Sign a copy of the bill of lading to accept the delivery.

3.2 **Enter Receipt into Accounting Systems (Receiving Staff)**

3.2-1. Access the authorizing purchase order on the corporate computer system and record both the received quantity and the warehouse location in which they will be stored. If portable barcode scanners are used, then record this transaction at the time the warehouse move is made.

3.2-2. Store a copy of the bill of lading in an indexed file.

3.2-3. Forward a copy of the bill of lading to the accounting department or digitize the image in a scanner and enter the document into the corporate accounting system.

Procedure 3: Track Inbound Consignment Inventory

The following procedure describes the labeling and documentation required to identify incoming inventory owned by a third party.

Policy/Procedure Statement	Retrieval Number	INV-03
[Company Name]	Page:	1 of 1
	Issue Date	10/28/05

Subject: Track Inbound Consignment Inventory

1. PURPOSE AND SCOPE

This procedure is used by the warehouse staff to properly track consignment inventory owned by other parties but stored in the company's warehouse.

2. RESPONSIBILITIES

Warehouse Staff

3. PROCEDURES

3.1 **Label Consigned Inventory (Warehouse Staff)**

3.1-1. Upon receipt of consigned inventory, prominently label the inventory with a colored tag, clearly denoting its status.

3.1-2. Record the inventory in the computer system using a unique part number to which no valuation is assigned. If a consignment flag is available in the database, flag the part number as being a consignment item.

3.1-3. Store the item in a part of the warehouse set aside for consigned inventory.

3.2 **Review Consigned Inventory (Warehouse Staff)**

Include the consigned inventory in a review by the materials review board (see "Review Inventory for Obsolescence" procedure), which should regularly determine the status of this inventory, and arrange for its return if there are no prospects for its use in the near future.

Procedure 4: Kit Inventory

The following procedure describes the steps required to obtain kitting information, assemble kits, forward them to the production area, and process any returned items.

Policy/Procedure Statement	Retrieval Number	INV-04
[Company Name]	Page: Issue Date	1 of 1 10/28/05

Subject: Kit Inventory

1. PURPOSE AND SCOPE

This procedure is used by the warehouse staff to assemble inventory for production jobs, and to process any returns from the shop floor.

2. RESPONSIBILITIES

Warehouse Staff

3. PROCEDURES

3.1 **Collect Parts Kitting Information (Warehouse Staff)**

The materials management department issues a parts request form to the warehouse for each new job to be produced. Upon receipt, set up a pallet on which to store the requested items.

3.2 **Kit Inventory Items (Warehouse Staff)**

1. Collect the requested items from the warehouse, checking off each completed part number on the list and noting the quantity removed and the location from which they were removed.
2. Access the inventory database record for each removed item and log out the quantities taken from the appropriate warehouse locations.
3. Deliver the filled pallet to the production floor.

3.3 **Process Returned Items (Warehouse Staff)**

1. If any parts remain after the production job is complete, accept them at the warehouse gate using the Inventory Sign-Out and Return Form (see Exhibit 12.3), log them back into the computer system, and notify the materials management department of the overage, so they can adjust the bill of materials for the products being produced.
2. If any parts are returned in a damaged condition, record them on the Scrap/Rework Transaction Form (see Exhibit 12.4), log them in with a damaged code, and store them in the review area where the materials review board can easily access them. Periodically print out a report listing all items stored in this area, and forward it to the materials review board, so they will be aware that items require their attention.

Exhibit 12.3 *Inventory Sign Out and Return Form*

Description	Part No.	Quantity Issued	Quantity Returned	Job No.	Date

Exhibit 12.4 *Scrap/Rework Transaction Form*

7403

Date: _____

Item Number: _____

Description: _____

Scrapped	**Sent to Rework**
Quantity Scrapped: _____	Quantity to Rework: _____
Reason: _____	Reason: _____
_____	_____
_____	_____
Signature: _____	Signature: _____

Procedure 5: Cycle Count Inventory

The following procedure describes the steps needed to select inventory items for a cycle count, conduct the count, and investigate the reasons for any variances discovered.

Policy/Procedure Statement	Retrieval Number	INV-05
[Company Name]	Page:	1 of 1
	Issue Date	10/28/05

Subject: Cycle Count Inventory

1. PURPOSE AND SCOPE

This procedure is used by the warehouse staff to ensure that a perpetual inventory's computer records match the physical inventory.

2. RESPONSIBILITIES

Warehouse Staff

3. PROCEDURES

3.1 **Verify Cut-off Controls (Warehouse Staff)**

Ensure that all inventory transactions related to the items to be counted have been entered. To do so, verify with the warehouse manager that all tracking sheets from the day before have been logged into the computer system. Also, conduct the cycle count at the beginning of the day, before any new inventory transactions have been initiated.

3.2 **Collect Cycle Counting Information (Warehouse Staff)**

Print a portion of the inventory report, sorted by location (see Exhibit 12.5). Block out a portion of the physical inventory locations shown on the report for cycle counting purposes.

3.3 **Compare Physical Inventory to Book Records (Warehouse Staff)**

1. Go to the first physical inventory location to be cycle counted and compare the quantity, location, and part number of each inventory item to what is described for that location in the inventory report. Mark on the report any discrepancies between the on-hand quantity, location, and description for each item.

2. Use the reverse process to ensure that the same information listed for all items on the report matches the items physically appearing in the warehouse location. Note any discrepancies on the report.

3.4 Enter Changes in Accounting Database (Warehouse Staff)

1. Verify that the noted discrepancies are not caused by recent inventory transactions that have not yet been logged into the computer system.
2. Correct the inventory database for all remaining errors noted.

3.5 Initiate Corrective Actions (Warehouse Staff)

1. Calculate the inventory error rate and post it in the warehouse (see Exhibit 12.6).
2. Call up a history of inventory transactions for each of the items for which errors were noted, and try to determine the cause of the underlying problem. Investigate each issue and recommend corrective action to the warehouse manager, so the problems do not arise again.

Exhibit 12.5   *Cycle Counting Report*

Location	Item No.	Description	U/M	Quantity
A-10-C	Q1458	Switch, 120V, 20A	EA	
A-10-C	U1010	Bolt, Zinc, $3 \times \frac{1}{4}$	EA	
A-10-C	M1458	Screw, Stainless Steel, $2 \times \frac{3}{8}$	EA	

Exhibit 12.6 *Inventory Accuracy Report*

Aisles	Responsible Person	2 Months Ago	Last Month	Week 1	Week 2	Week 3	Week 4
A-B	Fred P.	82%	86%	85%	84%	82%	87%
C-D	Alain Q.	70%	72%	74%	76%	78%	80%
E-F	Davis L.	61%	64%	67%	70%	73%	76%
G-H	Jeff R.	54%	58%	62%	66%	70%	74%
I-J	Alice R.	12%	17%	22%	27%	32%	37%
K-L	George W.	81%	80%	79%	78%	77%	76%
M-N	Robert T.	50%	60%	65%	70%	80%	90%

Procedure 6: Perform Physical Inventory Count

The following procedure describes the multitude of tasks required to organize a physical count, manage the counting process, and enter any resulting variances in the inventory database.

Policy/Procedure Statement	Retrieval Number	INV-06
[Company Name]	Page: Issue Date	1 of 1 10/28/05

Subject: Perform Physical Inventory Count

1. PURPOSE AND SCOPE

This procedure is used to create a structured approach to a physical inventory count.

2. RESPONSIBILITIES

    Controller
    Count Teams

3. PROCEDURES

3.1 **Preparation for the Count (Controller)**

Take the following steps one week before the physical count:

1. Contact the printing company and order a sufficient number of sequentially numbered count tags. The first tag number should always be "1000." The tags should include fields for the product number, description, quantity count, location, and the counter's signature.
2. Review the inventory and mark all items lacking a part number with a brightly colored piece of paper. Inform the warehouse manager that these items must be marked with a proper part number immediately.
3. Clearly mark the quantity on all sealed packages.
4. Count all partial packages, seal them, and mark the quantity on the tape.
5. Prepare "Do Not Inventory" tags and use them to mark all items that should not be included in the physical inventory count.
6. Issue a list of count team members, with a notice regarding where and when they should appear for the inventory count.

3.2 **One Day Before the Count (Controller)**

1. Remind all participants that they are expected to be counting the next day.
2. Notify the warehouse manager that all items received during the two days of physical counts must be segregated and marked with "Do Not Inventory" tags.

3. Notify the manager that no shipments are allowed for the duration of the physical count.
4. Notify the warehouse manager that all shipments for which the paperwork has not been sent to accounting by that evening will be included in the inventory count on the following day.
5. Notify the warehouse manager that all shipping and receiving documentation from the day before the count must be forwarded to the accounting department that day, for immediate data entry. Likewise, any pick information must be forwarded at the same time.
6. Notify all outside storage locations to fax in their inventory counts.

3.3 **Morning of the Physical Inventory Count (Controller)**

1. Enter all transactions from the previous day.
2. Assemble the count teams. Issue counting instructions to them, as well as blocks of tags, for which they must sign. Give each team a map of the warehouse with a section highlighted on it that they are responsible for counting. Those teams with forklift experience will be assigned to count the top racks; those without this experience will be assigned the lower racks.
3. Call all outside storage warehouses and ask them to fax in their counts of company-owned inventory.
4. The count supervisor assigns additional count areas to those teams that finish counting their areas first.
5. The tag coordinator assigns blocks of tags to those count teams that run out of tags, tracks the receipt of tags, and follows up on missing tags. All tags should be accounted for by the end of the day.
6. The data entry person enters the information on the tags into a spreadsheet, and then summarizes the quantities for each item and pencils the totals into the cycle count report that was run earlier in the day.
7. The count supervisor reviews any unusual variances with the count teams to ensure that the correct amounts were entered.
8. Review the test count with an auditor, if necessary. Give the auditor a complete printout of all tags, as well as the cycle counting spreadsheet, showing all variances.

3.4 **Job Descriptions (Controller)**

- The count supervisor is responsible for supervising the count, which includes assigning count teams to specific areas and ensuring that all areas have been counted and tagged. This person also waits until all count tags have been compared to the quantities listed in the computer, and then checks the counts on any items that appear to be incorrect.
- The tag coordinator is responsible for tracking the blocks of count tags that have been issued, as well as for accounting for all tags that have been returned. When distributing tags, mark down the beginning and ending numbers of each block of tags on a tracking sheet, and obtain the signature of the person who receives the tags. When the tags are returned, put them

in numerical order and verify that all tags are accounted for. Once the verification is complete, check off the tags on the tracking sheet as having been received. Once returned tags have been properly accounted for, forward them to the extension calculation clerk.

- The extension calculation clerk is responsible for summarizing the amounts on the tags (if there are multiple quantities listed) to arrive at a total quantity count on each tag. This person also compares the part numbers and descriptions on each tag to see if there are any potential identification problems. This person forwards all completed tags to the data entry person.
- The data entry person is responsible for entering the information on all count tags into the computer spreadsheet. When doing so, enter all the information on each tag into a spreadsheet. Once a group of tags has been entered, stamp them as having been entered, clip them together, and store them separately. Once all tags are entered in the spreadsheet, sort the data by part number. Print out the spreadsheet and summarize the quantities by part number. Transfer the total quantities by part number to the cycle count report. If there are any significant variances between the counted and cycle count quantities, bring them to the attention of the count supervisor for review.

3.5 Time and Place (Count Teams)

The count begins at 7:30 A.M. and ends at 4:30 P.M. on the first day of the count. If the count continues to a second day, it will begin at the same time, and count teams will be released whenever the counts have been completed. On both days, all count teams should meet at the warehouse gate.

3.6 Counting Responsibility (Count Teams)

1. Count the bin locations assigned to you. These will be marked on a map of the warehouse with a highlighter. When you have counted all of the items in your assigned area, return to the count supervisor, who will assign additional count areas to you.
2. For each item counted in a separate bin location, enter the product code and date on the part of the inventory tag that is labeled "Pallet" and tape it to the inventory item. Rip off the other part of the tag and mark on it the product code, description, location, and quantity counted. Also initial the tag or list the number of your count team. Keep this part of the tag and return it to the tag coordinator when you run out of tags. This person will ensure that all of the tags assigned to you have been returned. If some are missing, you must locate and return them to the tag coordinator.
3. If there are many boxes of the same item to count, list the individual amounts on a tag, and an extensions calculation person will add them up for you. For example, if there are 18 boxes of 300 and a partial box of 12, just enter $(18 \times 300) + 12$ on the tag.

3.7 General Information (Count Teams)

- Do not count any item that has a "Do Not Inventory" tag on it.

- Scales will be provided to all count teams. The warehouse supervisor is available for training in the use of scales.
- Use a pen (not a pencil) to enter information on count tags. To make a quantity correction, put a line through the old quantity, write the new quantity next to it, and initial the change.
- *All* tags must be accounted for! If you do not use some, return them to the tag coordinator.

Procedure 7: Calculate Period-End Inventory

The following procedure notes the steps a cost accountant must follow to determine the correct period-end inventory valuation.

Policy/Procedure Statement	Retrieval Number	INV-07
[Company Name]	Page:	1 of 1
	Issue Date	10/28/05

Subject: Calculate Period-End Inventory

1. PURPOSE AND SCOPE

This procedure is used by the cost accountant to ensure that the inventory valuation created by a computerized accounting system is accurate, as well as to update it with the latest overhead costs.

2. RESPONSIBILITIES

Cost Accountant

3. PROCEDURES

3.1 **Verify Inventory Quantities and Costs (Cost Accountant)**

1. Following the end of the accounting period, print out and review the computer change log for all bills of materials and labor routings. Review them with the materials manager and production engineer to ensure their accuracy. Revise any changes made in error.
2. Go to the warehouse and manually compare the period-end counts recorded on the inventory report for the most expensive items in the warehouse to what is in the warehouse racks. If there are any variances, adjust them for any transactions that occurred between the end of the period and the date of the review. If there are still variances, adjust for them in the inventory database.

3. Print a report that sorts the inventory in declining extended dollar order and review it for reasonableness. Be sure to review not only the most expensive items on the list but also the least expensive, since this is where costing errors are most likely to be found. Adjust for any issues found.

3.2 **Verify Overhead Costs and Allocations (Cost Accountant)**

1. Review all entries in the general ledger during the reporting period for costs added to the cost pool, verifying that only approved costs have been included. Also investigate any unusually large overhead entries.
2. Verify that the overhead allocation calculation conforms to the standard allocation used in previous reporting periods, or that it matches any changes approved by management.
3. Verify that the journal entry for overhead allocation matches the standard journal entry listed in the accounting procedures manual.

3.3 **Review Variances from Prior Period (Cost Accountant)**

Print out the inventory valuation report and compare its results by major category to those of the previous reporting period, both in terms of dollars and proportions. Investigate any major differences.

Procedure 8: Calculate Lower of Cost or Market Value

This procedure notes the steps a cost accountant must follow in order to periodically test the lower of cost or market value for a company's inventory.

Policy/Procedure Statement	Retrieval Number	INV-08
[Company Name]	Page:	1 of 1
	Issue Date	10/28/05

Subject: Calculate Lower of Cost or Market Value

1. PURPOSE AND SCOPE

This procedure is used by the cost accountant to periodically adjust the inventory valuation for those items whose market value has dropped below their recorded cost.

2. RESPONSIBILITIES

Cost Accountant

3. PROCEDURES

3.1 **Identify High-Value Inventory Items (Cost Accountant)**

Export the extended inventory valuation report to an electronic spreadsheet. Sort it by declining extended dollar cost, and delete the 80% of inventory items that do not comprise the top 20% of inventory valuation. Sort the remaining 20% of inventory items by either part number or item description. Print the report.

3.2 **Conduct Market Price Review (Cost Accountant)**

1. Send a copy of the report to the materials manager, with instructions to compare unit costs for each item on the list to market prices, and be sure to mutually agree on a due date for completion of the review.
2. When the materials management staff has completed its review, meet with the materials manager to go over its results and discuss any major adjustments. Have the materials management staff write down the valuation of selected items in the inventory database whose cost exceeds their market value.

3.3 **Document Change in Valuation (Cost Accountant)**

1. Have the accounting staff expense the value of the write-down in the accounting records.
2. Write a memo detailing the results of the lower of cost or market calculation. Attach one copy to the journal entry used to write down the valuation, and issue another copy to the materials manager.

Procedure 9: Reorder Supplies with a Visual Review System

The following procedure describes the steps required to periodically inspect and reorder inventory items that are not tracked through a perpetual inventory database.

Policy/Procedure Statement	Retrieval Number	INV-09
[Company Name]	Page:	1 of 1
	Issue Date	10/28/05

Subject: Reorder Supplies with a Visual Review System

1. PURPOSE AND SCOPE

This procedure is used by the purchasing staff to place orders for supplies not tracked through the inventory system.

2. RESPONSIBILITIES

Purchasing Clerk

3. PROCEDURES

3.1 Discuss Visual Review Parameters (Purchasing Clerk)

1. Meet with the production manager and discuss any revisions to the bin sizes and reorder lines used in the current two-bin ordering system.

2. If necessary, alter the bin sizes used or move the reorder line marked inside the bins.

3.2 Visually Review Supply Stock Levels (Purchasing Staff)

1. If a two-bin reordering system is in use, note on a reorder form the part number of any item for which its replenishment bin is empty.

2. If a single-bin reordering system is in use, note on a reorder form the part number of any item for which the inventory level has dropped below the reorder line.

3. Refer to the standard order quantity summary for each part to be reordered, and note the quantity on the reorder form next to each part number requiring replenishment.

3.3 Reorder Required Supplies (Purchasing Clerk)

1. Obtain a purchase order number for all items shown on the reorder form.

2. Enter the purchase order number at the top of the form.

3. Fax the reorder form to the single-source parts supplier.

4. Call the supplier to confirm receipt of the fax, and obtain an expected delivery date from the supplier.

5. Enter the delivery date in the purchase order record in the computer system.

6. File the reorder form.

Procedure 10: Receive Sales Returns

This procedure describes the steps required by several departments to process any goods being returned by customers, ranging from initial authorization of a return, through inspection of the received items, to the processing of any credits due to customers.

Policy/Procedure Statement	Retrieval Number	INV-10
[Company Name]	Page: Issue Date	1 of 1 10/28/05

Subject: Receive Sales Returns

1. PURPOSE AND SCOPE

This procedure is used by the accounts receivable clerk to calculate the correct amount of credit to apply to a sales return.

2. RESPONSIBILITIES

Accounts Receivable Clerk
Receiving Clerk
Quality Assurance Clerk

3. PROCEDURES

3.1 Assign Sales Return Authorization Number (Accounts Receivable Clerk)

Upon receipt of a sales return inquiry from a customer, assign the customer a unique sales return authorization number. Enter this number on the Sales Return Authorization Form (see Exhibit12.7), as well as quantity, product number, and description of the items being returned. In addition, enter one of the standard reason codes on the form into the "Reason for Return" field. Store a copy of the form in the sales return file, sorted by date. Send another copy to the receiving department.

3.2 Accept Sales Return (Receiving Clerk)

1. When a customer returns a product to the receiving dock, compare the sales return authorization number listed on the package to the list of open sales return authorization numbers. Accept the delivery if there is a numerical match and the product quantity and type is the same. If the number does not exist, or the product type is incorrect, or the quantity is too large, reject the order.
2. If the order is acceptable, log it into the inventory database in the "Requires Review by Quality Assurance" category. Notify quality assurance that it needs to inspect returned product. Forward the shipping information attached to the delivery to the accounting department, and enter the receipt into the receiving log.

3.3 Determine Damage Credit (Quality Assurance Clerk)

Upon receipt of notification from the receiving staff, the quality assurance clerk must inspect the returned goods, verifying the condition of the packaging, documentation, and product. If any of these items require replacement, complete a Product Repair Ticket and attach it to the returned goods. Send a copy of the Ticket to the accounting department.

3.4 **Calculate Sales Return Credit (Accounts Receivable Clerk)**

1. Upon receipt of the shipping information attached to the sales return, the accounts receivable clerk uses the Sales Return Credit Calculation Form (see Exhibit 12.8) to determine the correct amount of credit to be granted to the customer.
2. Enter the product number, quantity returned, product description, unit price, and extended price for each item returned on the form.
3. Calculate the amount of damage credit to enter on the form by multiplying the required product repairs listed on the Product Repair Ticket by the standard product cost listed in the computer system for each item.
4. Reduce the amount of credit by a ___% restocking fee, and also subtract a $___ transaction fee.
5. Calculate the net credit granted.
6. Sign and date the form.
7. File one copy of the form in the customer file, sorted by date. Forward another copy to the clerk who processes credits (see the "Issue Customer Credits" procedure).

Exhibit 12.7 *Sales Return Authorization Form*

Company Name

Sales Return Authorization Form

Customer Name: _____ Date: _____

Sales Return Authorization Number: _____ **(Required)**

Product Being Returned			Reason for
Number	**Quantity**	**Description**	**Return**
_____	_____	_____	_____
_____	_____	_____	_____
_____	_____	_____	_____
_____	_____	_____	_____

Standard Reason Codes:

1 = Product damaged in transit   4 = Incorrect quantity shipped

2 = Product quality below required level   5 = Shipment made to wrong location

3 = Incorrect product shipped   6 = Other (describe below)

Other reasons for return: _____

_____

_____

Exhibit 12.8 *Sales Return Credit Calculation Form*

Company Name

Sales Return Credit Calculation Form

Customer Name: _____ Date: _____

Sales Return Authorization Number: _____

Product Number	Quantity	Description	Unit Price	Extended Price	Damage Credit
_____	_____	_____	_____	_____	_____
_____	_____	_____	_____	_____	_____
_____	_____	_____	_____	_____	_____
_____	_____	_____	_____	_____	_____
_____	_____	_____	_____	_____	_____

Totals _____ _____

Less:

20% Restocking Fee _____

Total Damage Credit _____

$25 Transaction Fee $25 _____

Net Credit Granted _____

_____   _____

Clerk Signature   Clerk Name

Procedure 11: Review Inventory for Obsolescence

The following procedure describes the steps one should follow to identify and process any inventory items considered to be obsolete.

Policy/Procedure Statement	Retrieval Number	INV-11
[Company Name]	Page:	1 of 1
	Issue Date	10/28/05

Subject: Review Inventory for Obsolescence

1. PURPOSE AND SCOPE

This procedure is used by the warehouse staff to periodically review the inventory for obsolete items and account for items considered to be obsolete.

2. RESPONSIBILITIES

Warehouse Staff
General Ledger Accountant

3. PROCEDURES

3.1 **Determine Disposition of Inventory (Warehouse Staff)**

1. Schedule a meeting of the materials review board, to meet in the warehouse.
2. Prior to the meeting, print enough copies of the Inventory Obsolescence Review Report (see Exhibit 12.9) for all members of the committee.
3. Personally review all items on the report for which there appear to be excessive quantities on hand.
4. Determine the proper disposal of each item judged to be obsolete, including possible returns to suppliers, donations, inclusion in existing products, or scrap.

3.2 **Dispose of Inventory (Warehouse Staff)**

1. Have the warehouse staff mark each item as obsolete in the inventory database.
2. Issue a memo to the materials review board, summarizing the results of its actions.

3.3 **Write Down Inventory (General Ledger Accountant)**

Have the accounting staff write down the value of each obsolete item to its disposal value.

Exhibit 12.9 *Inventory Obsolescence Review Report*

Description	Item No.	Location	Quantity on Hand	Last Year Usage	Planned Usage	Extended Cost
Subwoofer case	0421	A-04-C	872	520	180	$9,053
Speaker case	1098	A-06-D	148	240	120	1,020
Subwoofer	3421	D-12-A	293	14	0	24,724
Circuit board	3600	B-01-A	500	5,090	1,580	2,500
Speaker, bass	4280	C-10-C	621	2,480	578	49,200
Speaker bracket	5391	C-10-C	14	0	0	92
Wall bracket	5080	B-03-B	400	0	120	2,800
Gold connection	6233	C-04-A	3,025	8,042	5,900	9,725
Tweeter	7552	C-05-B	725	6,740	2,040	5,630

13

Inventory Measurements

After having implemented any of the best practices noted in the previous chapters, one should determine the extent of any resulting changes. This chapter* contains 32 measurements related to inventory that can selectively be used to track changes in new product design, computer files, receiving, putaway, production, picking, shipping, and inventory storage—in that sequential order.

Don't feel compelled to use all 32 measurements. Instead, use only those measurements needed to track the most important parts of the inventory process flow. Too many measurements constitute an overflow of information, and certainly require an excessive amount of effort to calculate. The measurements discussed are shown in Exhibit 13.1.

13.1 Percentage of New Parts Used in New Products

A continuing problem for a company's logistics staff is the volume of new parts that the engineering department specifies for each new product. This can result in an extraordinary number of parts to keep track of, which entails additional purchasing and materials handling costs. From the perspective of saving costs for the entire company, it makes a great deal of sense to encourage engineers to design products that share components with existing products. This approach leverages new products from the existing workload of the purchasing and materials handling staffs, and has the added benefit of avoiding an investment in new parts inventory. For these reasons, the percentage of new parts used in new products is an excellent choice of performance measurement.

---

*Selected measurements in this chapter are used with permission from Bragg, *Business Ratios and Formulas*, John Wiley & Sons, 2002.

Exhibit 13.1 *Summary of Inventory Measurements Best Practices*

13.1	Percentage of New Parts Used in New Products
13.2	Percentage of Existing Parts Reused in New Products
13.3	Bill of Material Accuracy
13.4	Item Master File Accuracy
13.5	On-Time Parts Delivery Percentage
13.6	Incoming Components Correct Quantity Percentage
13.7	Percentage of Receipts Authorized by Purchase Orders
13.8	Percentage of Purchase Orders Released with Full Lead Time
13.9	Putaway Accuracy
13.10	Putaway Cycle Time
13.11	Scrap Percentage
13.12	Average Picking Time
13.13	Picking Accuracy for Assembled Products
13.14	Average Picking Cost
13.15	Order Lines Shipped per Labor Hour
13.16	Shipping Accuracy
13.17	Warehouse Order Cycle Time
13.18	Inventory Availability
13.19	Delivery Promise Slippage
13.20	Average Back Order Length
13.21	Dock Door Utilization
13.22	Inventory Accuracy
13.23	Inventory Turnover
13.24	Percentage of Warehouse Stock Locations Utilized
13.25	Storage Density Percentage
13.26	Inventory per Square Foot of Storage Space
13.27	Storage Cost per Item
13.28	Average Pallet Inventory per SKU
13.29	Rate of Change in Inactive, Obsolete, and Surplus Inventory
13.30	Obsolete Inventory Percentage
13.31	Percentage of Inventory > XX Days Old
13.32	Percentage of Returnable Inventory

Divide the number of *new* parts in a bill of materials by the *total* number of parts in a bill of materials. Many companies may not include fittings and fasteners in the bill of materials, since they keep large quantities of these items on hand at all times, and charge them off to current expenses. If so, the number of parts to include in the calculation will usually decline greatly, making the measurement much easier to complete. The formula is:

$$\text{Percentage of new parts used in new products} = \frac{\text{Number of new parts in bill of materials}}{\text{Total number of parts in bill of materials}}$$

Engineers may argue against the use of this measurement on the grounds that it provides a disincentive for them to locate more reliable and/or less expensive parts with which to replace existing components. Though this measure can act as a block to such beneficial activities, a measurement system can avoid this problem by also focusing on long-term declines in the cost of products, or increases in the level of quality. A combined set of these measurements can be an effective way to focus on the most appropriate design initiatives by the engineering department.

13.2 Percentage of Existing Parts Reused in New Products

The inverse of the preceding measurement can be used to determine the proportion of existing parts that are used in new products. However, as the formula reveals, this measurement is slightly different from an inverse measurement. Companies that have compiled an approved list of parts that are to be used in new product designs, which is a subset of all existing parts, use this variation. By concentrating on the use of an *approved* parts list in new products, a company can incorporate high-quality, low-cost components in its products.

Divide the number of approved parts in a new product's bill of materials by the total number of parts in the bill. If there is no approved components list, then the only alternative is to use the set of all existing components from which to select items for the numerator, which will likely result in a higher percentage. The formula is:

$$\text{Percentage of existing parts used in new products} = \frac{\text{Number of approved parts in bill of materials}}{\text{Total number of parts in bill of materials}}$$

Since a complex product will probably contain one or more subassemblies rather than individual components, one should verify that selected subassemblies are also on the approved parts list; otherwise, subassemblies will be rejected for the purposes of this measurement.

13.3 Bill of Materials Accuracy

The engineering department is responsible for the release of a bill of materials for each product that it designs. The bill of materials should specify exactly what components are needed to build a product, plus the quantities required for each part. The logistics staff uses this information to ensure that the correct parts are available when the manufacturing process begins. At least a 98 percent accuracy rating is needed for this measurement in order to manufacture products with a minimum of stoppages due to missing parts.

To calculate the measurement, divide the number of accurate parts (defined as the correct part number, unit of measure, and quantity) listed in a bill of materials by the total number of parts listed in the bill. The formula is:

$$\frac{Bill\ of\ materials}{accuracy} = \frac{Number\ of\ accurate\ parts\ listed\ in\ bill\ of\ materials}{Total\ number\ of\ parts\ in\ bill\ of\ materials}$$

Though the minimum acceptable level of accuracy is 98 percent, this is an area where nothing less than a 100 percent accuracy level is required in order to ensure that the production process runs smoothly. Consequently, a great deal of attention should be focused squarely on this measurement.

The timing of the release of the bill of materials is another problem. If an engineering staff is late in issuing a proper bill of materials, then the logistics group must scramble to bring in the correct parts in time for the start of the production process. Measuring the timing of the bill's release as well as its accuracy can avoid this problem by focusing the engineering staff's attention on it.

13.4 Item Master File Accuracy

The item master file contains all the descriptive information about each inventory item, such as its unit of measure and cubic volume. This information must be correct, or else a number of downstream materials planning functions will issue incorrect results. Consequently, one should conduct a periodic audit of the file, and report its accuracy to management.

To calculate the item master file accuracy, conduct an audit of a random sample of all item master records, verifying each field in the selected batch. Then divide the total number of records containing 100 percent accurate information by the total number of records sampled. The calculation follows:

$$Item\ master\ file\ accuracy\ =\ \frac{Total\ number\ of\ records\ reviewed\ having\ 100\ percent\ accurate\ information}{Total\ number\ of\ records\ sampled}$$

An alternative approach is to divide the total number of accurate fields within the records by the total number of fields reviewed. However, this tends to result in an extremely high accuracy percentage, since there are many fields within each record, most of which are probably accurate. Since the point of using the measurement is to highlight problem areas, it is best to base the calculation on records reviewed, rather than fields, so that a lower accuracy percentage will be more likely to initiate corrective action by management.

13.5 On-Time Parts Delivery Percentage

One of the key performance measures for rating a supplier is its ability to deliver ordered parts on time, since a late delivery can shut down a production line. Furthermore, a long-standing ability to always deliver on time gives a company the ability to reduce the level of safety stock kept on hand to cover potential parts shortages, which represents a clear reduction in working capital requirements. Consequently, the on-time parts delivery percentage is crucial to the logistics function.

Subtract the requested arrival date from the actual arrival date. If one's intent is to develop a measurement that covers multiple deliveries, then one can create an average by summarizing this comparison for all the deliveries and then dividing by the total number of deliveries. Also, if an order arrives prior to the requested arrival date, the resulting negative number should be converted to a zero for measurement purposes; otherwise, it will offset any late deliveries, when there is no benefit to the company of having an early delivery. Because a company must pay for these early deliveries sooner than expected, they can even be treated as positive variances by stripping away the minus sign. Any of these variations are possible, depending on a company's perception of the importance of not having early deliveries. The basic formula is:

$$\frac{On\text{-}time\ parts\ delivery}{percentage} = Actual\ arrival\ date - Requested\ arrival\ date$$

This is an excellent measurement, but it does not address other key aspects of supplier performance, such as the quality of the goods delivered or their cost. These additional features can be measured alongside the on-time delivery percentage, or melded into an overall rating score for each supplier.

13.6 Incoming Components Correct Quantity Percentage

If the quantity of items received in comparison to the amount ordered is too low, the company may be faced with a parts shortage in its production operation. If the quantity is too high, then it may find itself with more inventory than it can use. Also, if an odd lot size is received, it may be difficult for the receiving staff to find a location in the warehouse in which to store it. For these reasons, the incoming components correct quantity percentage is very commonly used.

Divide the number of orders to suppliers for which the correct quantity is delivered by the total quantity of orders delivered. This measurement is commonly subdivided into individual suppliers, so the performance of each one can be measured. A variation on the formula is to include in the numerator only those orders received for which the entire order amount is shipped; this approach is used by companies that do not want to deal with multiple partial orders from their suppliers, due to the increased cost of receiving and related paperwork. The formula is:

$$\frac{Incoming\ components\ correct}{quantity\ percentage} = \frac{Total\ quantity\ of}{orders\ delivered}$$

The formula can result in a very low correct quantity percentage if the quantity received is only off by one unit. This may seem harsh if an order of 10,000 units is incorrect by one unit. Consequently, it is common for companies to consider an order quantity to be accurate if the quantity received is within a few percent of the ordered amount. The exact percentage used will vary based on the need for precision and the cost of the components received, though 5 percent is generally considered to be the maximum allowable variance.

13.7 Percentage of Receipts Authorized by Purchase Orders

One of the most difficult tasks for the receiving staff is to decide what to do with orders that are received with no accompanying purchase order. Since the orders are not authorized, the staff could simply reject them. However, they run the risk of rejecting some items that may have been bought on a priority basis, and which will cause undue trouble for the logistics manager when projects in other parts of the company are held up. Accordingly, these orders are frequently set to one side for a few hours or days, while the receiving staff tries to find out who ordered them. This can be a significant waste of receiving time and storage space, and is worth measuring on a trend line to see if the problem is worsening.

The receiving department should maintain a receiving log, on each line of which is recorded the receipt of a single product within an order. Using the line items in the receiving log that correspond to the dates within the measurement period, summarize the number of receipt line items authorized by open purchase orders by the total number of receipt line items in the log. The formula is:

$$\text{Percentage of receipts authorized by purchase order} = \frac{\text{Receipt line items authorized by open purchase orders}}{\text{Total receipt line items}}$$

This is an excellent measurement, since the use of purchase orders is one of the best controls over unauthorized buying, and the measurement clearly shows the extent of control problems in this area. However, it does not include other types of purchases that never run through the receiving area, such as services, subscriptions, or recurring lease payments. These other types of costs can constitute the majority of all nonpayroll costs in services industries; consequently, the measurement is of most use in businesses dealing in tangible goods.

13.8 Percentage of Purchase Orders Released with Full Lead Time

If the purchasing department is not preparing purchase orders on time, they will be forcing suppliers to deliver in less than standard lead times or incur expensive overnight air freight to bring items in on time. This may be a problem with an inefficient purchasing staff, or be caused by sudden near-term changes in the production schedule. Whatever the reason may be, one should track the proportion of purchase orders released with full lead time, and investigate those that are not.

To calculate the proportion of purchase orders released with full lead times, have the computer system summarize all purchase order lines in the measurement period for which there were full lead times, and divide this by the total number of purchase order lines released during the period. The calculation is:

$$\begin{matrix} \textit{Percentage of} \\ \textit{purchase orders} \\ \textit{released with full} \\ \textit{lead time} \end{matrix} = \frac{\textit{Purchase order lines released with full lead time}}{\textit{Total purchase order lines released}}$$

Given the quantity of purchase order lines involved, the summarization of data almost certainly will require a report from the computer system—manual summarization is *not* recommended! One should also use an additional report that itemizes each order line released with less than the full lead time, so that management can investigate the problem.

This measurement is not intended to apply in cases where a company orders standard parts for its manufacturing processes through the use of rolling schedules or just-in-time systems. In these instances, there should be no purchase orders at all.

13.9 Putaway Accuracy

The ability of the receiving staff to accurately put received items away into stock locations correctly, including the proper recording of the transaction, is critical to all subsequent inventory transactions. If a putaway is done incorrectly, it is very difficult to find an item, or verify that an incorrect part number or quantity has been used. An incorrect putaway also impacts the materials planning staff, which now has incorrect information about how much stock is on hand.

The basic putaway issue can be quantified with the putaway accuracy measurement. To calculate it, divide the total number of putaway transactions during the measurement period into the number of items for which an accurate putaway transaction was recorded. The formula is:

$$Putaway\ accuracy = \frac{Number\ of\ accurate\ putaway\ transactions}{Total\ number\ of\ putaway\ transactions}$$

From a practical perspective, it is usually easier to determine the number of incorrect putaways than the number of correct ones, so the numerator can be modified to be the total number of putaway transactions, less the number of putaway errors. This percentage is most easily calculated by periodically testing a sample of all inventory items.

This measurement should be clearly posted for the warehouse staff to read, thereby driving home to them the importance of a correct putaway. One should also include it in the performance reviews of the warehouse staff, for the same reason.

13.10 Putaway Cycle Time

The accuracy of a putaway, as noted in the last measurement, is certainly important, but can take so long that it impacts the ability of a company to turn around items for shipment to customers or delivery to the shop floor. Consequently, one must also track the average putaway cycle time to ensure that this is being done in as short a period as possible. It is best to report the putaway cycle time and putaway accuracy measurements together in order to obtain an overall picture of the putaway function.

To measure putaway cycle time, subtract the arrival time of each receipt from its putaway time, summarize this information for all receipts during the measurement period, and divide it by the total number of receipts in the period. The calculation is:

$$Putaway\ cycle\ time = \frac{\begin{array}{c}Sum\ for\ all\ receiving\ transactions\\ (Putaway\ date\ /\ Time - Receipt\ date\ /\ Time)\end{array}}{Number\ of\ receipts\ during\ the\ measurement\ period}$$

Given the large number of receiving transactions for all but the smallest warehouses, this measurement is best calculated via the materials management database. Also, since the measurement is based on the *time* of receipt and putaway (i.e., the number of minutes and seconds elapsed between these two events), the only way to obtain accurate transaction stamping is to use on-line, real-time data entry, which calls for the use of portable terminals linked to the materials management database. If this data collection system is not available, the measurement should not be used.

One more problem is the likely presence at the end of each measurement period of receipts that have not yet been put away. If one ignores these transactions for purposes of calculating the measurement, the average putaway cycle time will almost certainly be too low, since the items causing putaway problems are not being included. A better approach is either to delay the calculation until the unfinished transactions are completed or to revise the calculation a month later when the next periodic measurement is made.

13.11 Scrap Percentage

The amount of scrap generated by a production operation is of great concern to the production manager, for it can be indicative of a number of problems—poor training of the direct labor work force, improper machine setup, materials handling problems, or even the ordering of substandard raw materials. Another reason for keeping a close watch over the scrap percentage is that inordinate amounts of scrap may require extensive revisions to the production schedule in order to produce extra goods, which in turn will require short-term changes to the purchasing schedule in order to bring in the required raw materials. For these reasons, the scrap percentage is one of the most closely watched performance measurements in the factory.

The amount of scrap that a company produces is difficult to measure, because it can be produced in many parts of a facility, and in many cases is not accumulated for measurement purposes. If this is the case, the best approach is to subtract the standard cost of goods sold from the actual cost of goods sold, and divide the result by the standard cost of goods sold. By using this approach, one can compare the aggregate cost of what was produced to what should have been produced, without having to resort to a detailed count of each item scrapped. The formula is:

$$\frac{Scrap}{percentage} = \frac{(Actual\ cost\ of\ goods\ sold - Standard\ cost\ of\ goods\ sold)}{Standard\ cost\ of\ goods\ sold}$$

A variation on this formula is to track only the scrap generated by the bottleneck production operation. This is especially important, because the scrap lost through this operation must be manufactured again, which may interfere with the production of other goods that must pass through the same operation, thereby possibly reducing the total amount of gross margin generated by the factory.

There are several problems with comparing the actual cost of goods sold to the standard amount, and assuming that the difference is scrap. One problem is that there may be a standard scrap value already included in the bills of materials that comprise the standard cost of goods sold, so these values must be extracted from the standard in order to determine the actual amount of scrap. Another problem is that there may be other variances contained within the actual cost of goods sold, such as a price variance on raw materials purchased. These variances must be calculated and removed from the actual cost of goods sold before the amount of scrap can be determined. Another problem is that many of the costs that make up the cost of goods sold are related to overhead, rather than the direct cost associated with scrap. To avoid this problem, one can include in the cost of goods sold only the direct labor and direct materials costs associated with production, removing all overhead costs. Finally, the inherent assumption in this formula is that standard costs are reasonably accurate; if not, the resulting scrap calculation will be incorrect.

13.12 Average Picking Time

A great many best practices in this book involve the attainment of a high level of order picking speed. Since some of the advocated changes involve a considerable capital investment or at least major changes in the scheduling or movement of the picking staff, would it not be useful to see if the changes are making a difference? The measurement of average picking time is a good way to do so, though one must be aware of its shortcomings.

To measure the average picking time at the most detailed level, one can subtract the time at which an order was completed from the time when a picker received the order. Since this approach to the measurement clearly involves a massive amount of nonvalue-added timekeeping, one can do it only if wireless, real-time terminals are being used, so the computer system automatically tracks order duration. In the absence of such a system, the best approach is to divide the total number of orders completed during the measurement period by the total person-hours of picking time during the period. The calculation is:

$$\frac{Average}{picking\ time} = \frac{Total\ number\ of\ orders\ completed}{(Total\ person\text{-}hours\ worked\ by\ picking\ staff}{+ Total\ person\text{-}hours\ worked\ by\ contract\ staff)}$$

The denominator includes hours worked by both in-house and contract staff; some warehouses employ contract staff whose hours do not appear in the normal payroll system, so their hours must be added from the accounts payable system in order to obtain a full picture of the total hours being worked in the picking function.

Though this measure gives a good summary-level view of picking efficiency, it can be misinterpreted. The main issue is variations in the size of orders picked; if a larger proportion of single-line orders are processed in one month than in the next, then efficiency levels will appear to have declined, because orders are easier to fill when they contain only a single line. This problem is most common in low-volume environments when a small number of unusually large or small orders can significantly alter the measurement. However, when there are a great many orders to be picked, variations in order size tend to average out over the measurement period. If the measurement appears to be skewed by this issue, it may be possible to have the computer system summarize the total number of order lines picked during the period, and use this figure in the numerator of the measurement; this approach is usually too labor-intensive to attempt manually.

13.13 Picking Accuracy for Assembled Products

When a company ships disassembled products to customers, it is extremely important that the kits shipped out have exactly the correct number of the right parts. If the number is too high, then the company will be increasing its materials costs more than necessary. If the number is too low, then the company faces a significant customer relations problem, as well as added costs to locate and ship missing parts to customers. For these reasons, the picking accuracy of assembled products is considered very important for those companies that ship kits.

To calculate this measurement, conduct an audit of a sample of completed kits, counting as an error every kit where the quantity of parts is incorrect, as well as an error for every kit where the quantity is correct, but the types of parts included are incorrect. Once a kit is considered incorrect for either reason, it cannot be counted as an error again (thereby avoiding double counting). Then divide the total number of errors by the total number of product kits sampled. Finally, subtract the resulting percentage from 100 percent. The formula is:

$$\text{Picking accuracy for assembled products} = 100\% - \frac{\text{Number of quantity errors} + \text{Number of part errors}}{\text{Total number of product kits sampled}}$$

If the company feels that the key issue is avoiding customer complaints, then it may be justified in not bothering to count a part overage as an error. This is especially common when counting fittings and fasteners, which are usually the least expensive parts of a product kit.

13.14 Average Picking Cost

Even if a company has achieved an extremely high level of picking efficiency and accuracy, it should not have done so at an inordinately high cost. Consequently, it is best to measure the picking cost per order line alongside efficiency and accuracy measurements in order to gain a complete picture of a company's picking capability.

To measure the average picking cost, divide the total picking cost by the number of order lines picked. The total picking cost should include the fully burdened labor cost of the picking staff, plus the depreciation on any incremental improvements in warehouse equipment or racking specifically intended to improve picking efficiency or accuracy. The calculation follows:

$$\text{Average picking cost} = \frac{(\text{Fully burdened picking staff wages} + \text{Depreciation on picking equipment and storage})}{\text{Total order lines picked}}$$

Obtaining the total number of order lines picked is best achieved by having the computer system summarize this information for the measurement period. Determining picking staff wages can be difficult if the warehouse staff switches among tasks, rather than having dedicated pickers; though one can use timesheets to track how much time was spent on each activity, this is a nonvalue-added activity, so the only alternative may be an occasional sample study of worker time. The depreciation on picking equipment and storage should be included in the numerator, because a company may invest heavily in such expensive assets as automated storage and retrieval systems or carousels in order to improve the efficiency of its picking operations. If there are such assets, use straight-line depreciation over the useful life of each asset rather than the accelerated depreciation system that may be used for accounting purposes. The straight-line method more accurately reflects the periodic expense of these assets.

13.15 Order Lines Shipped per Labor Hour

The ability to ship orders is a determinant of the efficiency of a warehouse staff. Though there are many other transactions involved in warehouse activities, it must be able to reliably ship to customers on time, since this is a service issue directly experienced by customers. A warehouse manager could simply overstaff the shipping department to ensure that all possible orders are shipped on time, but this negatively impacts profits.

The best way to determine the efficiency of the shipping function is to compare the number of order line items filled to the total labor hours expended in this activity. To measure it, divide the total number of order lines shipped by the total labor hours expended to fill orders. The calculation is:

$$\frac{Order\ lines\ shipped}{per\ labor\ hour} = \frac{Total\ order\ lines\ shipped}{Total\ labor\ hours\ used\ to\ ship\ orders}$$

The numerator cannot be the total number of orders, since some orders may contain multiple line items, thereby artificially making the shipping staff look less efficient than it really is. Also, the denominator must include all labor involved in the order fulfillment process, including all picking, packing, and shipping tasks. It is generally easiest to include in the denominator the total hours worked by all persons assigned to these tasks, so there is no chance of undercounting labor hours.

13.16 Shipping Accuracy

Though the preceding "Order Lines Shipped per Labor Hour" measurement (13.15) gives a gross measure of the efficiency of the shipping function, it yields no information about the accuracy of the orders shipped—it does no good to ship with astonishing efficiency if the wrong items go to the customer! Accordingly, one should report that measure alongside a shipping accuracy percentage in order to gain a total perspective on the shipping function.

Shipping accuracy information comes from the customer, who lodges complaints about incorrect order fulfillment. This information becomes the numerator in the shipping accuracy measurement when subtracted from the total order lines shipped. If divided by the total order lines shipped, one can derive the measure as a percentage. The calculation is:

$$Shipping\ accuracy\ =\ \frac{(Total\ order\ lines\ shipped\ -\ Incorrect\ order\ lines\ reported\ by\ customers)}{Total\ order\ lines\ shipped}$$

The problem with this measurement is linking the timing of the order line complaint from the customer to the order line volume for the period in which the order was delivered. Though there may be a difference of only a few days between the shipment and complaint dates, it is still common to mismatch a reported shipment error to shipment volume from a different period. The best way to resolve the issue is to record the order number over which a complaint has been lodged, and have the computer system track down the date on which that order was shipped. This approach correctly matches a shipping error to the volume of items shipped during a specific period.

13.17 Warehouse Order Cycle Time

One of the primary customer service measures involving the warehouse is its ability to ship an order as rapidly as possible (as well as accurately—see measurement 13.15, "Order Lines Shipped per Labor Hour"). Constant attention to the interval required from receipt of a customer order to its delivery is necessary, both to bring the order cycle time up to acceptable standards and to ensure that it does not dip below unacceptable levels.

To calculate the warehouse order cycle time, subtract the date and time of the order receipt into the company order entry system from the delivery date and time of the last line item left open on the order. The calculation is:

$$\begin{matrix} \textit{Warehouse order} \\ \textit{cycle time} \end{matrix} = \begin{matrix} \textit{Date and time of last line item delivery} \\ - \textit{Date and time of order receipt} \end{matrix}$$

There are several ways to interpret this measurement. First, consider breaking down the set of orders from which it is derived, so that the slowest 20 percent of all deliveries are measured separately. One should print a detailed report of each of these slow orders, so the management team can focus its attention not only on the gross time interval required to ship the slowest orders, but also on the specific orders in this subset. Second, as noted in the original measurement description, be sure to measure based on delivery of the *last* order line item to be shipped—it makes no sense to measure a successful order as one for which just a few items are shipped; by doing so, management essentially chooses to ignore items placed on backlog, which is precisely where its attention should be most intensely focused. Third, if the warehouse order cycle time is initially quite long, do not bother to measure the time of delivery within a day—that can wait until the average cycle time has been driven down to just a day or two, after which management's measure of success will be small improvements in time intervals.

13.18 Inventory Availability

One of the primary reasons for having inventory is to satisfy customer demand in a timely manner. Maintaining a high level of inventory availability is usually cited as the primary reason why companies keep such high levels of finished goods and service parts on hand. Given this logic, one should measure a company's success in filling orders to see if high inventory retention is working as a policy.

To measure inventory availability, divide the total number of completed orders received by customers no later than their required date during the measurement period by the total number of completed orders that customers should have received during the measurement period. The calculation is:

$$\text{Inventory availability} = \frac{\text{Total number of completed orders received by customer by required date}}{\text{Total number of orders that should have been completed}}$$

The measurement emphasizes a successful order fulfillment as one *received* by the customer on time, since the customer is not being properly served if the order was merely shipped as of the required due date. Most company systems have no provision for tracking customer receipt dates. To avoid this problem, a company can train the order entry staff to subtract shipping time from a customer's required date on receipt of the order, and enter the shortened date in the order entry system.

A company can falsely assume that it has a high availability rate if it counts any sort of partial shipment as a completed order in the numerator, possibly on the grounds that it has successfully shipped nearly all of an order. This measurement approach certainly is not the view of the customer, who may very well stop using the company on the basis of a "completed" order, which it sees as a failure.

13.19 Delivery Promise Slippage

An extremely common occurrence is for the customer support staff to convince a customer to take a delivery later than the original promise date, and then enter the revised promise date in the computer system as though it were the original promise date. Then, when the order is finally delivered, the delivery is measured as being on time, because it matched the revised promise date. Management is therefore unaware of any problem with customer satisfaction resulting from continual slippage problems. The solution is to track the slippage in the delivery promise date.

There are two ways to measure delivery promise slippage. The first is to subtract the final promise date from the original promise date for all orders, and divide by the total number of orders. This approach assumes that the final promise date matches the actual shipment date, which may not be the case. The second approach, which avoids this problem, is to subtract the delivery date from the original promise date for all orders, and divide by the total number of deliveries. The calculation is:

$$\text{Delivery promise slippage} = \frac{\substack{\text{Sum for all delivery transactions} \\ \text{(Delivery date/time – Original promise date/time)}}}{\text{Total number of deliveries}}$$

This measurement requires the presence of a field in the order entry database reserved for the original promise date, which is not available in some less-expensive software packages. Also, it is best if the original promise date field can be locked, so there is no chance of meddling with dates in order to attain a better delivery promise slippage measurement.

One problem is the likely presence at the end of each measurement period of promised orders that have not yet been delivered. If one ignores these transactions for purposes of calculating the measurement, the average delivery promise slippage will almost certainly be too low, since the items causing slippage problems are not being included. A better approach is either to delay the calculation until the unfinished transactions are completed or to revise the calculation a month later when the next periodic measurement is made.

13.20 Average Back-Order Length

When a company focuses solely on the inventory availability measurement just described, the status of any items placed on back order tends to fall off the map. If a customer cannot receive a shipment on time, it at least wants to receive it as soon thereafter as possible, so a company should also track the average length of its back-ordered items to ensure that customers are not excessively dissatisfied.

To measure the average back-order length, compile a list of all customer orders that were not shipped on time and summarize from this list the total number of days that each order has gone past the customer receipt date without being shipped. Then divide this total number of days by the total number of back-ordered customer orders. The calculation is:

$$\text{Average back-order length} = \frac{\substack{\text{Sum of the [Number of days past the required} \\ \text{customer receipt date for each order]}}}{\text{Total number of back-ordered customer orders}}$$

Though the measurement is useful enough by itself, management will probably want to see an accompanying list of the oldest back-ordered items, so it can resolve them as soon as possible.

13.21 Dock Door Utilization

A warehouse may contain a great many dock doors, each of which must be backed by a significant amount of floor space to allow for proper materials movement and related shipping and receiving equipment. Thus, dock doors represent a considerable amount of nonvalue-added floor space, and so must be heavily utilized in order to release as much space as possible for other applications. One should track dock door utilization to determine if the current number of doors is optimal.

To measure dock door utilization, multiply the average dock time per trailer by the number of trailers docked during the measurement period. Then divide the result by the total number of hours in the period, multiplied by the number of dock doors. The calculation is:

$$\frac{Dock\ door}{utilization} = \frac{(Average\ dock\ time\ per\ trailer \times Number\ of\ trailers\ docked)}{(Number\ of\ hours\ in\ measurement\ period \times Number\ of\ dock\ doors)}$$

Proper formulation of this measurement requires tracking of all trailers docked during the measurement period, which one can back into by summarizing all shipping and receiving transactions through the computer system, or by manually tracking this information. The key flaw in this measurement is the average dock time per trailer, which can seriously impact the measurement's accuracy if it is incorrectly formulated. One should schedule on the warehouse activities calendar a periodic reformulation of the average dock time, based on all trailers docked during a sample period.

13.22 Inventory Accuracy

If a company's inventory records are inaccurate, timely production of its products becomes a near-impossibility. For example, if a key part is not located at the spot in the warehouse where its record indicates it should be, or its indicated quantity is incorrect, then the materials handling staff must frantically search for it and probably issue a rush order to a supplier for more of it, while the production line remains idle, waiting for the key raw materials. To avoid this problem, a company must ensure not only that the quantity and location of a raw material is correct, but also that its units of measure and part number are accurate. If any of these four items is wrong, there is a strong chance that the production process will be negatively impacted. Thus, inventory accuracy is one of the most important materials handling measurements.

Divide the number of accurate test items sampled by the total number of items sampled. The definition of an accurate test item is one whose actual quantity, unit of measure, description, and location match those indicated in the warehouse records. If any one of these items is incorrect, then the test item should be considered inaccurate. The formula is:

$$Inventory\ accuracy\ =\ \frac{Number\ of\ accurate\ test\ items}{Total\ number\ of\ items\ sampled}$$

It is extremely important to conduct this measurement using all four of the criteria noted in the formula derivation. The quantity, unit of measure, description, and location must match the inventory record. If this is not the case, then the reason for using it—ensuring that the correct amount of inventory is on hand for production needs—will be invalidated. For example, even if the inventory is available in the correct quantity, if its location code is wrong, then no one can find it in order to use it in the production process. Similarly, the quantity recorded may exactly match the amount located in the warehouse, but this will still lead to an incorrect quantity if the unit of measure in the inventory record is something different, such as dozens instead of eaches.

13.23 Inventory Turnover

Inventory is frequently the largest component of a company's working capital; in such situations, if inventory is not being used up by operations at a reasonable pace, then a company has invested a large part of its cash in an asset that may be difficult to liquidate in short order. Accordingly, keeping close track of the rate of inventory turnover is a significant function of management. Turnover should be tracked on a trend line in order to see if there are gradual reductions in the rate of turnover, which can indicate that corrective action is required to eliminate excess inventory stocks.

The simplest turnover calculation is to divide the period-end inventory into the annualized cost of sales. One can also use an *average* inventory figure in the denominator, which avoids sudden changes in the inventory level that are likely to occur on any specific period-end date. The formula is:

$$\frac{Cost\ of\ goods\ sold}{Inventory}$$

A variation on the preceding formula is to divide it into 365 days, which yields the number of days of inventory on hand. This may be more understandable to the layperson; for example, 43 days of inventory is clearer than 8.5 inventory turns, even though they represent the same situation. The formula is:

$$Inventory\ turnover\ = 365\ /\ \left(\frac{Cost\ of\ goods\ sold}{Inventory}\right)$$

The preceding two formulas use the entire cost of goods sold in the numerator, which includes direct labor, direct materials, and overhead. However, only direct materials costs directly relate to the level of raw materials inventory. Consequently, a cleaner relationship is to compare the value of direct materials expense to raw materials inventory, yielding a raw materials turnover figure. This measurement can also be divided into 365 days in order to yield the number of days of raw materials on hand. The formula is:

$$\frac{Inventory\ turnover}{formula\ 2} = \frac{Direct\ materials\ expense}{Raw\ materials\ inventory}$$

This formula does not yield as clean a relationship between direct materials expense and work-in-process or finished goods, since these two categories of inventory also include cost allocations for direct labor and overhead. However, if these added costs can be stripped out of the work-in-process and finished goods valuations, then there are reasonable grounds for comparing them to the direct materials expense as a valid ratio.

The turnover ratio can be skewed by changes in the underlying costing methods used to allocate direct labor and especially overhead cost pools to the inventory. For example, if additional categories of costs are added to the overhead cost pool, then the allocation to inventory will increase, which will reduce the reported level of inventory turnover—even though the turnover level under the original calculation method has not changed at all. The problem can also arise if the method of allocating costs is changed; for example, it may be shifted from an allocation based on labor hours worked to one based on machine hours worked, which can alter the total amount of overhead costs assigned to inventory. The problem can also arise if the inventory valuation is based on standard costs, and the underlying standards are altered. In all three cases, the amount of inventory on hand has not changed, but the costing systems used have altered the reported level of inventory costs, which impacts the reported level of turnover.

A separate issue is that the basic inventory turnover figure may not be sufficient evidence of exactly where an inventory overage problem may lie. Accordingly, one can subdivide the measurement, so that there are separate calculations for raw materials, work-in-process, and finished goods (and perhaps be subdivided further by location). This approach allows for more precise management of inventory-related problems.

13.24 Percentage of Warehouse Stock Locations Utilized

One should periodically obtain a quantification of the amount of warehouse space currently being used to store stock. This is very useful during the annual budgeting process, since the management team needs to know if projected inventory levels for the coming year can be contained within the existing warehouse space. The information also shows the before-and-after results of having cleared out obsolete or rarely used inventory.

To measure the percentage of warehouse stock locations utilized, divide the number of stock locations containing any amount of inventory by the total number of stock locations in the warehouse. The calculation is:

$$\text{Percentage of warehouse stock locations utilized} = \frac{\text{Number of utilized stock locations}}{\text{Total number of stock locations in the warehouse}}$$

If inventory records are stored in a computer database, as well as cross-referenced to a file listing all possible inventory locations, it is easy to derive the proportion of registered warehouse locations currently being utilized.

If there is no inventory database, one can usually determine the total number of stock locations by walking through the warehouse and adding them up; this number does not change much, unless the warehouse is reconfigured, in which case a single walkthrough will yield the new total number of locations. If one must also walk through the warehouse to count the number of utilized stock locations, it is almost always easier to count the number of stock locations in which there is *no* inventory (since warehouses rarely suffer from underutilization), and then subtract this amount from the total number of stock locations.

The main problem with this measurement is that it does not give any indication of the cubic volume of space being filled. The measure considers any stock location containing even the smallest amount of inventory to be a fully utilized location, which may grossly misrepresent the amount of unused cubic space available.

13.25 Storage Density Percentage

Though every storage rack and bin in a warehouse may be filled to the brim, indicating a 100 percent utilization of all stock locations, this may not indicate the true storage capacity of the warehouse. It is entirely possible that existing storage systems are not making use of all horizontal or vertical storage capabilities within a warehouse, due to such factors as insufficiently high racks or excessively wide aisles. Consequently, it is useful to occasionally determine a warehouse's overall storage density percentage, which measures storage capacity per square foot.

To measure the storage density percentage, divide the cubic volume of all storage locations by the total warehouse square footage and the square footage for all external staging areas. The calculation is:

$$\text{Storage density percentage} = \frac{\textit{Cubic volume of available storage space}}{\textit{(Total warehouse square footage + External staging area square footage)}}$$

This is an easy calculation if a company maintains a storage location file that includes the cubic volume of each location.

This measurement can be misinterpreted, since one can create a warehouse with an excessively high storage density percentage. This can be accomplished by installing racking systems that are dangerously high, or by laying out aisles that are too narrow for efficient item movement.

13.26 Inventory per Square Foot of Storage Space

It is sometimes useful to gain an understanding of overall storage space utilization, particularly in comparison to benchmarked measurements obtained elsewhere. To this end, one can relate the amount of inventory on hand to the total square feet of space it occupies. The main problem is determining the numerator in the calculation—should it be based on the quantity, dollar value, or cubic volume of stock keeping units (SKUs) on hand? If the quantity of SKUs is used, a large number of very small items can skew the measurement in favor of showing a very large amount of inventory per square foot. The same logic applies to the inventory dollar value. This leaves the cubic volume of inventory on hand, which best represents space utilization.

To measure the amount of inventory per square foot of storage space, divide the cubic volume of all inventory on hand by the total warehouse square footage, plus the square footage of all external staging areas. The calculation is:

$$\text{Inventory per square foot of storage space} = \frac{\textit{Cubic volume of inventory on hand}}{\textit{(Total warehouse square footage + External staging area square footage)}}$$

The cubic volume of inventory on hand can be difficult to calculate manually. The best approach is to add the cubic volume for each item to the item master file, so this information can be automatically calculated by the computer system. If this approach is used, be sure to match the cubic volume figure to the unit of measure entered in the item master file. Otherwise, an incorrect cubic volume figure will result.

A possible area of contention in this measurement is the use of total warehouse square footage in the denominator. One might be tempted to use only the square footage of actual storage racks, but doing so ignores the efficient use of other space in the warehouse. For example, one could limit the denominator to square footage occupied by existing racks to obtain an excellent result, but it would hide the existence of excessively wide aisles that could be narrowed to yield additional storage space.

13.27 Storage Cost per Item

Items can languish in the warehouse for years. During that time, one can forget their presence on the assumption that they are accumulating no costs, and so can be safely ignored. Unfortunately, inventory accumulates more costs every day in the form of rack space taken, insurance coverage expenses, the opportunity cost of invested funds, and so on. One must be aware of these costs or be ignorant of a major portion of a company's cost structure.

There are several ways to measure the storage cost of an inventory item. At a summary level, one can simply divide the total number of SKUs actually on hand into all warehouse costs, which is comprised of the fully burdened wages of all warehouse staff, depreciation on all fixed assets, inventory insurance coverage, utilities, obsolescence, scrap costs due to damaged goods, and the corporate cost of capital on funds invested in inventory. At this simplified level, the calculation looks like this:

$$\textit{Storage cost per item} \ = \ \frac{\textit{Total warehouse expenses}}{\textit{Total stock keeping units on hand}}$$

The problem with this calculation is that not all SKUs incur the same costs. For example, a high-value item should be charged a higher proportion of insurance costs, while perishable goods must be charged with a higher proportion of obsolescence costs. Thus, a better approach is to adopt an activity-based costing (ABC) approach to measuring the storage cost per item. Under ABC, costs are accumulated by activity (such as by putaway or picking transaction), and then costs are charged out to individual SKUs based on their use of these transactions. Though the ABC calculation can be lengthy, a typical finding is that a large proportion of all SKUs on hand are costing a company far more than they earn on the gross margin from their eventual sale.

13.28 Average Pallet Inventory per SKU

When planning storage requirements in a warehouse, it is extremely useful to determine in advance the likely pallet inventory required for each SKU, so a sufficient space can be set aside for each one.

To measure the average amount of pallet space required for each SKU, first divide the forecasted unit sales by the historical or planned turnover for each SKU, yielding the average number of units on hand at any time. Then divide this by the number of units per pallet, yielding the average number of pallets on hand. The calculation is:

$$\text{Average pallet inventory per SKU} = \frac{(\textit{Forecasted SKU unit sales / Turnover})}{\textit{Units per pallet}}$$

One can take the measurement a step further by dividing the average pallet inventory by the number of storage levels available in the pallet storage area in order to derive the storage requirement per square foot.

There are three problems with this measurement. First, it relies heavily on an accurate forecast from the marketing department. Second, it assumes that an average inventory level is sufficient for year-round demand, when in fact there may be considerable demand spikes requiring much higher storage levels. Third, the measurement should be used at the SKU level, which can require a prohibitive amount of calculations unless the underlying data are available on a computer for automatic calculations.

13.29 Rate of Change in Inactive, Obsolete, and Surplus Inventory

The header for this best practice refers to three types of inventory: parts having no forecasted usage (inactive), parts no longer incorporated into any current product (obsolete), and parts with quantities exceeding forecasted usage (surplus). For brevity, we will refer to all three categories of inventory as "IOS."

The accounting staff can have a difficult time quantifying its ongoing obsolescence reserve for IOS inventory. In a typical company, a team of reviewers periodically designates specific items in the warehouse as obsolete, at which point the accounting staff adjusts its obsolescence reserve to match the total amount of identified obsolete stock. This tends to result in sudden and large changes in the obsolescence expense that can skew reported financial results. In order to make a more gradual adjustment in the obsolescence reserve, one can use the following formula to arrive at a smaller incremental monthly adjustment in the reserve, based on the monthly growth rate in the IOS:

$$\begin{array}{c} \textit{Rate of change in} \\ \textit{inactive, obsolete, and} \\ \textit{surplus inventory} \end{array} = \frac{\begin{array}{c}\textit{(Current IOS inventory balance} \\ - \textit{(Beginning IOS balance} \\ - \textit{Actual write-off in the period))}\end{array}}{\textit{Number of months covered by calculation}}$$

Though this approach will result in fewer massive increases in the obsolescence reserve, such adjustments are still possible. The formula is based on historical changes in obsolescence, not any forward-looking adjustments that may include substantial writedowns related to such events as a product termination. Consequently, one can use this formula to make incremental adjustments to the obsolescence accrual, but also adjust these entries for estimated changes in the future rate of obsolescence.

13.30 Obsolete Inventory Percentage

A company needs to know the proportion of its inventory that is obsolete, for several reasons. First, external auditors will require that an obsolescence reserve be set up against these items, which drastically lowers the inventory value and creates a charge against current earnings. Second, constantly monitoring the level of obsolescence allows a company to work on eliminating the inventory through such means as returns to suppliers, taxable donations, and reduced-price sales to customers. Finally, obsolete inventory takes up valuable warehouse space that could otherwise be put to other uses; monitoring it with the obsolete inventory percentage allows management to eliminate these items in order to reduce space requirements.

Summarize the cost of all inventory items having no recent usage, and divide by the total inventory valuation. The amount used in the numerator is subject to some interpretation, since there may be occasional usage that will eventually use up the amount left in stock, despite the fact that it has not been used for some time. An alternative summarization method for the numerator that avoids this problem is to include only those inventory items that do not appear on any bill of materials for a currently produced item. The formula is:

$$\text{Obsolete inventory percentage} = \frac{\text{Cost of inventory items with no recent usage}}{\text{Total inventory cost}}$$

A high level of obsolete inventory does not reflect well on the logistics manager, who is responsible for maintaining a high level of inventory turnover. If this person has any influence over the calculation, it is possible that he or she will attempt to alter the amount listed in the numerator, either by defining "recent usage" as anything within a very long time period, or by ensuring that all inventory items are included on some sort of bill of materials, which is generally considered evidence that it may eventually be used. To avoid this problem, the calculation should be given to someone outside of the logistics department.

13.31 Percentage of Inventory > XX Days Old

A company may not have any obsolete inventory, but it may have a sufficient amount of older inventory that it is concerned about the possibility of obsolescence at some point in the future. By determining the amount of inventory that is older than a certain fixed date, the logistics staff can determine which items should be returned to suppliers (see measurement 13.32) or which items should be sold off at a reduced price.

Settle on a number of days after which inventory is considered to be old enough to require liquidation action. Then determine the dollar value of all items whose age exceeds this number of days. Divide that total by the total dollar value of inventory. The measurement should be accompanied by a report that lists the detailed amounts and locations of each inventory item in the numerator, so that the logistics staff can review them in detail. The formula is:

$$\text{Percentage of inventory} > XX \text{ days old} = \frac{\text{Dollars of inventory} > XX \text{ days old}}{\text{Total dollars of inventory}}$$

The measurement can give some idea of the total amount of inventory that may require liquidation, but it gives no visibility into the raw materials usage requirements of the production schedule, which may be scheduled to use these items during an upcoming production run. One can tell if this is the case only by comparing the old inventory list to the production requirements report.

If this report is used to determine the proportion of old finished goods, it yields a better idea of what products may need to be sold off. However, it also requires some knowledge of the timing of the sales season for each product on the list. For example, an article of clothing may appear to be old, but if its prime selling season were just starting, then it would make sense to leave it alone through much of the season to see if it could be sold at its full retail price before considering any type of price discounting.

13.32 Percentage of Returnable Inventory

Over time, a company will tend to accumulate either more inventory than it can use, or inventory that is no longer used at all. These overaccumulations may be caused by an excessively large purchase, or the scaling back of production needs below original expectations, or perhaps a change in a product design that leaves some components completely unnecessary. Whatever the reason may be, it is useful to review the inventory occasionally in order to determine what proportion of it can be returned to suppliers for cash or credit.

Summarize all inventory items for which suppliers have indicated that they will accept a return in exchange for cash or credit. For these items, one may use in the numerator either the listed book value of returnable items or the net amount of cash that can be realized by returning them (which will usually include a restocking fee charged by suppliers). The first variation is used when a company is more interested in the amount of total inventory that it can eliminate from its accounting records, while the second approach is used when it is more interested in the amount of cash that can be realized through the transaction. The denominator is the book value of the entire inventory. The formula is:

$$\text{Percentage of returnable inventory} = \frac{\textit{Dollars of returnable inventory}}{\textit{Total dollars of inventory}}$$

Even though a large proportion of the inventory may initially appear to be returnable, one must also consider that near-term production needs may entail the repurchase of some of those items, resulting in additional freight charges to bring them back into the warehouse. Consequently, the underlying details of the measurement should be reviewed in order to ascertain not only which items can be returned, but also more specifically which ones can be returned that will not be needed in the near term. This will involve the judgment of the logistics staff, perhaps aided by a reorder quantity calculation, to see if it is cost justifiable to return goods to a supplier that will eventually be needed again. A reduced version of the measurement that avoids this problem is to include in the numerator only those inventory items for which there is no production need whatsoever, irrespective of the time line involved.

Summary of Inventory Best Practices

This appendix includes the title and reference number for every best practice listed in the book, and serves as a quick reference guide. In addition, the formulas for all the measurements noted in Chapter 13 are listed at the end of the appendix.

Chapter 2   Inventory Purchasing

2.1	Include Suppliers in the New Product Design Process
2.2	Avoid Designing Risky-Procurement Items into Products
2.3	Reduce Safety Stock by Shrinking Supplier Lead Times
2.4	Purchase Supplier Capacity
2.5	Reduce Safety Stocks by Accelerating the Flow of Internal Information
2.6	Buy from Suppliers Located Close to the Company
2.7	Eliminate Approvals of Routine Purchases
2.8	Purchase Based on Material Requirements Planning
2.9	Compare Open Purchase Orders to Current Requirements
2.10	Freeze the Short-Term Production Schedule
2.11	Obtain Direct Links into Customer Inventory Planning Systems
2.12	Require Frequent Deliveries of Small Quantities
2.13	Arrange for Inbound Split Deliveries
2.14	Arrange for Phased Deliveries
2.15	Adopt Rolling Schedules
2.16	Adopt Just-In-Time Purchasing
2.17	Implement Stockless Purchasing
2.18	Designate Major Suppliers as Lead Suppliers

4.5   Assign Unique Location Codes to All Inventory Storage Locations

4.6   Reduce the Number of Inventory Bin Locations Assigned to the Same Product

4.7   Assign Fixed Inventory Locations to High-Volume Items

4.8   Segregate Customer-Owned Inventory

4.9   Allocate Warehouse Areas to Specific Customers

4.10   Segregate Inventory by ABC Classification

4.11   Store High-Volume Items in Order Fulfillment Zones

4.12   Adjust Case Height to Match Cubic Storage Capabilities

4.13   Adjust Case Stacking or Width to Avoid Pallet Overhang

4.14   Combine Out-and-Back Inventory Moves

4.15   Use Different Storage Systems Based on Cubic Transactional Volume

4.16   Use Modular Storage Cabinets for Low-Storage-Volume Items

4.17   Use Carousels to Increase Picking Efficiency

4.18   Use Moveable Racking Systems

4.19   Use Multistory Manual Picking Systems

4.20   Use Gravity-Flow Racking for FIFO Picking

4.21   Use Pallet-Flow Racks for Pallet FIFO Picking

4.22   Create Double-Deep Racking or Stacking Lanes for Large SKU Pallet Volumes

4.23   Use Push-Back Racks for Multiple Pallet Storage

4.24   Eliminate Cross Bracing in Low-Weight Storage Configurations

Chapter 5   Inventory Picking

5.1   Group Single-Line Orders and Pick in Order by Location

5.2   Use Single-Order Picks for Emergency Orders

5.3   For Manual Systems, Pick from the Source Document

5.4   Implement Forward Picking

5.5   Use Wave Picking by Grouping to Consolidate Transactions

5.6   Use Zone Picking to Consolidate Total Transactions

5.7   Use Zone Picking with Order Forwarding

Chapter 7   Inventory Transactions

7.1   Reduce the Number of Stored Data Elements

7.2   Record Inventory Transactions with Bar Codes

7.3   Record Inventory Transactions with Radio Frequency Communications

7.4   Track Inventory with Radio Frequency Identification

7.5   Eliminate All Paper from Inventory Transactions

7.6   Use the Kanban System to Pull Transactions through the Facility

7.7   Eliminate All Transaction Backlogs

7.8   Verify that Receipts are Entered in the Computer System at Once

7.9   Have Customers Order by Part Number

7.10   Audit All Inventory Transactions

7.11   Compare Recorded Inventory Activity to On-Hand Inventories

7.12   Immediately Review All Negative Inventory Balances

7.13   Replace the Physical Count Process with Cycle Counts

7.14   Streamline the Physical Count Process

7.15   Install a Warehouse Management System

Chapter 8   Inventory Planning and Management

8.1   Include Materials Managers in the New Product Design Process

8.2   Reduce the Number of Product Options

8.3   Reduce the Number of Products

8.4   Design Products with Lower Tolerances

8.5   Require Formal Review and Approval of Engineering Change Orders

8.6   Forecast Demand by Product Families

8.7   Centralize Responsibility for Inventory Planning

8.8   Delay the Order Penetration Point as Long as Possible

8.9   Use a Material Requirements Planning System to Model Alternative Lot Sizes, Safety Stocks, and Lead Times

8.10   Use Variable Safety Stocks for Fluctuating Demand

8.11   Eliminate Expediting

8.12   Develop a Product Substitution System

Chapter 9   Warehouse Layout

11.5   Eliminate Redundant Part Numbers

11.6   Standardize Parts

11.7   Review Inventory Returned to the Warehouse

11.8   Use Bills of Materials to Find Inventory Made Obsolete by Product Withdrawals

11.9   Identify Inactive Inventory in the Product Master File

Chapter 12   Inventory Policies and Procedures

12.1   Create a Policies and Procedures Manual

12.2   Train the Warehouse and Accounting Staffs in Inventory Procedures

12.3   Cross-train for Mission-Critical Activities

12.4   Train Using Training Teams

Chapter 13   Inventory Measurements

13.1 $\text{Percentage of new parts used in new products} = \dfrac{\text{Number of new parts in bill of materials}}{\text{Total number of parts in bill of materials}}$

13.2 $\text{Percentage of existing parts used in new products} = \dfrac{\text{Number of approved parts in bill of materials}}{\text{Total number of parts in bill of materials}}$

13.3 $\text{Bill of materials accuracy} = \dfrac{\text{Number of accurate parts listed in bill of materials}}{\text{Total number of parts in bill of materials}}$

13.4 $\text{Item master file accuracy} = \dfrac{\text{Total number of records reviewed having 100 percent accurate information}}{\text{Total number of records sampled}}$

13.5 $\text{On-time parts delivery percentage} = \text{Actual arrival date} - \text{Requested arrival date}$

13.6 $\text{Incoming components correct quantity percentage} = \text{Total quantity of orders delivered}$

13.7 $\quad$ Percentage of receipts authorized by purchase order $= \dfrac{\text{Receipt line items authorized by open purchase orders}}{\text{Total receipt line items}}$

13.8 $\quad$ Percentage of purchase orders released with full lead time $= \dfrac{\text{Purchase order lines released with full lead time}}{\text{Total purchase order lines released}}$

13.9 $\quad$ Putaway accuracy $= \dfrac{\text{Number of accurate putaway transactions}}{\text{Total number of putaway transactions}}$

13.10 $\quad$ Putaway cycle time $= \dfrac{\text{Sum for all receiving transactions (Putaway date / Time – Receipt date / Time)}}{\text{Number of receipts during the measurement period}}$

13.11 $\quad$ Scrap percentage $= \dfrac{(\text{Actual cost of goods sold – Standard cost of goods sold})}{\text{Standard cost of goods sold}}$

13.12 $\quad$ Average picking time $= \dfrac{\text{Total number of orders completed}}{(\text{Total person-hours worked by picking staff + Total person-hours worked by contract staff})}$

13.13 $\quad$ Picking accuracy for assembled products $= 100\% - \dfrac{\text{Number of quantity errors + Number of part errors}}{\text{Total number of product kits sampled}}$

13.14 $\quad$ Average picking cost $= \dfrac{(\text{Fully burdened picking staff wages + Depreciation on picking equipment and storage})}{\text{Total order lines picked}}$

13.15 $\quad$ Order lines shipped per labor hour $= \dfrac{\text{Total order lines shipped}}{\text{Total labor hours used to ship orders}}$

13.16 Shipping accuracy $= \dfrac{\text{(Total order lines shipped} - \text{Incorrect order lines reported by customers)}}{\text{Total order lines shipped}}$

13.17 Warehouse order cycle time $= \text{Date and time of last line item delivery} - \text{Date and time of order receipt}$

13.18 Inventory availability $= \dfrac{\text{Total number of completed orders received by customer by required date}}{\text{Total number of orders that should have been completed}}$

13.19 Delivery promise slippage $= \dfrac{\text{Sum for all delivery transactions (Delivery date/time} - \text{Original promise date/time)}}{\text{Total number of deliveries}}$

13.20 Average back-order length $= \dfrac{\text{Sum of the [number of days past the required customer receipt date for each order]}}{\text{Total number of back-ordered customer orders}}$

13.21 Dock door utilization $= \dfrac{\text{(Average dock time per trailer} \times \text{Number of trailers docked)}}{\text{(Number of hours in measurement period} \times \text{Number of dock doors)}}$

13.22 Inventory accuracy $= \dfrac{\text{Number of accurate test items}}{\text{Total number of items sampled}}$

13.23 Inventory turnover $= 365 \Big/ \left(\dfrac{\text{Cost of goods sold}}{\text{Inventory}} \right)$

13.23 Inventory turnover formula 2 $= \dfrac{\text{Direct materials expense}}{\text{Raw materials inventory}}$

13.24 $\text{Percentage of warehouse stock locations utilized} = \dfrac{\text{Number of utilized stock locations}}{\text{Total number of stock locations in the warehouse}}$

13.25 $\text{Storage density percentage} = \dfrac{\text{Cubic volume of available storage space}}{(\text{Total warehouse square footage} + \text{External staging area square footage})}$

13.26 $\text{Inventory per square foot of storage space} = \dfrac{\text{Cubic volume of inventory on hand}}{(\text{Total warehouse square footage} + \text{External staging area square footage})}$

13.27 $\text{Storage cost per item} = \dfrac{\text{Total warehouse expenses}}{\text{Total stock keeping units on hand}}$

13.28 $\text{Average pallet inventory per SKU} = \dfrac{(\text{Forecasted SKU unit sales} / \text{Turnover})}{\text{Units per pallet}}$

13.29 $\text{Rate of change in inactive, obsolete, and surplus inventory} = \dfrac{\begin{array}{c}(\text{Current IOS inventory balance} \\ - (\text{Beginning IOS balance} \\ - \text{Actual write-off in the period}))\end{array}}{\text{Number of months covered by calculation}}$

13.30 $\text{Obsolete inventory percentage} = \dfrac{\text{Cost of inventory items with no recent usage}}{\text{Total inventory cost}}$

13.31 $\text{Percentage of inventory} > XX \text{ days old} = \dfrac{\text{Dollars of inventory} > XX \text{ days old}}{\text{Total dollars of inventory}}$

13.32 $\text{Percentage of returnable inventory} = \dfrac{\text{Dollars of returnable inventory}}{\text{Total dollars of inventory}}$

Glossary

ABC inventory classification A method for dividing inventory into classifications, either by transaction volume or cost. Typically, category A includes that 20 percent of inventory involving 60 percent of all costs or transactions, while category B includes the next 20 percent of inventory involving 20 percent of all costs or transactions, and category C includes the remaining 60 percent of inventory involving 20 percent of all costs or transactions.

Accumulation bin A location in which components destined for the shop floor are accumulated prior to delivery.

Advance materials request Very early orders for materials prior to the completion of a product design, given the long lead times required to supply some items.

Aggregate planning A budgeting process using summary-level information to derive various budget models, usually at the product family level.

Automated storage/retrieval system A racking system using automated systems to load and unload the racks.

Backflush The subsequent subtraction from inventory records of those parts used to assemble a product, based on the number of finished goods produced.

Barcode Information encoded into a series of bars and spaces of varying widths, which can be automatically read and converted to text by a scanning device.

Batch picking Picking for a number of summarized orders at the same time, thereby reducing the total number of required picks. The combined picks must still be separated into their constituent orders, typically at some central location.

Bill of materials A listing of all parts and subassemblies required to produce one unit of a finished product, including the required number of units of each part and subassembly.

Bin A storage area, typically a subdivision of a single level of a storage rack.

Bin transfer A transaction to move inventory from one storage bin to another.

Blend off The reintroduction of a faulty product into a process production flow by adding it back in small increments.

Bottleneck A resource whose capacity is unable to match or exceed that of the demand volume required of it.

Breeder bill of materials A bill of materials that accounts for the generation and cost implications of byproducts as a result of manufacturing the parent item.

Byproduct A material created incidental to a production process, which can be sold for value.

Carrying cost The cost of holding inventory, which can include insurance, spoilage, rent, and other expenses.

Component Raw materials or subassemblies used to make either finished goods or higher levels of subassembly.

Configuration audit A review of all engineering documentation used as the basis for a manufactured product to see if the documentation accurately represents the finished product.

Configuration control Verifying that a delivered product matches authorizing engineering documentation. This also refers to engineering changes made subsequent to the initial product release.

Consigned stocks Inventories owned by a company, but located on the premises of its agents or distributors.

Cost of goods sold The charge to expense of the direct materials, direct labor, and allocated overhead costs associated with products sold during a defined accounting period.

Cut-off control A procedure for ensuring that transaction processing is completed prior to the commencement of cycle counting.

Cycle counting The frequent, scheduled counting of a subset of all inventories, with the intent of spotting inventory record inaccuracies, investigating root causes, and correcting those problems.

Delivery policy A company's stated goal for how soon a customer order will be shipped following receipt of that order.

Departmental stocks The informal and frequently unauthorized retention of excess inventory on the shop floor, which is used as buffer safety stock.

Discrete order picking A picking method requiring the sequential completion of each order before one begins picking the next order.

Distribution center A branch warehouse containing finished goods and service items intended for distribution directly to customers.

Distribution inventory Inventory intended for shipment to customers, usually comprised of finished goods and service items.

Earmarked materials Inventory that has been physically marked as being for a specific purpose.

Ending inventory The dollar value or unit total of goods on hand at the end of an accounting period.

Engineering change A change to a product's specifications as issued by the engineering department.

Enterprise resource planning system A computer system used to manage all company resources in the receipt, completion, and delivery of customer orders.

Expedite To artificially accelerate an order ahead of its regularly scheduled counterparts.

Explode The multiplication of component requirements itemized on a bill of materials by the number of parent items required to determine total parts usage.

Failure analysis The examination of failure incidents to identify components with poor performance profiles.

Field warehouse A warehouse into which service parts and finished goods are stocked, and from which deliveries are made directly to customers.

Finished goods inventory Completed inventory items ready for shipment to customers.

First in, first out (FIFO) An inventory valuation method under which one assumes that the first inventory item to be stored in a bin is the first one to be used, irrespective of actual usage.

Fixed-location storage An inventory storage technique under which permanent locations are assigned to at least some inventory items.

Floor stocks Low-cost, high-usage inventory items stored near the shop floor, which the production staff can use at will without a requisition, and which are expensed at the time of receipt, rather than being accounted for through a formal inventory database.

Fluctuation inventory Excess inventory kept on hand to provide a buffer against forecasting errors.

Forward buying The purchase of items exceeding the quantity levels indicated by current manufacturing requirements.

Hedge inventory Excess inventories kept on hand as a buffer against contingent events.

Inactive inventory Parts with no recent prior or forecasted usage.

Indented bill of materials A bill of materials reporting format under which successively lower levels of components are indented further away from the left margin.

Interplant transfer The movement of inventory from one company location to another, usually requiring a transfer transaction.

In-transit inventory Inventory currently situated between its shipment and delivery locations.

Inventory Those items categorized as either raw materials, work-in-process, or finished goods, and involved in the creation of products or service supplies for customers.

Inventory adjustment A transaction used to adjust the book balance of an inventory record to the amount actually on hand.

Inventory diversion The redirection of parts or finished goods away from their intended goal.

Inventory issue A transaction used to record the reduction in inventory from a location, due to its release for processing or transfer to another location.

Inventory receipt The arrival of an inventory delivery from a supplier or other company location.

Inventory returns Inventory returned from a customer for any reason. This receipt is handled differently from a standard inventory receipt, typically into an inspection area, from which it may be returned to stock, reworked, or scrapped.

Inventory turnover The number of times per year that an entire inventory or a subset thereof is used.

Item master file A file containing all item-specific information about a component, such as its weight, cubic volume, and unit of measure.

Item number A number uniquely identifying a product or component.

Just-in-time A cluster of manufacturing, design, and delivery practices designed to continually reduce all types of waste, thereby improving production efficiency.

Kit A group of components needed to assemble a finished product that has been clustered together for delivery to the shop floor.

Last in, first out (LIFO) An inventory valuation method under which one assumes that the last inventory item to be stored in a bin is the first one to be used, irrespective of actual usage.

Lean production The technique of stripping all nonvalue-added activities from the production process, thereby using the minimum possible amount of resources to accomplish manufacturing goals.

Locator file A file identifying where inventory items are situated, by bin location.

Make to order A production scheduling system under which products are only manufactured once a customer order has been received.

Make to stock A production scheduling system under which products are completed prior to the receipt of customer orders, which are filled from stock.

Manufacturing resource planning An integrated, computerized system for planning all manufacturing resources.

Mass customization High-volume production runs of a product, while still offering high variability in the end product offered to customers.

Material requirements planning A computerized system used to calculate material requirements for a manufacturing operation.

Materials requisition A document listing the quantities of specific parts to be withdrawn from inventory.

Materials review board A company committee typically comprised of members representing multiple departments, which determines the disposition of inventory items that will not be used in the normal manufacturing or distribution process.

Matrix bill of materials A bill of materials chart listing the bills for similar products, which is useful for determining common components.

Maximum inventory An inventory item's budgeted maximum inventory level, comprised of its preset safety stock level and planned lot size.

Minimum inventory An inventory item's budgeted minimum inventory level.

Mix ticket A list of the ingredients required for a blending operation.

Modular bill of materials A bill of materials format in which components and subassemblies are clustered by product option, so one can more easily plan for the assembly of finished goods with different configurations.

Move The movement of inventory among various locations within a company.

Multilevel bill of materials An itemization of all bill of materials components, including a nested categorization of all components used for subassemblies.

Net inventory The current inventory balance, less allocated or reserved items.

Nonconforming material Any inventory item that does not match its original design specifications within approved tolerance levels.

Nonsignificant part number An identifying number assigned to a part that conveys no other information.

Obsolete inventory Parts not used in any current end product.

Offal materials The waste materials resulting from a production process.

On-hand balance The quantity of inventory currently in stock, based on inventory records.

Order penetration point The point in the production process when a product is reserved for a specific customer.

Order picking The process of moving items from stock for shipment to customers.

Outbound stock point A designated inventory location on the shop floor between operations where inventory is stockpiled until needed by the next operation.

Overrun A manufactured or received quantity exceeding the planned amount.

Packing slip A document attached to a customer shipment, describing the contents of the items shipped, as well as their part numbers and quantities.

Pallet ticket A document attached to a pallet, showing the description, part number, and quantity of the item contained on the pallet.

Part A specific component of a larger assembly.

Part number A number uniquely identifying a product or component.

Parts requisition An authorization to move a specific quantity of an item from stock.

Parts standardization The planned reduction of similar parts through the standardization of parts among multiple products.

Periodic inventory A physical inventory count taken on a repetitive basis.

Perpetual inventory A manual or automated inventory tracking system in which a new inventory balance is computed continuously whenever new transactions occur.

Phantom bill of materials A bill of materials for a subassembly not normally kept in stock, since it is used at once as part of a higher-level assembly or finished product.

Physical inventory A manual count of the on-hand inventory.

Picking list A document listing items to be removed from stock, either for delivery to the shop floor for production purposes or for delivery to a customer.

Picking transaction Withdrawing parts or subassemblies from stock in order to manufacture subassemblies or finished products.

Point-of-use delivery A delivery of stock to a location in or near the shop floor adjacent to its area of use.

Point-of-use storage The storage of stock in a location in or near the shop floor adjacent to its area of use.

Primary location A storage location labeled as the primary location for a specific inventory item.

Process flow production A production configuration in which products are continually manufactured with minimal pauses or queuing.

Product Any item intended for sale.

Projected available balance The future planned balance of an inventory item, based on the current balance and adjusted for planned receipts and usage.

Pull system A materials flow concept in which parts are withdrawn only after a request is made by the using operation for more parts.

Push system A materials flow concept in which parts are issued based on planned material requirements.

Putaway The process of moving received items to storage and recording the related transaction.

Rack A vertical storage device in which pallets can be deposited, one over the other.

Radio frequency identification (RFID) The basis for small radio transmitters that emit an RFID to receiver devices. The transmitter is a tiny tag, storing a unique product identification code that is transmitted, and which is used for inventory tracking.

Random-location storage The technique of storing incoming inventory in any available location, which is then tracked in a locator file.

Raw materials Base-level items used by the manufacturing process to create either subassemblies or finished goods.

Reconciling inventory The process of comparing book to actual inventory balances, and adjusting for the difference in the book records.

Record accuracy The variance between book and on-hand quantities, expressed as a percentage.

Remanufactured parts Parts that have been reconstructed to render them capable of fulfilling their original function.

Repair bill of materials A special bill itemizing changes needed to refurbish an existing product.

Replacement parts Parts requiring some modification before being substituted for another part.

Reprocessed materials Materials that have been reworked and returned to stock.

Requirements explosion The component-level requirements for a production run, derived by multiplying the number of parent-level requirements by the component requirements for each parent, as specified in the bill of materials.

Reserved materials Materials that have been reserved for a specific purpose.

Rework The refurbishment of a faulty part.

RFID See *radio frequency identification.*

Safety stock Extra inventory kept on hand to guard against requirements fluctuations.

Scrap Faulty material that cannot be reworked.

Scrap factor An anticipated loss percentage included in the bill of materials, and used to order extra materials for a production run, in anticipation of scrap losses.

Seasonal inventory Very high inventory levels built up in anticipation of large seasonal sales.

Shelf life The time period during which inventory can be retained in stock, and beyond which it becomes unusable.

Shelf-life control Deliberate usage of the oldest items first, in order to avoid exceeding a component's or product's shelf life.

Shrinkage Any uncontrolled loss of inventory, such as through evaporation or theft.

Shrinkage factor The expected loss of some proportion of an item during the production process, expressed as a percentage.

Significant part number An identifying number assigned to an item that conveys additional embedded information.

Single level bill of material A list of all components used in a parent item.

Single sourcing Using a single supplier as the only source of a part.

SKU (stock keeping unit) An item used at a single location.

Slow-moving item An inventory item having a slower rate of turnover than the average turnover for the entire inventory.

Split delivery The practice of ordering large quantities on a single purchase order, but separating the order into multiple smaller deliveries.

Stackability The ability to safely stack multiple layers of the same SKU on top of each other.

Staging Picking parts from stock for an order before they are needed, in order to determine parts shortages in advance.

Standard containers Common-sized containers used to efficiently move, store, and count inventory.

Stock Any item held in inventory.

Stock keeping unit See *SKU*.

Stockless purchasing The purchase of material for direct delivery to the production area, bypassing any warehouse storage.

Stockout The absence of any form of inventory when needed.

Stockpoint An inventory storage area used for short-term inventory staging.

Subassembly A group of assembled components used in the assembly of a higher-level assembly.

Summarized bill of materials A bill of materials format showing the grand total usage requirement for each component of a finished product.

Supplies General supplies used throughout a company, and expensed at the time of acquisition.

Surplus inventory Parts for which the on-hand quantity exceeds forecasted requirements.

Traceability The ability to track the components used in production through their inclusion in a finished product and from there to specific customers.

Two-bin system A system in which parts are reordered when their supply in one storage bin is exhausted, requiring usage from a backup bin until the replenishment arrives.

Unit of measure The summarization unit by which an item is tracked, such as a box of 100 or an each of 1.

Unplanned receipt A stock receipt for which no order was placed, or for which an excess quantity was received.

Vendor-managed inventory The direct management and ownership of selected on-site inventory by suppliers.

Visual control The visual inspection of inventory levels, enabled by the use of designated locations and standard containers.

Visual review system Inventory reordering based on a visual inspection of on-hand quantities.

Warehouse demand The demand for a part by an outlying warehouse.

Wave picking The practice of grouping the priority of pick lists so that groups of picked orders can be delivered at the same time, such as a set of orders being delivered to a single customer on a single truck departing at a specific time.

Where-used report A report listing every product whose bill of materials calls for the use of a specific component.

Withdrawal The release of items from storage.

Work-in-process Any items being converted into finished goods, or released from the warehouse in anticipation of beginning the conversion process.

Zone picking The practice of picking by area of the warehouse, rather than by order, requiring an additional consolidation step from which picking by order is completed.

Index